SALESM[...] GOLDE[...]

If you can sell yourself on yourself . . .

if you can sell others on you and what you have to offer . . .

if you can make adversity work for you, not against you, and spot and seize opportunity wherever and however it appears . . .

if you can follow Napoleon Hill's time-tested techniques and step-by-step instructions, and gain inspiration from the true stories of men and women who did it and reaped the rewards . . .

then you can—

SUCCEED AND GROW RICH THROUGH PERSUASION
Napoleon Hill's most valuable guide to wealth and happiness

Newly revised and updated for the 1990s

SUCCEED AND GROW RICH THROUGH
PERSUASION

REVISED EDITION

Napoleon Hill

with an Introduction by
W. Clement Stone

Edited by
Samuel A. Cypert

A SIGNET BOOK

SIGNET
Published by New American Library, a division of
Penguin Putnam Inc., 375 Hudson Street,
New York, New York 10014, U.S.A.
Penguin Books Ltd, 80 Strand,
London WC2R 0RL, England
Penguin Books Australia Ltd, Ringwood,
Victoria, Australia
Penguin Books Canada Ltd, 10 Alcorn Avenue,
Toronto, Ontario, Canada M4V 3B2
Penguin Books (N.Z.) Ltd, 182–190 Wairau Road,
Auckland 10, New Zealand

Penguin Books Ltd, Registered Offices:
Harmondsworth, Middlesex, England

First published by Signet, an imprint of New American Library,
a division of Penguin Putnam Inc.

First Printing (Revised Edition), May 1992
20 19 18 17

CONTENTS

SUCCEED AND GROW
RICH THROUGH
PERSUASION

INTRODUCTION

We are all salespeople. Some of us who have made careers of calling on customers and clients to sell a product or service are more overt, but everyone is selling something—an idea, a dream, or a point of view.

The source of that thought is Wally Armbruster, an advertising man who reached the top of his profession and created campaigns that have become part of the American lexicon. Armbruster has received countless awards for his creativity and he holds many impressive titles, but his passion is salesmanship. In his book, *Where Have All the Salesmen Gone?* he writes: "Supersalesmanship, I think, belongs up there with the arts. It's surely a *practical* art. And maybe the very highest form of human endeavor."

If you have nothing to sell, Armbruster says, you'd better check your pulse—you're probably dead.

PERSISTENCE PAYS OFF

I began my career as a salesman at age six, hawking newspapers on Chicago's tough South Side. It was not a job for the meek. I was often yelled at and threatened by older, bigger boys who wanted the busy street corners for themselves.

Although I didn't realize it at the time, it was there that I learned the meaning of one of Napoleon Hill's favorite phrases: "In every adversity there is the seed of an equivalent or greater benefit." Of necessity I learned to turn lemons into lemonade.

After a few altercations with the older boys, I started to think there might be a better way to sell newspapers. Near the corner where I tried to work—and kept experiencing problems with aggressive competitors—was Hoelle's Restaurant. It was a very frightening prospect for a child of six, but I went inside and started peddling papers.

The owner threw me out in short order, but not before I sold three papers. When Mr. Hoelle wasn't watching I went back inside and sold another and got a dime tip from a friendly customer who apparently liked my determination. The third time I went back in, the customers told the owner to leave me alone. He did and I stayed until I sold all my papers.

I went back inside Hoelle's again the next day and he escorted me out the door again, but when I kept coming back, he threw his hands in the air in exasperation and said, "What's the use?" We eventually became great friends and I regularly sold my newspapers in his restaurant.

From that experience I learned that when you set out to sell a certain amount of something, you can do it. The only way to reach a goal is to set one for yourself and never give up until you reach it. That lesson was continually reinforced throughout my life.

I used the techniques I learned selling newspapers to launch my career in the insurance business. I got in the business of selling accident insurance quite by accident. When I was about to enter high school, my mother entered the insurance business by pawning the only two diamonds she owned to open an insurance agency in Detroit. I attended high school in Chicago and spent the summers with her. It was there I started to develop my own sales techniques.

The first day on the job, I studied the policy I was about to sell to the unsuspecting Detroit public. My instructions were to canvass the Dime Bank Building, calling on every office except the office of the building. As

I began, I was more than a little frightened, but I remembered the rule I set for myself as a newsboy: *When you set out to do something, don't come back until you've done it.*

Many people gave me advice along the way—some good, some only well-intentioned—and from that advice and my own experience, I gradually began to develop a system that has never failed me.

First and foremost, I went where the prospects were. I worked in large office buildings where I could call on twice as many people in half the time. That technique I had learned as a six-year-old newsboy selling papers in Hoelle's Restaurant.

Of course I was frightened and insecure. I was a teenager calling on successful business people in plush offices! As I stood outside the door of an office, not knowing what was on the other side, I searched for reasons to go inside. Because I searched, I found them. I told myself: *Success is achieved only by those who try. When there is nothing to lose and everything to gain by trying—by all means try it!*

The idea made sense, but it still didn't address the emotional resistance to walking through a door and risking rejection by a total stranger. Fortunately for me, I hit upon another self-motivator that I use to this day: *Do it now!* I have so cultivated that three-word phrase that has become an inseparable part of myself. Everyone who knows me knows those words and has probably heard me use them on more than one occasion.

THE VALUE OF ENTHUSIASM

I also learned something else during those early years: the value of enthusiasm. I knew that if someone was going to buy something from me, I would have to be sold on the product myself. I would have to be convinced that I was selling them something they needed and at a fair price. I would have to excite them about my product or service through my infectious enthusiasm.

As Ralph Waldo Emerson said, "Nothing great was ever achieved without enthusiasm." Andrew Carnegie knew its value well. He told Napoleon Hill that the reason he paid Charles Schwab a million dollars a year to run his steel mills was Schwab's ability to arouse the enthusiasm of workers. Schwab himself said, "A man can succeed at almost anything for which he has unlimited enthusiasm."

My personal discovery about enthusiasm is that it can be taught. Anyone can learn how to generate it within themselves. In fact, the definition implies that it must come from within. The word itself comes from the Greek words: *theos* (God) and *en* (in).

Most of us have an innate timidity that must be overcome before we can achieve success in sales. I found that the only way I could overcome that frightened feeling was by mastering control of my voice. I then discovered that voice control was the key to the whole process of developing enthusiasm.

I discovered that no prospective client could tell I was sweating and trembling on the inside when I employed a commanding, enthusiastic tone of voice. This discovery led me to five rules that I have since used and trained thousands of others to use to great advantage:

1. *Talk loudly.* Speak up so others can hear you and clearly see what they perceive to be a self-confident individual.
2. *Talk rapidly and concentrate on your subject.* Maintain eye contact with your subject to inspire confidence and keep your thoughts in order.
3. *Pause and emphasize.* Hesitate where there is a comma or a natural break and stress important words.
4. *Keep a smile in your voice.* A gruff or unfriendly tone will soon kill enthusiasm. You make your mind think you are cheerful when you keep a smile.
5. *Modulate your voice.* A monotonous delivery is boring and objectionable. Lower your voice from time to time so your listener has to strain to hear you, then abruptly raise your voice on a few key words before returning to your normal pitch.

Although these are simple rules, they employ a well-known psychological principle: Emotions can be controlled by action.

You can be enthusiastic about everything you do. When you shake hands with someone, do it with enthusiasm. When you talk on the phone, work in a cheerful thought. Send a feeling of vitality across the wires to make the person on the other end feel better for having talked to you.

Enthusiasm is like a pump: first you have to prime it, but once it is flowing, it goes right on flowing. Practice priming your own enthusiasm and watch it flow magically from others.

> You've got to prime the pump,
> You must have faith and believe;
> You've got to give of yourself,
> 'Fore you're worthy to receive.
> Drink all the water you can hold,
> Wash you face, cool your feet,
> But leave the bottle full for others.
> Thank you kindly, Desert Pete.
> (from the folk song "Desert Pete")

THE POWER OF THE SUBCONSCIOUS

Although I didn't fully realize it at the time, I was beginning to employ the technique of autosuggestion to get myself going. Words are far more than a collection of characters in a language; they are the symbols of ideas. When you hear and understand them, you are subject to the power of suggestion. When you use them, you employ the power of conscious autosuggestion.

For example, when you utter a negative phrase such as "I can't," follow through with another negative, such as "I can't fail!" You are then using autosuggestion to develop a positive mental attitude, because a double negative becomes a positive.

Make it a habit when you hear suggestions that are harmful to you to question immediately the words you hear. Employ a positive thought even though you may not express it verbally. For example, when someone says, "You can't do it!" Think, "Maybe you can't, but I can. I may not know how at this moment, but I can and will find a way!" You can repel negative suggestion with applied positive autosuggestion.

I have developed an inventory of self-motivating phrases that have become such a part of me that the response is instantaneous and automatic—for example, to neutralize fear . . . face problems more directly . . . turn advantages into disadvantages . . . strive for higher achievement . . . solve serious problems . . . or control my emotions. When the need arises, I use one of these favorites:

- God is always a good God.
- You have a problem . . . That's good!
- With every adversity there is a seed of an equivalent or greater benefit.
- What the mind can conceive and believe, the mind can achieve.
- Find one good idea that will work and work with that one good idea!
- Do it now!
- To be enthusiastic . . . act enthusiastic!

Even when you are sleeping, your subconscious is hard at work. If you have ever awakened in the middle of the night with a brilliant idea or the solution to a problem, that's the subconscious at work. When your conscious mind was at rest, your subconscious worked out the problem. You can deliberately employ this great resource to your advantage. By filling your mind with positive thoughts, you are conditioning yourself for success.

When you visualize a goal you plan to achieve, you are convincing yourself through your subconscious that you will reach your goal. When you repeat something to yourself often enough, your subconscious will accept the statement as fact. If you set a reasonable, reachable goal for yourself that doesn't violate the laws of God or the rights of your fellow man, your subconscious will help you achieve it.

For example, let's say you wish to sell a million dollars worth of real estate this year. Every morning, look at

yourself in the mirror and say aloud: I am going to sell
a million dollars of real estate this year. I am going to
sell $100,000 of real estate this month. (Use the other
two months for vacations, holidays, studying, and improving your skills.) Repeat this goal fifty times each
morning and each night pray for guidance.

Of course, you have to do all the right things to reach
your goal. You have to prospect, make sales calls, work
referrals, and all the other good sales techniques that are
quickly learned. Your subconscious will then help you
turn your desires into their physical counterpart.

Napoleon Hill once told me a story that is a great
illustration of the effective use of self-suggestion: when
he finished the manuscript for his second book, he gave
it the working title *The Thirteen Steps to Riches*. The
publisher, however, wanted a livelier title, one that
would capture the prospective buyer's fancy. He wanted
a million-dollar name for the book. He called Hill every
day for the new title, but even though Hill had tried
about six hundred possibilities, none of them felt right.

One day the publisher called and said, "I've got to
have a title by tomorrow. If you don't have one, I do,
and it's a humdinger: *Use Your Noodle and Get the
Boodle.*"

"You'll ruin me. That title is ridiculous," Hill shouted.

"Well, that's it, unless you get me a better one by
tomorrow morning," the publisher responded.

That night, Hill addressed his subconscious: "You and
I have gone a long way together. You've done a lot of
things for me, and some things to me. But I've got to
have a million-dollar title, and I've got to have it tonight.
Do you understand that?" For several hours he engaged
in thinking time, and then he went to bed.

About two in the morning, he awoke as though shaken
by someone. As he came out of sleep, a phrase glowed
in his mind. He jumped to his typewriter and put the
phrase on paper. Then he grabbed the phone and called
his publisher. "We've got our million-dollar selling title!"
he shouted.

He was right! *Think and Grow Rich*, a classic in the

self-help field, has sold thirty million copies in the past fifty years.

You can employ the same techniques to tap the hidden powers of your own subconscious.

PREPARE YOURSELF

In order to tap into the powers that are available to you as Napoleon Hill did, you must first be prepared to accept and apply the information.

If you believe the principles of success will work for you as they have for others, regardless of your past experiences, lack of education, environment, or physical health, they will. Conversely, if you believe you are destined to fail and there is nothing you can do about it, you will certainly fail.

The mind has a wonderful capacity to translate our thoughts into their physical counterpart. If you allow your mind to dwell on thoughts of poverty and failure, you can be sure that will become your destiny. But if you focus on positive thoughts, develop a belief in yourself, and seek opportunities, you will become a success. As Napoleon Hill and I have said in all our writings: "Whatever the mind can conceive and believe, it can achieve."

You are the product of your heredity, environment, physical body, conscious and subconscious mind, experience in thought and action, your particular position and direction in time and space and something more . . . including powers known and unknown.

You are the most important living person as far as you and your life are concerned. You have the potential power to affect, use, control, or harmonize all of them. For you have a brain and a nervous system, and through them you can develop the habit of following through with the proper actions in applying what you have learned through your conscious mind to affect your subconscious.

You are a mind with a body. Your mind consists of dual, invisible potential powers—your conscious and subconscious—which have enormous powers when properly used. The power created by the conscious mind directing the subconscious is almost unlimited.

The old saying "Knowledge is power" is only partly correct. Knowledge is only potential power. It becomes power only when you use it, just as a gallon of gasoline in your car is only potential power until you turn on your ignition and use it. When the conscious and subconscious minds work in harmony, they can affect, use, control, or harmonize with all known and unknown powers.

You can double your productivity through the use of this power. Can you conceive of accomplishing twice as much as you usually do in the same amount of time? What would it involve? Write it down on a sheet of paper: "Tomorrow I will . . ."

Now relax for fifteen minutes and open your mind to ideas as to how you will go about achieving these written objectives. Jot down your ideas as they occur, but don't worry about organizing them in logical form or assigning priorities. Try to keep the flow of ideas going. It may help to visualize "logic gates" in your mind. Concentrate on keeping these gates open and letting the ideas emerge from your subconscious.

If after thirty minutes of free-flowing thought your paper is a hodgepodge of scribbled ideas, go ahead and arrange them in logical order. If you haven't yet arrived at a concept of how to go about doubling your productivity, keep trying. Some persons require several weeks of daily practice before they master this process. I never go to bed at night without first taking time for thinking, study, and planning. I recommend that you develop this habit, too. It is essential to making the most of your abilities.

THE POWER OF PRAYER

There is a source of everyday power that at best most of us have only the most cursory understanding. We know that there is a power generation station out there somewhere to which our individual homes are connected and that we plug in our appliances and computers and they work. They open cans, process words and food, perform complex mathematical calculations, and wash dishes.

Yet if most of us were asked to prove there is power in electricity—or even that it exists at all—we probably couldn't, even with the help of an engineer. We can't see electricity; we can only see the results.

The same is true with prayer. We can't quantify or measure its power; we can only see its results. It can't be proven scientifically that prayer has the power to change the course of civilization, prevent war, cure physical and mental illness, and to turn failures into successful, productive people. Yet we have seen prayer accomplish these things and more many times throughout history. It is a matter of record.

I have had the opportunity to study these things for a good number of years and to discuss such thoughts with many of the leading thinkers on the subject. The more I study, the more I learn, and the more I study the lives of successful people, the more I am convinced that our greatest power lies in the power of prayer. It has been proven to me time and time again.

Over the years I have received countless letters from people who have read my books, articles, and columns. Many have taken the time to tell me that my writings inspired them or motivated them to achieve something they had previously thought impossible. Those letters are gratifying indeed, but the ones that mean the most to me are from readers who are motivated to return to their churches or seek divine guidance to save their own lives or have successfully used prayer to regain physical, mental, or moral health.

It is not even important to understand how prayer works—only that it does. There are many mysteries in the cosmos that we may never understand, but we do know that there are certain universal laws that always apply. Through the power of prayer we can use those universal laws to direct our own lives into positive, productive channels. No one on earth can stop you.

You must remember, however, that prayer is participatory, not passive. It isn't enough to ask for guidance, you have to take action. Anything worth praying for is worth working for. The success cycle is prayer . . . action

. . . work. You can achieve any goal you set for yourself by following this cycle.

We all have a preference for the times we like to pray. I recommend praying both in the morning and at night when things are quiet and peaceful, but any time will work as long as you set aside time for thoughtful and reverent prayer. We could learn something from other cultures that take their prayers more seriously than any business commitment and take time to pray during every working day. The inner peace and harmony that comes from daily prayer will pay great dividends.

I have found that in addition to memorized prayers, it is helpful to follow the approach of one America's wisest leaders—Benjamin Franklin—and pray for wisdom. Focus on the ideals and attributes that will empower you to be your best. And pray for others, including every member of your family.

When you pray, follow this rule: Pray as though everything depends upon God, then act as though everything depends on you. If you do, you will truly harness the greatest power known to mankind—the power of prayer.

BELIEVE IN YOURSELF

After you conceive what you wish to achieve and what you must do to attain it, you must *believe* it can be done—by you. This may be more difficult.

Such belief requires self-discipline and self-confidence. Psychologist M. Scott Peck says in his book *The Road Less Travelled* that self-discipline is self-caring. "If we believe ourselves to be valuable, then we will feel our time to be valuable, and if we feel our time to be valuable, we will want to use it well."

Peck believes that the feeling of being valuable, the cornerstone of self-discipline, is a direct product of parental love. "Such a conviction must be gained in childhood; it is extremely difficult to acquire in adulthood," he says. "Conversely, when children have learned through the love of their parents to feel valuable, it is almost impossible for the vicissitudes of adulthood to destroy their spirit."

I know Peck is correct because I had a loving mother who taught me self-esteem. It was the basis of my success. If you did not have such an upbringing, however, it isn't too late. You can learn self-esteem by reading self-help, action books such as this one and many others.

Once you have mastered the ability to conceive and believe, you *can* double your productivity. I did and you can, too. It may not happen immediately, but I can tell you unequivocally that when I used the process outlined here I doubled my sales, then doubled them again and again.

I asked myself, "Why not sell as much in a day as I have been selling in a week? Why not?" And I did. Then I decided to sell as much in a week as others sold in a month. Finally I sold as much in a month as others did in a year.

THE R2A2 FORMULA

I have always made it a personal rule when training salespeople that I would never tell a person *what* to do unless I could tell him or her *how* to do it. I follow the same rule in my writings. If you are ready to use these principles, here are two that will guarantee your success:

1. Recognize, Relate, Assimilate, and Apply principles, systems, techniques, and methods from what you see, hear, read, and experience that can help you attain your desires and goals. This is what I call the R2A2 Formula. As you have, no doubt, already determined, R2 stands for *Recognize* and *Relate*, A2 for *Assimilate* and *Apply*.

2. Invoke the power of your subconscious mind so as to direct your thoughts, control your emotions, and ordain your destiny by motivating yourself at will and motivating others to motivate themselves to achieve worthwhile goals.

To use this formula, you must keep your goals constantly in mind and be *ready* to accept useful information. When you have a burning desire to reach the goal you have set for yourself, you will view the world in terms of your goals. Everything you learn from any field, every action you take, will either move you closer to your goal or it won't. Having the goal firmly in mind helps you make priority decisions easily, and helps you focus on what is important to you.

For example, as you read a self-help book, concentrate on the meanings of the thoughts and words in terms of your own goals. Read as if the author were a close personal friend who was writing to you and you alone.

Read the *entire* book—the dedication, the introduction, even the index and bibliography, as well as each page in sequence. If you own the book, *underscore* or *highlight* sentences or passages that you feel are important, especially those that you may wish to memorize.

Put question marks next to statements you don't understand. Write short notes in the margins of pages and make longer entries in a notebook when you have inspiring ideas or when potential solutions to problems flash in your mind as a result of your reading.

Another example of focus would be listening to a lecture, a sermon, or a motivational speaker. Since ideas often come from unexpected places, it is important to listen with a notepad at hand. Anything of interest (a flash of inspiration or a solution to a problem) should be jotted down.

Concentration is important in listening to a speaker, too, for you should constantly be asking yourself the question: "What does this mean to me?" With specific ideas in mind, you can approach the speaker after the talk with questions aimed at helping you R2A2 his or her answers.

The second part of the formula is most important, but it is the part many people tend to avoid or gloss over. You can identify such people quickly, because they are the ones who always make excuses.

NOTHING HAPPENED

A few years ago, the telephone rang in my office and Linda, my administrative assistant, answered. "I want to talk to Mr. Stone," a woman demanded angrily. Linda said, "Mr. Stone is out of the city right now. May I help you?"

During the course of the conversation, the caller revealed that she and her husband had been arguing over the money they had "wasted" on two of my books— *Success Through a Positive Mental Attitude* and *The Success System That Never Fails*. The woman told Linda that she had read both my books and that nothing happened.

"My husband is still out of work," she said, "and I'm still standing on my feet ten hours a day in that crummy restaurant! Mr. Stone wrote: 'Whatever the mind of man can conceive and believe, the mind can achieve.' A promise is a promise and a deal is a deal!"

"But what action did you take as a result of reading Mr. Stone's books?" Linda asked the woman.

There was a long pause and then the response, "I waited."

Linda told the woman what she has often heard me say: "A writer of self-help action literature judges his or her work by what action readers take as a direct result of what they have read. Why don't you read the books again? Don't look for a bit of magic to appear on the pages. Look for a principle or an idea that has particular meaning for you, and then follow through with *action*."

They talked awhile longer and Linda offered some specific suggestions for follow-through. The conversation ended on a pleasant note.

Several months later, the woman called back. "You probably don't remember me," she told Linda, "but I'm the woman who called a few months ago and you suggested that I reread Mr. Stone's books and do something about them. I just had to call and tell you what *has* happened."

The caller related that she and her husband had read the books again—together this time, with the motivation to follow through with action. She decided to take some business classes at night school. Although she was temporarily making less money at the restaurant because she was working fewer hours, she was investing in her future. She had already been told that she was being considered for three jobs that would be available to her when she finished night school, and at a salary double that of what she was earning as a waitress.

"We still have a long way to go," she said, "but we are on our way. I wanted to call and thank you. You were right. The answers were in the books, but the bit of magic you referred to is inside me."

I haven't heard from the woman in a while, but if I were to speculate, I would guess that she is doing just fine. When she began to put the information she had learned into action, she began to change her life for the better.

Entrepreneur Del Smith founded his extraordinarily successful Evergreen International Aviation, Inc. on the premise that "Performance is the only thing that counts," and I think it is a good motto for any one of us to adopt. Good ideas are like good intentions. They will come to nothing unless they are put into action!

Even though the action part of the formula is most important, it won't work without the first part. To R2 an idea, you discover it and relate it to your own situation or needs. You then assimilate it or absorb and make it your own.

Ideas may be difficult to assimilate. Doing so is usually a three-step process:

1. Understanding—meaning that you see the idea and all its implications and ramifications. If you truly understand the idea, you will be able to explain it to someone else.
2. Testing—trying out the idea to see whether you are comfortable with it. Suppose, for example, you have R2'd my method of using self-motivaters. You would test it by repeating a self-motivater such as "Do it now!" to yourself over and over again for several days to see how it works and to determine how this fits your personal style.
3. Affirming—saying "yes, this idea or method is part of my personal approach to life," and making it one of your habit patterns.

Like any formula, R2A2 has two functions, descriptive and prescriptive. There is something satisfying about the descriptive aspect, but simply knowing the meaning of

$E = MC^2$ is a long way from using that formula to manufacture a nuclear reactor. The same is true of the R2A2. Individuals who understand the principle but fail to put it into action will remain on the sidelines, theoretical achievers taking refuge in excuses.

Taking action involves risk, of course, but you can reduce the amount of risk by thinking your actions through carefully and invoking the power of your subconscious to make sure you are employing all the assets you have at your disposal to ensure success.

THE MAGIC INGREDIENT

As I began planning what I would write in this Introduction, I reflected on the work Napoleon Hill and I did together, and I browsed through some of my old records of our work. I recalled our excitement about new findings about vitamins back in 1955.

We decided to come up with our own vitamin discovery, which we labeled Vitamin I. By now you know a great deal about Vitamin A, B, B_1, the B complexes, C, D, E, and K, but if you haven't heard about Vitamin I, let me elaborate. Vitamin I is the "Inspiration Vitamin."

We all know that the body will only absorb the quantity of vitamins it can use. What it can't use, it eliminates as waste. You may over the course of a lifetime spend large sums of money for obtaining vitamins in foods and food supplements because we must replenish the source of those vitamins.

Vitamin I, on the other hand, can be absorbed from the same sources over and over without diminishing the source of supply. It can be generated from within, and it can be stimulated from without by selecting beneficial external influences to help you achieve the inspiration you are seeking.

The subconscious reacts if exposed long enough and frequently enough to external influences that are inspiring. Select environmental influences that cause you to react just as carefully as you select food and vitamin supplements for the body. Because your subconscious mind reacts to your inspiring thoughts quicker and with greater effectiveness than external influence—think inspiring thoughts.

Just as vitamins must be taken regularly for a healthy body, Vitamin I must be taken for a healthy mind. Inspiration without action is beautiful but valueless. It is short-lived and extinguished like a flame—often never to return. The mind is affected by the physical condition of the body to an extent, but the body is more affected by the condition of your mind. Select your daily supply of Vitamin I.

THE ART OF SELF-MOTIVATION

The greatest power we human beings have is the power to choose. But to choose, we must make a decision. And decisions are sometimes painful, often difficult. Those of us who have made it a practice to study behavioral patterns and how to persuade people to change their behavior for their own benefit have arrived at some inescapable conclusions. One fundamental rule is this: You and I have inherited instincts, emotions, feelings and tendencies. We develop moods, habits, and impulses. Even the most logical of us does not act from reason alone. We act on our emotions and feelings as well as logic.

One of the wonderful things about our fantastic brain and nervous system is that we can use both reason and emotion to motivate ourselves at will. But to do so requires a small leap of faith. We have to accept as fact that there are powers known and unknown that we can use to our advantage—forces that motivate us.

Motivation, after all, is simply defined as that which induces action or determines choice. It is that which provides a motive. Your motives are the inner urges that are yours alone. They are the things within you that incite you to action such as an idea, emotion, desire, or impulse. It is the hope or other force which starts you in action in an attempt to produce specific results.

Much has been written about the fundamental conflict that seems to reside in us all. The battle between good and evil is the stuff of high drama and pulp fiction, and we recognize some of the same conflicts when we attempt to motivate ourselves. We all have complex and often conflicting emotions, but successful people are those who learn to manage them. They overcome a natural tendency to fail by motivating themselves to do something unnatural—to succeed!

If you understand how motivation works in yourself, you can go a long way toward understanding others. When you can determine what motivates someone else, you will be a better manager because you can inspire your employees to set and reach higher and higher goals. You will also be a better parent because you will be better equipped to help your children realize their potential, and if you understand what motivates a prospective buyer, you can sell him or her your ideas, your products, or your services.

A TRIBUTE TO A MASTER MOTIVATOR

A few years ago, I was quite surprised to see the "discovery" of Napoleon Hill by *Inc.* magazine. The article was titled "Napoleon Who?" and though its lack of knowledge about Hill's work was a little unsettling, it did conclude that *Law of Success* should be required reading for entrepreneurs.

What was really surprising to me was that the article labeled Hill's writings as "underground classics." To my way of thinking, that's backward. What could be more mainstream than the American Publisher's Association list of all-time best sellers? It puts *Think and Grow Rich* at the top among business books. Few writers can claim a following as diverse as that of Hill's. Inventor Thomas Edison, automobile magnate Henry Ford, and superstar Michael Jackson can be counted among his fans. F. W. Woolworth, whose ideas revolutionized retailing, said his chain was built on the principles of success that Hill expounded. He declared, "I presume it would be no exaggeration of fact if I said that the Woolworth Building might properly be called a monument to the soundness of these principles."

Michael Jackson's interest in Hill seems to stem from

the fact that one of his heroes is Thomas Edison, whom Hill knew well and wrote about at length. Jackson has a large collection of Edison memorabilia which he showed me recently when I had dinner at his home in California.

Although Jackson had called me and chatted on the telephone several times, this was our first meeting in person, and I was struck by his understanding of the common thread that links men and women who achieve great things in life. His public persona masks a tough, philosophical bent. I would guess that few, if any, of his millions of fans have the vaguest notion of his great interest in the sources of human motivation and achievement.

Jackson and I found that we have a lot of ideas in common, and I wasn't surprised that Napoleon Hill's work was what brought us together. Hill had a facility for communicating thoughts that virtually everyone can identify with.

Napoleon Hill's philosophy so closely coincided with my own that in 1937 I sent a copy to each of my sales representatives. *Bingo!* I hit the jackpot. Sales went through the roof.

More than twenty years later, I persuaded Hill to come out of retirement and resume lecturing and writing. He agreed on one condition: that I act as his general manager. I did so for ten years, and the Master Mind Alliance that Hill and I formed was one of the most rewarding experiences of my life.

He devoted his life to helping others realize their potential, and today the foundation that bears his name continues to spread his message. It has been my pleasure to serve as chairman of the foundation for many years and to see the results brought about by this philosophy.

The words you are about to read can positively change your life in ways that you cannot now imagine—if you are ready to receive them and act upon them.

—W. Clement Stone

SUCCEED
AND GROW RICH
THROUGH PERSUASION

CHAPTER ONE

POSITIVE MENTAL
ATTITUDE

The Power of Positive Persuasion will show you how to define and acquire the things you desire from life, with ample power to transform every adversity into a richer, more desirable opportunity. This power can help you find a better self, even when you think you have applied your very best talents. During your study of this book, I hope to stimulate and bring into focus all the greater powers that are within you. When the written word brings new understanding and direction, stop where you are and take notes so that you can review and develop the habit of applying this new power.

You will find that many of the great powers are already within you. They may need awakening and refining in order to develop your greatest potential. It is impossible for the author to know where or when each reader will discover the needed principle that will close his individual gap between success and mediocrity.

A positive mental attitude is basic to all achievement. Having set out on your self-study toward a more successful way of life, begin by considering your habits of thinking. Your mental attitude determines your reaction to whatever situation confronts you. You act favorably or unfavorably, constructively or destructively, positively or negatively. Our mental attitude defines our personality. Men and women of great achievement have learned the art of keeping their minds positive. They have learned

25

the art of keeping their minds directed to that which they
desire from life.

THE CHOICE IS YOURS

At some point in life most individuals are made
keenly, even painfully, aware that they must always be
making choices—choices that determine their destiny. It
is as though at birth they were given two sealed enve-
lopes, each of which contained orders by which their
lives were to be governed. One envelope would contain
a long list of the blessings the individual could enjoy if
he recognized the power of his own mind, took possession of it, made it positive, and directed it carefully to
ends of his own choice, without violating the rights of
others. The other envelope would contain an equally
long list of the penalties the individual must pay if he
did not recognize this power and use it constructively.

Our mind is the only thing we can control. Either we
control it, or we relinquish control to other forces, and
our minds and our wills become as chips in a puddle of
water, being swept one way, then another and never
coming to any satisfactory conclusions, easily falling prey
to any negative wind that blows.

Without control the mind looses its powerful effectiveness and is as a withered arm. With control, exercise,
and direction, the mind gains power.

Any situation that confronts man must be dealt with.
There is no such thing as not reacting to a situation. The
situation is a fact. Whether the situation is positive or
negative depends on your reaction. The wise individual
reacts in a consciously thoughtful manner, beneficial to
his particular situation. He makes the choice of reacting
thoughtfully, with purpose and in the manner most suited
to his best interests. This is mastery of a situation. The
positive thinker is aware of this choice. The positive
thinker is the realist.

Achievement is a result of controlling the mind. Practice insures control at all times. Even when the situation
seems disastrous, there is the possibility of a positive
attitude.

This is best exemplified in the story of a strong and healthy farmer who was stricken with double paralysis. Discouraged and apparently helpless, he faced the reality that his days of farming were over forever. He remembered having read a book in which the author stated, "Every adversity carries with it the seed of an equivalent or greater benefit." He searched for that seed and he found it.

Calling his family together, he announced that he wanted every acre of his farm planted in corn. He wanted the corn fed to hogs, and he wanted the young pigs made into little sausages. Milo Jones became a millionaire from the products of the same small farm that had once afforded only a modest living. Today, Jones Farm Sausages are a favorite all over America and the company Jones founded employs thousands of people.

Brownie Wise was a discouraged widow without a job or money to support her invalid child, when she came across a copy of *Think and Grow Rich*. Fascinated by what she read, she began moving toward a better life. She organized Tupperware home parties and began to train women to sell Tupperware kitchen utensils. In a single year her sales climbed to more that $30 million, and Tupperware's headquarters near Orlando, Florida, have become a showplace.

There are countless examples of individuals who have found the "seed of an equivalent benefit" in that form of adversity which enslaves other men and women for life in a negative mental attitude. Adversity will come at some time to every man and woman. How you meet it, what you make of it and what you allow it to take from you or give to you are determined by your mental habits. All experiences will do something FOR you—or something TO you.

MOVE TOWARD YOUR GOAL

A positive mental attitude is something you cannot acquire in any manner whatsoever except by building it, step by step, through your own conscious decision. The very first building block out of which you may shape a positive mental attitude is the habit of moving with definiteness and purpose toward your goal.

If you do not yet know what you desire from life, if it is still a hazy, changeable, unnamed goal, you should define it. Without a purpose, without adequate plans for the fulfillment of whatever goal you may have, your mind is left wide open to negative, lazy mental attitudes. Successful men and women are those who set a positive goal, plan the means by which they expect to achieve that goal, and set out a timetable for the achievement of their goal. Right now, while it is fresh in your mind, write down a clear outline of everything you desire within a definite length of time, perhaps for the next five years.

Write down the amount of income you desire and an equally clear statement of what you intend to give to earn this income, since there is no such reality as something for nothing. The statement should name the amount you intend to acquire each week, each month, and each year.

Write a complete description of the sort of home you desire to live in and, if possible, an architect's plan of the building. Post it where you can see it daily. Note the approximate amount of money you intend to put into the home.

Write a description of the automobile or automobiles you desire to drive. Clip a picture of the car you desire, and keep it on your desk.

If you are not married, write a description of the person you desire as your mate. Include a detailed outline of every trait of character, every habit, and every physical quality you wish your mate to possess. Then list the traits of character and other qualifications you have or intend to acquire to entitle you to the sort of mate you have described. Remember, the sacred partnership of marriage is a two-way street and both parties are entitled to an equal share of the road.

Make a list of how you intend to use the twenty-four hours of time you have at your disposal each day. You have approximately three periods of eight hours each— one period is devoted to sleep, one to your business, profession, or calling, and the third, a period of "free time," can be used as you please.

Write out a description of your occupation, business, or professional calling. Then select the most successful person you know in a related field and similar position, and make up your mind to become as successful as he—or more—within a given length of time.

Set aside one hour of your eight hours of "free time" each day, and devote it entirely to reading that will inspire you to keep your mind positive. Your reading material should be related to your occupation or in some way help you with your career.

Last, but perhaps most important, express a prayer of gratitude at least twice daily, just before retiring at night and just after rising in the morning, for the blessings you now possess as well as for the things you expect to attain in the future. As you pray, picture in your mind all your goals and desires, and pray that when you attain them you will remember to be as fervent in gratitude.

FORM A COOPERATIVE ALLIANCE

The second building block for a positive mental attitude is the establishment of a harmonious cooperative alliance with other people: "Inasmuch as lieth in you . . . live peacefully with one another."

You and you alone are the proper person to determine what you desire from life, but the choice you make may be of such magnitude that you will need the help of others in acquiring it. The more successful people are those who have discovered how to attract other people to work with them, so that they benefit by other persons' education, experience, influence and, sometimes, their financial aid.

Thomas A. Edison, for example, had only three months of formal schooling, but he chose a profession that required him to make use of many of the sciences, such as chemistry, electronics, physics, mathematics, and engineering. He solved this problem by surrounding himself with people who had the education and training he lacked.

Henry Ford ushered in the great automobile age by associating himself in friendly business alliances with men who could supply him with what he needed for the manufacture of automobiles. He found men like the Dodge brothers, who had great ability in mechanics, and James Couzens, who had money of his own, and he acquired additional funds from others for use in the business.

Remember this when you form your cooperative alliance: No one ever does anything without a motive. Make sure that each member of your alliance receives some form of compensation equivalent to the amount of service he renders you. If you fail in this, you will have defections from your group, and some of these may turn up later as competitors.

Andrew Carnegie paid one of his mastermind allies, Charles M. Schwab, a salary of $75,000 a year, a phenomenal salary at the time. On some occasions, Carnegie paid as much as $1 million at the end of the year as a bonus for service that Schwab had rendered. When asked if it was necessary for him to give Schwab such a large sum when it had not been promised, Carnegie replied, "No, it was not necessary, but it seemed better than running the risk of his leaving my service and becoming my competitor."

When pressed for a further explanation, Carnegie replied, "I pay him $75,000 a year for what he does personally, and a much larger sum as a bonus for what he induces others to do by inspiring them to work with a positive mental attitude."

This gives you an idea of the value Carnegie placed on men who exercised a positive mental attitude.

GO THE EXTRA MILE

As building block number three in the creating of a positive mental attitude, cultivate the habit of doing more than you are paid, or expected, to do. Form the habit of going the extra mile, giving service that is not expected, for this attracts friends, clients, and supporters in many ways.

There is much to be said for the old cliché "Service

with a smile." If your attitude outwardly and inwardly is positive, and you go the extra mile, give extra service over and above that prescribed by your job description, then you are well on your way to worthwhile relationships that can be not only pleasant but often splendidly rewarding in speeding you toward the achievement of your highest goals.

The habit of giving more and better service than you are paid for brings rewards in many forms. It will attract the favorable attention of the right people—who will provide you with opportunities for self-advancement. Very often the returns will come from an entirely unexpected source—not from the person you initially helped. The law of increasing returns will go to work for you: the extra seeds of service you sow will come back to you, greatly multiplied in one form or another.

You need not ask permission to do more than is expected—either in manner or in deed. If you work for wages, the habit of doing more than required gives you a perfect right to expect pay increases and promotions; nothing else gives you that right. If you are rendering only enough service to justify the pay you receive, then you have a very poor case if you ask for or expect a raise. If you render less service than is required, then by the law of diminishing returns, the market for your particular services will eventually dwindle away. Remember this: The quality of the service you give—plus the quantity of the service and the mental attitude in which you give it—determine the pay you will receive.

Remember this also: If your mental attitude is negative, if you complain and find fault with others, it will offset whatever you do, even if you do more than you are paid to do. No one wants to be associated with a person whose mind is habitually negative. No one enjoys buying anything from the salesman who is a sour individual. No one wants to live with a mate whose mind is negative and whose words and deeds are sharp-edged and vitriolic.

There is power in the hands of people who do a job consistently well, with a pleasant attitude toward those around them, and who remember always to give just a little more than is expected of them.

ENTHUSIASM!

Block number four is concentrating on the habit of putting enthusiasm into your words and deeds.

"Nothing great," said Emerson, "was ever created without enthusiasm."

Enthusiasm is a magnetic force that attracts those who come under its influence. It is the keystone to the arch in the sales technique of the Master Salesperson.

We become enthusiastic by injecting strong emotional feeling into our words and deeds and by thinking always in enthusiastic terms and acting in the same manner.

Luther Burbank was so conscious of the power of enthusiasm that he claimed to have used it effectively in talking to the flowers and shrubs with which he worked as a horticulturist. He said he could pick out any plant, talk to it in enthusiastic praise of its beauty, and the plant would actually grow faster, outshining its relatives in the same soil. This would have seemed incredible if such a statement had come from any man other than Burbank.

Salesmen seldom sell anything without applying enthusiasm at some point in the transaction.

BELIEVE IN YOURSELF

An enduring capacity for faith is the fifth building block. That brief quotation, "Whatever the mind of man can conceive and believe, it can achieve," is no mere assemblage of words. The revelations of science, particularly in recent years, lead to the inevitable conclusion that man's only limitation is that which he sets up in his own mind, or what he accepts in the circumstances he meets from day to day. Thus, faith in a personal God is essential to achievement.

Man has invented telescopes so powerful that we can now look into space, seeing objects which are millions of light years removed from our earth; we can analyze the size and contents of the sun, and have developed the means to conquer outer space. Man has proved that there are no limits to the power of the mind—only temporary obstacles which he can remove at will.

The first and perhaps the most important step to take in using the vast powers of the mind is to discover the power of self-suggestion that can harness the mind and believe whatever the individual desires it to.

This power is sometimes called auto-suggestion; but regardless of the name by which it is known, it is an irresistible force that enables man to cut through the lines of resistance and perform things that might at first seem impossible.

How does one translate fear, doubt, and hopelessness into the power of belief?

The procedure is simple. You work by continuous repetition of a positive idea, plan, or purpose, until it is accepted by the subconscious mind. There, by some imponderable means, it makes contact with the power that translates belief into its physical counterpart.

The power of self-suggestion can render the word "impossible" so impotent that eventually it will become obsolete in your vocabulary.

One of the oldest books, the Bible, is rich in promises that every man has the power to move from where he is to wherever he desires to be. But generation after generation, men and women have read these promises and said to themselves, "This is not for me." Yet, a few people in every generation have said, "This is definitely for me." They have grasped the true nature of their own minds and pushed ahead until they have lifted man to his present state of civilization.

Science has isolated, analyzed, and harnessed almost every power available to man except the power of faith. Despite this fact, enough has been learned about this profound power so that everyone who wishes to can harness it and direct it to ends of his or her own choice.

These five principles can provide you with powers achievement that work as if they were magic. In a series of lectures delivered at the Harvard School of Business, one of the students asked Dr. Hill if this power might be dangerous in the hands of an unscrupulous person.

His reply was this: "Ability in any form which is not counterbalanced by honesty of purpose and sound character may become a tool for evil instead of good. But this is no argument against the use of the power of the mind, since every good is capable of being converted into evil. For example, nuclear energy is a benefit when it is understood and applied constructively, but it can also destroy life on an awesome scale."

Additional factors which may be used for the development and maintenance of a positive mental attitude are the following.

CONTROL AND DIRECTION OF THE EMOTIONS

Your emotions must be under control before you can be sure of maintaining a positive mental attitude. Without this control, you are like a person on a runaway horse who cannot grasp the reins.

Control over your emotions must include both the negative and the positive emotions described below:

The Seven Positive Emotions	*The Seven Negative Emotions*
1. Love	1. Fear (there are six basic fears)
2. Sex	2. Jealousy
3. Hope	3. Hatred
4. Faith	4. Revenge
5. Enthusiasm	5. Greed
6. Loyalty	6. Anger
7. Desire	7. Superstition

Emotions are your action-producing forces. They can lift you to the highest plane of achievement in your chosen calling, or lower you to the depths of failure, depending upon the extent of your control over them.

If you believe that only your negative emotions need control, dismiss this idea immediately. Your positive emotions can also lead you into excesses that destroy the power of a positive mental attitude. The emotions of love and sex require careful guidance, because they are the most powerful of all the emotions, and are the ones which get out of control most often.

CONTROL OF YOUR DOMINATING THOUGHT HABITS

Form the habit of keeping your mind occupied with what you desire, and keeping it off that which you do not desire. Your thoughts tend to manufacture the circumstances that occupy your mind most often. Think about prosperity, plan to attain it, believe you will achieve it, and your thoughts will lead you in the direction of opulence.

LEARN TO TRANSMUTE ADVERSITY INTO A BENEFIT

Every adversity, every unpleasant experience, every failure, carries with it the seed of an equivalent or greater benefit. Search for this seed when you meet with any form of defeat. Examine every adversity carefully. You will discover that it has a potential benefit for you far in excess of that which you lost through the experience. Explore this benefit, make the most of it, and you will discover one of the most profound of all the success principles. You will have learned how to convert stumbling blocks into stepping stones.

LEARN THE ART OF TRANSMUTATION OF
THE SEX EMOTION

The word *transmute* means, quite simply, to change one element or form of energy into another. In this philosophy, the art of sex transmutation means using your sex appeal for purposes more noble than the purely physical.

The sex drive is one of the most powerful of human emotions. When driven by it, people develop courage, imagination, willpower, persistence, and creativity that is unknown to them at other times. So strong is the desire for sexual contact that people at times risk their lives and reputations to indulge in it. When harnessed and redirected along other lines, this motivating force can employ the creativity and energy it generates to achieve any goal you set for yourself. It can fill the mind with lofty ideals and plans, and provide the means of carrying them to a successful conclusion.

The transmutation of sex energy requires willpower, to be sure, but the reward is certainly worth the effort. This is not to suggest that the inborn desire for sexual expression should be repressed or eliminated. But it should be given an outlet through forms of expression that enrich the body, mind, and spirit. If it is not given this form of outlet through transmutation, it will seek outlets that are purely physical.

Proper expression of the sex drive can create a passion for life that permeates the entire being. It gives one more energy, more enthusiasm, and a zest for life that is unparalleled. Without it, life can be routine, bland, and boring.

FOLLOW THE HABIT OF PRAYER

Prayer, if properly understood, can become the greatest of all the factors which help you develop and keep a positive mental attitude. It can give you peace of mind where everything else may fail. It can reveal to you the means that can draw upon the powers of the universe and use them for the attainment of your desires.

Do not wait until you are in need before going to prayer, but condition your mind through prayers of gratitude for the blessings you now have, so that when you do need guidance, you will have earned the right to request it.

And close your prayer with these words: "I ask not for more blessings, but for more wisdom to make better use of the blessings I now possess through my unchallengeable right to direct my mind to whatever ends I desire."

People who go to prayer only when emergency overtakes them, or when they are sorely in need, usually go with the haunted feeling that their prayers will not be answered.

When you make up your list of blessings for which you intend to express gratitude, do not forget these:

1. Your privilege of freedom of speech and action in a country that is rich in every form of blessing that your mind can conceive.
2. Your inalienable right to the full and complete control and direction of your own mind to whatever ends you desire.
3. The loyalty of your friends and loved ones, whose influence inspires you to seek the respect of yourself and all mankind.
4. Your power to transmute adversity, opposition, and defeat into a creative force that can help you in your search for peace of mind, and whatever else you are seeking from life.
5. Your privilege of forgiving those who may offend or injure you.
6. Your power to control all your emotions and transmute them into a motivating force that can aid you in the realization of your aims and purposes.
7. Very special mention of those who might have come to your aid in emergencies, when you had exhausted your own resourcefulness to solve your problems.
8. The soundness of your physical body, the resourcefulness of your imagination.

These are some of the blessings for which you should offer gratitude. Add to the list any others you may choose.

"Gratitude" is a powerful and profound word. It represents a feeling very closely associated with a positive mental attitude. Therefore, cultivate it as a permanent foundation stone of your habits of prayer.

You now have a description of the most important factors with which to develop and maintain a positive mental attitude, without which the Power of Persuasion cannot be mastered:

1. Define your goals and move toward them.
2. Establish a cooperative alliance with other people.
3. Learn to "go the extra mile."
4. Put enthusiasm into your words and deeds.
5. Develop your capacity for faith.
6. Control and direct your emotions.
7. Control your dominating thought habits.
8. Learn to transmute adversity into a benefit.
9. Transmute sex emotion.
10. Follow the habit of prayer.

Before beginning Chapter Two, give yourself a rating test on these factors by writing "OK" after those on which you rate satisfactorily, and "X" after those on which you are in doubt, or know yourself to be deficient.

You can follow this plan more effectively if you copy the factors on a separate sheet of paper and mark off twelve columns at the right of the sheet, heading them "First Week," "Second Week," and so on to the twelfth column. Then give yourself a careful analysis and a grading once each week for three months. Make up your mind before you begin that in the twelfth column there will be no "X's"—nothing but "OK's."

If you have weaknesses which interfere with your positive mental attitude, this procedure will help you to discover them. You will make discoveries about yourself that can change your life and lead you to whatever goals you may set for attainment.

HOW OTHERS HAVE SUCCEEDED

In the chapters which follow, you will be provided with the success formulas that others have used to lift themselves to great heights of personal achievement.

You will be introduced to methods by which successful men and women have learned to make contact with and to use invisible sources of power, performing seemingly miraculous tasks.

A man whom Dr. Hill observed on many occasions and counted as a friend accomplished great things in perpetuating the cause of the American free-enterprise system. His message was always positive and enthusiastic. He understood and used the power of persuasion to rekindle love of country and the brotherhood of man.

The late Dr. Kenneth McFarland, who has been called the nation's most eloquent and effective exponent of what is commonly called the American system, through his avid interest in America and its way of life, built a remarkably successful career in public speaking.

To his concept of basic Americanism he has given the label "progressive conservatism." He was ambitious, he said, to conserve constitutional government, to conserve free competitive enterprise, and to conserve individual freedom under both.

Dr. McFarland declared that America is the land that "literally dumps the horn of plenty on the common man." But the system is not foolproof. It is not self-operating. It must be intelligently applied by people who understand and have faith in it. Dr. McFarland described the kind of people who are qualified to run the free-enterprise vehicle, and showed how these qualifications make an individual successful under the system.

Dr. McFarland was a guest lecturer for several of the nation's largest corporations and trade associations, and at one time served in the same capacity for *Reader's Digest.*

His phenomenal success in "selling America to Americans" caused the National Sales and Marketing Executives in 1957 to designate him for its annual award of Outstanding Salesman of America.

Dr. McFarland earned his bachelor's degree from Pittsburg State Teachers College in Kansas, his master's degree at Columbia University in New York, and his doctorate was earned at Stanford University, Palo Alto, California.

Dr. McFarland was an educator for twenty-four years and, in addition to his public speaking tours, was guest lecturer for General Motors Corporation and Educational Director for American Trucking Associations, Inc.

In early 1968 Dr. McFarland was chosen to receive the Freedom Leadership Medal of the Freedoms Foundation at Valley Forge, which cited Dr. McFarland "for his multitude of inspired patriotic speeches urging his audiences to be preservatives of the American way of life, and for his exemplary, unswerving faith in the values and virtues embodied in our precious American credo with freedom of choice and liberty under law . . . for his countless tiring travels crisscrossing the United States with the message that the responsibilities and the opportunities of constructive citizenship must be taught to our youth."

Dr. McFarland was widely heralded as an authority on the vital subject of law enforcement. His writings, studies, achievements, and speeches in his crucially important field won the acclaim of lawmen and laymen alike. He was an honorary member of the Fraternal Order of police.

Dr. McFarland was a 1968 Gold Plate winner of the American Academy of Achievement's Salute to Excellence.

Dr. McFarland exemplified and personified the kind of power that can be generated in the life of a man who lives by the principles of positive thinking, enthusiasm, patriotism, and self-discipline.

This chapter is only your introduction to the methods by which you, too, may tune in and draw upon powers you may have never utilized, and by which you may become whatever you desire. As you continue to study, you should discover principles that will assist you in mastering the Power of Persuasion.

Chapter Two

THE POWER OF
DIVINITY IN MAN

Every man possesses an element of genius. When realized and disciplined, it can enable him to accomplish worthwhile deeds and to achieve greater heights of service to mankind. When the great stores of untapped energy and ambition in every personality are unlocked and given expression and action, they can provide a tremendous force for success. When guided by a love of mankind and incorporated into character, the seeds of goodness and divinity within man empower him to live a life of value and significance.

Through the years, we have learned many of the secrets that reveal the divinity of man, unlock his energies, awaken his genius, and start the powers of persuasion which can actually turn negative into positive. In this book, many of the secrets that light the pathway of ambition and achievement will be revealed to all persons who desire a meaningful and useful life and are ready to accept guidance. You will see the Power of Positive Persuasion demonstrated in the life of a man who has obtained great financial wealth, but even greater spiritual understanding. The recognition and application of all the great powers discussed in this book are essential for financial success. They are equally important to those who have earned great fortunes and wish to share wisely with others. Philanthropy is an important responsibility, particularly when a person is capable of making funds or grants

41

available. There is always the possibility that a gift to an individual or an institution can be detrimental, making people dependent upon something for nothing, robbing them of the opportunity to develop their own best potential.

The powers described in this book should assist you in finding the pathway to happiness, developing a greater love of country and compassion for your fellow man, and rekindling the desire to perpetuate the American free-enterprise system. With these thoughts in mind, we want to introduce you to a man we know very personally, a man whose business ability we have witnessed on many occasions. He is an excellent example of someone who understands his responsibility to help mankind and has shared his life experience, financial means, and skill with the greatest number of people.

Many of the facts in this chapter were compiled by Napoleon Hill during a ten-year association with this man. Other material has been observed by the author and editor on various occasions, both privately and publicly. Various members of this man's staff supplied us with additional information. Regardless of the source of our information, we believe that the W. Clement Stone story is the best living example of the power of divinity in man—how it can work for the individual and benefit mankind.

ONE MAN'S ACHIEVEMENT

Early in life W. Clement Stone had a vision of who he was and what he wanted from life. He calls himself a salesman, and a salesman he is. For many years, Mr. Stone was president of Combined Insurance Company of America and its three wholly owned subsidiaries: Combined American Insurance Company, Dallas; Hearthstone Insurance Company of Massachusetts, Boston; and First National Casualty Company, Fond du Lac, Wisconsin. He is also a director of the Alberto-Culver Company. A few years ago, Mr. Stone merged Combined with Ryan Insurance to form the giant Aon Corporation, of which he is chairman. Mr. Stone is a Master Salesman;

but more than this, he is a man dedicated to the ideal of sharing. He delights in the sharing of spiritual and material wealth. He is not only a business executive but also a civic leader, a writer and editor, a publisher, and a lecturer.

A native Chicagoan, Stone and his wife live in suburban Winettka, Illinois. Mr. Stone's principle philanthropic concerns are in the fields of mental health and youth welfare. Much of his money and energy has been invested in the rehabilitation of delinquent youth and inmates of penitentiaries. Stone helps train social workers for youth work. Deeply religious, he was for two terms a trustee of the First Presbyterian Church of Evanston (the maximum consecutive period which the by-laws of the church permit for trustees). Mr. Stone holds the honorary degree of Doctor of Jurisprudence from Monmouth College and Doctor of Humanities from Interlochen Arts Academy.

Surely, you will agree this is an impressive degree of achievement. You will note that we did not discuss projects completed and future plans, for his current activities are more than ample to express our point. We do know that all of his philanthropic work is very thoroughly researched through the W. Clement and Jessie V. Stone Foundation.

We have found Mr. Stone to be a very warm, personable, and compassionate individual, who enjoys life to its fullest. His laugh is unique, infectious, and sincere to the last chuckle. True, this man has earned a lot of money, but his ability to earn the money has given him the wisdom and the power to use it properly for the benefit of the greatest number of people.

FIRST STEPS UP THE LADDER

Let's take a look into his early life to see if he inherited a great sum of money which helped him to build his huge empire. We want to study his inner thoughts to see if he depended on the "big break" or "lady luck." Did he believe that the world owed him a living, and that someday he would be the recipient of "something for nothing"? You will see first-hand how Mr. Stone climbed the ladder of success. His example may ignite the element of genius within you with power sufficient to achieve your goal and to attain overflowing abundance. His story can help you understand the necessity of helping others in proportion to the success you achieve. Certainly, this understanding will bring the joy of living a life of meaning, purpose, and significance.

Mr. Stone's father died when he was still young.

It was not an easy life for the young boy and his widowed mother. She became a seamstress, he a newsboy fighting for survival on street corners.

Bullied by older news vendors, the six-year-old newsboy tried selling his papers in Hoelle's, a South Side Chicago restaurant. Thrown out several times, he kept coming back. The restaurant owner so admired his persistence that he finally allowed the boy to make Hoelle's a regular stop.

Young Stone discovered he could sell papers in hospitals with even less effort than on street corners. He had realized it was more efficient and productive to sell to a large group of prospects concentrated in a single area.

Many years later he was to apply the same principle to selling insurance—"cold canvassing" in stores, offices, banks, and other large institutions. Notice that he used what he had learned.

He also had discovered something more important— the technique of extracting the principles of a given situation or problem and "relating and assimilating" them through "study time, thinking time, planning time" so that they would serve to meet other situations and problems.

Looking back, Mr. Stone says, "I believe that the basic principles of success were contained in my sales experience as a newsboy."

According to Mr. Stone, these principles are: (1) inspiration to action—self-motivation; (2) know-how; (3) activity knowledge.

Anyone who knows him in the slightest will agree that he applies these principles in all endeavors.

As Mr. Stone analyzes it in his books, the newsboy could not afford to lose the pennies invested in his newspapers; need inspired him to action. This is what he calls "inspirational dissatisfaction."

Finally, he had activity knowledge and know-how—selling his newspapers by repeating his previously learned successful techniques.

"The memory of those dim days is still with me," Stone writes in *The Success System that Never Fails*, "for it's the first time I can recall turning a disadvantage into an advantage. It's a simple story, unimportant now . . . and yet it was a beginning."

He believes, as do the authors, that every adversity contains within it the seed of an equivalent or greater benefit—and that all things are possible to those who cultivate a positive mental attitude or, as he calls it, PMA.

ACTION COMES FIRST!

Of the three parts of his success formula, he thinks inspiration to action is the most important. He also believes that this inspiration can be self-induced.

Stone has distributed millions of inspirational books, magazines, and records to young people, employees, company shareholders, schools, hospitals, veterans' organizations, and inmates of correctional institutions.

For example, in a single year, he personally donated more than one million books, records, magazines, and inspiration pamphlets.

His associates have observed, during their extensive travels for lectures, sales seminars, or humanitarian business for the Napoleon Hill Foundation, many outstanding and worthwhile reports of his labors. They have observed careful planning and organized effort which encourage other philanthropists to take a greater interest in our total society. Most important of all, none of his projects are designed for personal gain or commercial purposes.

You have heard the saying "stub your toe" as an expression for mistakes made. When asked to name some of his, he replied, "I soon ran out of toes, and just stumped my foot. With each mistake or setback, I organized my thinking and started doing something about the condition before it became a part of me. I am confident that temporary defeat is the reason I place so much importance on plans with action. When something goes wrong, sometimes it is necessary to review your plans. After this is done, your plan must have immediate action. May I humbly say that I believe the habit of 'do it now' is one of my greatest assets. This habit is so much a part of my life that I believe I exercise it today as efficiently as I did in the early days of a growing business. I am not referring to harebrained decisions. You must take time to gather all the facts; after this, there is no reason for procrastination. I still get a real thrill from the power of action. For action is a vital part of the power of persuasion for all human relations."

The history of his schooling relates how early success brought about a condition that would have greatly curtailed the development of his full talent. You will note that he recognized his error, changed his thinking, and put his findings into action.

Mr. Stone attended Senn High School in Chicago, where he was president of the Debating Club. Moving to Detroit, where his mother had bought a small insurance agency, he attended Northwestern High School during his junior year.

On summer vacation, at age sixteen, Mr. Stone sold his first insurance policy. The following school year, he left high school when he reasoned that he could make more money selling insurance than his teacher did teaching.

There are many great men of history who temporarily stopped their schooling, and then recognized the necessity of education.

"It was only a temporary interruption in my schooling," he says. "I soon realized the priceless value of education."

As a young insurance man, he continued his studies at YMCA schools, also attending Detroit College of Law for one year and Northwestern University for two and a half years.

As a teen-aged salesman, he had to work long hours, often late into the night with little time to call his own. Yet, as a young man, his heart turned to romance.

When he was twenty-one, Stone married his high-school sweetheart, Jessie Tarson. To make his marriage plans possible, he had formed his own insurance agency in Chicago at the age of twenty. The firm, Combined Registry Company, is still headed by Stone and has branched out into other fields.

Mr. Stone says, "Love is the greatest motivator of all."

He went into business for himself with a capital of $100, no debts, and desk space rented at $25 a month.

Mr. Stone in his career amassed a fortune of millions of dollars, much of which he gave away to worthy causes.

As his business prospered during the 1920's, he built a nation-wide sales force.

By 1931 the country was feeling the effects of the Great Depression—and so was he. Insurance sales were off and he was in debt.

Stone soon overcame this obstacle—he arranged to represent three additional insurance companies, urged his salesmen to sell a new, higher-premium policy, and developed an effective sales training program.

His sales force of 135 well-trained men was expanded to 1,000 salesmen, thoroughly indoctrinated in successful sales techniques. Volume increased and soon he was out of debt.

By 1939 he had perfected his "success system that never fails" and also had acquired what he calls a "living philosophy."

By 1956 Mr. Stone headed the largest accident and health insurance company of its kind in the United States.

Combined Insurance has shown consistent growth since then, and its entry into the life insurance field illustrates another of his principles: that every organism grows to maturity, levels off, and dies—unless there is rebirth through new life, new blood, new ideas, or new activity.

Every man has a philosophy. When asked to define his, this was his answer.

"First, God is always a good God.

"Second, truth will always be truth, regardless of lack of understanding, disbelief, or ignorance.

"Third, man is the product of his heredity, environment, physical body, conscious and subconscious mind, experience, and particular position and direction in time and space—and something more, including powers known and unknown. He has the power to affect, use, control, or harmonize with all of them.

"Fourth, man was created in the image of God, and he has the God-given ability to direct his thoughts, control his emotions, and ordain his destiny.

"Fifth, religious faith is a dynamic, living, growing experience. Its universal principles are simple and enduring. For example, the Golden Rule—do unto others as you would have others do unto you—is simple in its concepts and enduring and universal in its application. But it must be applied to become alive.

"Sixth, I believe in prayer and the miraculous power of prayer."

SHARING SUCCESS

For ten years Mr. Stone served as Napoleon Hill's business manager, an association that was valued by both men and obvious to all who knew them. What Mr. Stone felt about their association reveals much about himself. He said:

"*Think and Grow Rich* by Napoleon Hill was given to me in 1937. Its philosophy coincided with my own in so many respects that I sent *Think and Grow Rich* to all my representatives. Then wonderful things began to happen. My salesmen began to become super salesmen, they began to acquire wealth, they brought happiness into their homes, and they began to try to make their world a better place in which to live. This is understandable. For *Think and Grow Rich* has motivated more men and women to success than any book of its kind.

"In 1952, I met Napoleon Hill for the first time. I

encouraged him to come out of retirement for a period of five years. He agreed on one condition: that I become his general manager. I agreed. Although I was very busy building up my insurance enterprises, I realized that it is very seldom in the course of a lifetime that one man can affect the lives of the masses of the people of his generation and the multitudes of future generations for the better.

"For it's no longer true that if you build the best mousetrap, a path will be beaten to your door. Regardless of how good your service or product may be . . . it has to be sold. I am a salesman by vocation; therefore I felt that I could help spread the philosophy of American achievement as taught in Napoleon Hill's writings and thus render a real service to mankind. Now it always happens that *when you share with others a part of what you have, that which remains multiplies and grows*.

"In my effort to help others through my association with Napoleon Hill, I was blessed ten thousandfold . . . more than anyone might expect or deserve.

"It took us ten years to do the job we set out to do. During this period, my whole life was changed: my organizations prospered beyond the imagination of those who have not learned the art of motivation and the power of a positive mental attitude. I entered the fields of lecturing, writing, and teaching from a great philosopher and teacher—Napoleon Hill. But more important, I applied his principles.

Mr. Stone applied the principles of success with a fervor unmatched by few, if any, other persons. He also taught the principles to millions through his best-selling books, *Success Through a Positive Mental Attitude*, *The Success System That Never Fails*, and *The Other Side of the Mind*, through lectures to countless thousands, and through his tireless support of professional, civic, educational, philanthropic, and youth organizations.

He has been awarded nineteen honorary doctorates by leading colleges and universities and literally hundreds of organizations have bestowed special awards upon him. Mr. Stone has received humanitarian awards from Protestant, Catholic, and Jewish religious organizations alike,

as well as from American Red Cross. He has been nominated for the Nobel Peace Prize, he was awarded the
Navajo Nation's Medal of Honor, he is a recipient of
the Horatio Alger Award, and he is a member of the
council of trustees of the James S. Brady Presidential
Foundation.

Although the awards given to Mr. Stone and the organizations he has supported during a lifetime of helping
others number in the hundreds, the achievements of
which he is most proud are those resulting from his association with youth organizations and his work in America's prison system. Through those affiliations he touched
people who desperately needed positive encouragement,
people whose lives were forever changed for the better
because of his influence. He recalled:

"I saw poor students motivated to become good schol-
ars by applying the principles of success; I saw youngsters
in trouble with the law become fine decent citizens, and
I saw drug abusers turn their lives around.

"As a lecturer in prisons, I saw men and women motivated to change the course of their lives for the better.
Recidivism among those who have been motivated to
read inspirational self-help action books has been reduced to sixteen percent, while the records for the general prison population indicate that for every hundred
who are incarcerated and released, forty-nine will
return.

"In my work with mental health organizations such as
the Menninger Foundation and the National Association
for Mental Health, I have learned of human lives saved
by eliminating suicides among those who have such tendencies, and these fine organizations have given hope to
the hopeless in our inner cities; the underprivileged have
been motivated to achieve success and to encourage law
and order within their communities. But most of all, individuals have learned how to avoid mental illness and
maintain good mental health, *to seek divine guidance,
and to do the right thing because it is right.*

"Now the greatest service that I can render you, the
reader, or any individual is to motivate *you* to learn and
apply the principles to be found in this book. Memorize

the principles—and *apply them.* For the author, Napoleon Hill, has the power to motivate you to help yourself achieve any definite objectives you may have as long as these do not violate the laws of God and the rights of your fellowmen."

Chapter Three

PERVADING FAITH

GET ACQUAINTED WITH YOURSELF

The most important person you know is the person you are. The secret to the success of your relationship with every individual is found within your innermost self.

Your self-knowledge—the degree of your comprehension of your own powers, physical, intellectual, and spiritual, and the discipline with which you employ these powers—is the key to a satisfying, useful, and profitable life.

Considering that most of us often seem to be two people (or sometimes more) within our own minds, it is not unusual that many of us, at many times, are confused about who or what—and to what extent—WE ARE. To find one's real self is a priceless accomplishment. Never to find individuality is a tragic oversight. To become acquainted with the finest, strongest, most powerful being within us is a challenge, but an exciting and a rewarding one. If you can find and follow the instincts of your best self, all things can be yours. Your finest self can help to conquer fear, worry, indecision. It can lead you to a better understanding of the profound power of life, and can provide you with the mastery you need to be successful in whatever field you desire. Your best self is your most powerful ally.

To get to know the person you really are, to grasp the

knowledge of the most basic part of your personality, takes thought and concentration.

Find a quiet place and begin with the thought that you are going to be as completely honest with yourself as you can. Sort out the various things of your life and evaluate your present position and circumstances. Remember that you must try to be perfectly honest with yourself. Do not offer excuses and do not blame others if you feel that all is not well. Be objective, try to decide what you want most of all from life, from your job, from today. Decide on specific, definite things. Set these as your immediate and long-range goals. Take as long as you need to be truly alone, to sort out your thoughts, to think through your evaluation of your wants and your ambitions and desires. Determine that, with the help of the best self within you, you will achieve that success, gain that goal you so desire. Solitude is a good source of strength, a good ground for meeting our best self.

But how, in the midst of the busy, noisy world can one hold to any good resolutions, any strong inclinations? This takes another element—a basic ingredient called faith.

FAITH THAT WILL WORK

Faith is a state of mind, a positive mental attitude. Your mental attitude is the only thing over which you have complete, unchallengeable privilege of control. The exercise of this privilege carries with it amazing benefits. Think of this until you are determined to put faith and a positive mental attitude to work. This can be the beginning of a new and better way of life for you.

Applied faith is the basis of all self-confidence, all self-reliance. It is the moving spirit of personal initiative and enthusiasm. Until a man learns the basic fundamentals of applied faith, his accomplishments are very few.

The term *applied* faith is used here instead of just "faith," because before your spirit of faith can affect anything, it must be actively, positively directed. Faith must be willingness to act.

Faith is a state of mind that has been called the mainspring of the soul, through which one's aims, desires, plans, and purposes may be translated into their physical or financial equivalent. This is applied faith. Faith is a means by which you can put yourself in a frame of mind to tune in, and draw directly upon, the power that operates the whole universe.

Sam Z. Moore, whose remarkable record of success in the "Bible business" has been almost as amazing to him as to his associates, is an example of a man who chose a field that seemed at first more like a gamble than a sound business venture. Having a natural ability in the financial field, Mr. Moore graduated from college to find several opportunities open to him. A large bank, General Electric, and Westinghouse a extended job offers to him.

Sam had worked his way through college selling books and Bibles. He had met and talked with many people, in many walks of life. He was a native of Lebanon, but he loved America. And the more he saw of America and its people, the more he loved it. He saw the opportunities this country offers, and he saw the ideals and the philosophies that have made it great. He believed that he knew what Americans, particularly those in rural America, would like an opportunity to buy. So he took the experience he had had as a salesman, plus $1,000 he had saved and $1,000 which he borrowed, and began his own business in December of 1958. Today Mr. Moore heads the world's largest family Bible publishing company. His company also sells inspirational books, dictionaries, testaments, and related worship items. In ten years Mr. Moore built his company into a multimillion-dollar business. Five years later he made a public offering and added several hundred stockholders.

Here is a man who carefully took stock of his abilities, his fellowman, and the situation as he saw it. Exhibiting faith in his God, his country, its people, and his own best self, he set forth with a definite plan in mind. His enthusiasm, his skillful evaluation of supply and demand, and his open and fair attitude brought him undreamed-of success.

FUNDAMENTALS OF FAITH

Let us take a closer look at the ingredients necessary to faith.

1. DEFINITENESS OF PURPOSE supported by personal initiative or action. You will find that this principle of definiteness of purpose interlocks with almost every one of the other nine principles. All success begins with something definite that you fully intend to do.

2. A POSITIVE MENTAL ATTITUDE from which all negatives such as fear, envy, hatred, jealousy, and greed are removed. You can't have faith if the prevailing attitude of your mind is negative, no matter what may have caused the negative attitude.

3. A MASTERMIND ALLIANCE with one or more people who will radiate courage based on faith and who are suited mentally and spiritually to your needs. In other words, select your closest associates with exceeding care.

4. RECOGNITION OF THE FACT THAT EVERY ADVERSITY CARRIES WITH IT THE SEED OF AN EQUIVALENT OR GREATER BENEFIT and that temporary defeat is not failure. There is no such thing as failure until you have accepted it as such. And temporary defeats often turn out to be blessings in disguise—a stepping stone to extended wisdom for greater achievement.

5. THE HABIT OF AFFIRMING YOUR MAJOR DEFINITENESS OF PURPOSE IN THE FORM OF A PRAYER at least once daily and thanking your Creator for having granted you the view of your goal, the object of your major purpose, even before you start to attain it.

If you begin with an open mind and start affirming your purpose in prayer right away, such a tremendous change will take place in your relationship with people—and in your ralationship with yourself, your attitude toward yourself—that you will wonder why you didn't do this a long time ago.

All sincere prayers work. If you feel you get no results, consider this: We often go to prayer as a last resort. We don't expect our prayers to be answered. That's why prayers seem to fail—we pray with a negative mental attitude. If we pray for rain, we should carry our umbrella. Faith will thus be activated.

All-out faith is knowing in your heart that the thing you are seeking is entirely possible and that you're going to have it. You will be amazed at what can happen when you have a positive mental attitude and maintain it.

6. RECOGNITION OF THE EXISTENCE OF A CREATOR OF ALL THINGS who gives order to the entire universe. This book's whole philosophy is based upon this premise. It is the very starting point for the development and achievement of all our principles.

We must have faith in our Creator! Any intelligent thinking person knows there has to be a plan and a power controlling this universe. We know that the stars and planets do not keep in their accustomed places day in and day out, year in and year out, without a plan. We know there is something behind it, and we recognize that it is a power that affects every living creature on the face of the earth.

7. KNOW THYSELF is the next premise upon which this philosophy is based. We must recognize that the individual is a minute expression of the Creator of all things and, as such, we have no limitations except those accepted in our own minds.

The only limitations one has are self-imposed—limitations that we permit the circumstances of life to set up in our own minds. These limitations can be removed!

The Creator has provided every individual with a complete, unchallenged, and unchallengeable control over our minds. The individual can make the contact negative or positive. We can extend our own mind in all directions as far as we choose. Nobody can determine that for us. Nobody can lock up your mind except yourself. As sure as the sun rises in the east and sets in the west, your mental attitude determines your earthly destiny!

We must recognize as human beings that we're the only creatures on earth who can appropriate the power of the mind and direct it to ends of our own choice. No animal can do that. Animals have what is called instinct, but they cannot go one iota beyond that.

Recognizing the fact that as human beings we can direct the power of our minds to ends of our own choice, can we not therefore conclude that success is absolutely assured us? We have only to apply this faith in the Creator of our minds toward the achievement of our definite objective.

Jesus of Nazareth, as recorded in verses 7 and 9 of the seventh chapter of St. Matthew, said, "Ask, and it shall be given you! Seek, and ye shall find; knock, and it shall be opened unto you; for everyone that asketh, receiveth; and he that seeketh, findeth; and to him that knocketh, it shall be opened."

In the Epistle of Paul to the Hebrews we are told, "But without faith it is impossible to please him! for he that cometh to God must believe that he is, and that he is a rewarder of them that diligently seek him."

8. CAREFUL INVENTORY OF ONE'S PAST DEFEATS AND ADVERSITIES, from which it will become obvious that all difficult experiences do carry the seed of an equivalent or greater benefit. Go back into your past and analyze the times you have been defeated. Chances are that if you've gotten away from defeat long enough for the wound to heal, you are able to find the seed of an equivalent or greater benefit. Look for that seed, and you will be sure to find it sooner or later.

9. SELF-RESPECT EXPRESSED THROUGH HARMONY WITH ONE'S OWN CONSCIENCE. Conscience is a wonderful thing. It is your judge advocate. It sits over all your thoughts and over all your acts. It is an impartial and a just judge. You must not disregard its guidance.

10. RECOGNITION OF THE IMPORTANCE OF YOUR INDUSTRY to mankind is necessary in order for your occupation to become a labor of love.

SOME THINGS FAITH CAN DO

Faith is a prerequisite to positive power; it gives self-understanding, through the eyes of the honestly "ready" heart; it gives perspective, accurate analysis, and the ability to forge ahead.

For the individual seeking to develop a powerful, persuasive personality, there is no substitute for honest self-evaluation and faith.

Every man must have faith to achieve. A man without faith is a man without hope. Faith begins when there is born within the heart a strong conviction that there is Someone, Something, that is certain and can be trusted. This something must be personal in every way.

There is tremendous power in faith. Faith can get you where God intended you to be. Where you belong is as individual a place as you are an individual person. There is a special place, a special job for each of us. Yours is not your neighbor's, nor his yours.

Therefore, believing in God, you begin to believe in yourself. Faith is essentially thought; thus, every call to have faith is a call to trust in the power of your own thought about the Creator. The scriptures say, "According to your faith be it unto you." The law of man's individuality is, therefore, the law of liberty, and equally it is the gospel of peace; for when we truly understand the law of our own individual worth, we see that the same law finds its expression in everyone else; consequently, we shall revere the law in others, exactly in proportion as we value it in ourselves.

Then believing in God, believing in ourselves, we begin to believe in our fellowman. Then harmony may begin.

Chapter Four

THE PERSUASIVE
PERSONALITY

Having found the patterns which define the image of our own self, and having believed, through faith, that who we are and what we are is a valuable asset to be cultivated, stimulated, and enjoyed, then we begin to think about how we affect the individuals around us.

We all have what is called our own individual personality. We are endowed at birth with certain physical characteristics, and are exposed in life to a number of influences. Our personality evolves through our characteristic behavior and through education and projection. Our personality is how the world "sees" us through our behavior. The world observes our facial expressions, our alertness, our clothing, our manners, and our reactions to those about us. The world judges our personality by what is seen of us and heard of us. Do we smile while speaking, use tact in our conversation, and do we express sincerity, fairness, thoughtfulness, tolerance, patience? All these are expressions of our personality.

Personality is the sum total of a person's mental, spiritual, and physical traits and habits that distinguish him from all others. It is the factor which more than all others determines whether one is liked or disliked by others.

START WITH A POSITIVE MENTAL ATTITUDE

Self-analysis must begin with strict self-discipline based upon the courage to recognize one's faults and a sincere desire to eliminate them. Inasmuch as a positive mental attitude heads the list of traits of a pleasing personality, and also heads the list of the Twelve Great Riches of Life, let us now examine the qualities which lead to the development of this very desirable quality. What you look for in others, you find eventually mirrored in your own character; therefore, the habit of looking for the good in others leads to the development of good in yourself. Everyone must recognize the fact that nothing he worries about is worth the cost of worry, and that there are two types of worries: (1) those which one may correct, and (2) those over which one has no control. By deliberately filling the mind with positive thoughts and refusing space in the mind to negative thoughts, the individual creates a positive consciousness that inspires him to think in positive terms on all subjects.

Consider the need for flexibility of mind. Flexibility means adapting oneself to quickly changing circumstances without losing the sense of composure. The person who maintains a positive mental attitude will have no difficulty in maintaining flexibility of personality, because a positive mind is always under control and may be directed at will to any desired purpose.

Sincerity of purpose is one trait of personality for which no satisfactory substitute has ever been found, because it is something that reaches deeper into a human being than most qualities of personality. Sincerity begins with oneself and is a trait of sound character which reflects itself so visibly that none can fail to observe it. Be sincere first of all with yourself; be sincere with those to whom you are related by family ties; be sincere with your friends and acquaintances; and, of course, be sincere with your country and, above all, with the giver of all gifts to mankind.

Successful men reach decisions quickly. Many of them become annoyed by those who do not act promptly. Prompt decision-making is a habit which one must form through self-discipline. The person with the vision to recognize opportunity and the promptness of decision necessary to embrace it will get ahead.

Courtesy is respect for other people's feelings under all circumstances; the habit of going out of one's way, if need be, to help any less fortunate person whenever and wherever possible; and last but not least, the habit of controlling selfishness, greed, envy, and hatred.

SPEAKING—AND KEEPING QUIET

The spoken word is the medium by which you express your personality most often. The tone of voice, therefore, should be so definitely under control that it can be colored and modified to make it convey any desired meaning in addition to the words used. Since your voice is the most direct expression of your innermost self, you should be very careful to do yourself full justice with it.

The habit of smiling, like many others, is directly related to the individual's mental attitude and is the perfect means of identifying the nature of this attitude.

Muscles that control the lines of the face produce one arrangement while smiling, whereas a frown produces an entirely different arrangement, but each conveys with unerring accuracy the feeling that is taking place within the mind. The smile, the tone of the voice, and the expression on the face constitute open windows through which everyone may see and feel what takes place in a person's mind.

Tact is doing and saying the right thing at the right time. People display lack of tact in many ways, but these are among the more common:

1. Gruff and irritable voice tones, revealing the speaker's negative mental attitude or displeasure.
2. The habit of speaking when silence would be more appropriate.
3. Interrupting the other's speech.
4. Overworking the personal pronoun "I."
5. Volunteering opinions which have not been re-

quested and for which no reason exists, especially opinions on subjects with which one is not familiar.
6. Presuming upon friendship or acquaintance in asking favors one has not earned the right to request.
7. Expressing one's dislikes too freely.

Tolerance displays an open mind on all subjects toward all people at all times. In addition to being one of the more important traits of a pleasing personality, an open mind on all subjects is one of the Twelve Great Riches of Life.

Consider frankness in manner and speech. Men of sound character always have the courage to deal directly and openly with others, and they follow this habit even though it may at times be to their disadvantage. Perhaps their greatest compensation consists in their being able to maintain a clear conscience.

A well-developed sense of humor aids one in becoming flexible and adjustable to the varying circumstances of life. It also enables one to relax. A keen sense of humor, moreover, keeps you from taking yourself and life too seriously, a tendency toward which many people are inclined.

Faith in your Creator inspires faith in other matters as well. While doubt begets doubt, faith is the master gate through which one may give his brain free access to the great universal power of thought. It is inevitable that the subject of faith must be woven into every principle of the philosophy of individual achievement, because the intangible power of faith is the essence of every great achievement, no matter what its nature or source may be.

Justice, as the term is used here, has reference to intentional honesty. It is deliberate honesty that is adhered to so rigidly that the individual is motivated by it under all circumstances.

The English language is an extremely rich one, capable of expressing every conceivable shade of meaning; hence there can be no valid excuse for the common habit of using words which offend the sensibilities of others. The use of obscene profanity at any time or under any circumstance is inexcusable.

THE NEED FOR CONTROL

Control of the emotions can be achieved through self-discipline; and control is necessary if one is to enjoy the benefits of a pleasing personality. Some of the feelings which must be brought under control if one is to achieve a pleasing personality are: fear, hatred, anger, envy, greed, jealousy, revenge, irritability, and superstition. On the positive side are love, sex, faith, hope, desire, loyalty, sympathy, and optimism.

You can pay another person no greater compliment than to concentrate your attention upon his or her personal interests, and it is a well-known fact that it is a greater accomplishment to be an attentive listener when another is speaking than it is to be an able speaker.

We have only to observe carefully to find men and women who have risen to great heights of personal achievement because of their ability to sell themselves and their ideas through dramatization in speech. The most important factor in effective speech is a thorough knowledge of the subject on which one speaks. And the greatest of all rules of effective speaking can be stated in one sentence: Know what you wish to say, say it with all the emotional feeling at your command, then sit down.

The more popular people are usually very versatile. They have at least a cursory knowledge of many subjects. They are interested in other people and in their ideas and go out of their way to express that interest where it will inspire appropriate reaction.

It is inevitable that people who dislike others will, in turn, be disliked. Through the principle of telepathy, every mind communicates with all other minds within its range, and the person who wishes to develop an attractive personality must constantly control not only his words and deeds but, of course, his thoughts as well. A genuine fondness for people is a great asset.

If man lets his temper fly, he is sure to find it alighting where it will do him great injury on the rebound. An uncontrolled temper usually results in an uncontrolled tongue. Control of emotion, however, is one of the greatest powers at man's disposal.

People without an ambition and the hope of achieving it may be harmless to others, but they will never be popular. Nobody cares much about a person who shows clearly by his deeds or lack of deeds that he has abandoned hope of getting ahead in this world.

The man who lacks the necessary self-discipline to manage his personal habits instead of being controlled by them is never very attractive to others. This is especially true of the habits of eating and drinking, and sexual relationships. Excesses in relation to any of these destroy personal magnetism.

FURTHER PERSONALITY QUALITIES

This is a high-speed world in which we are living, and the tempo of human thoughts and deeds is so rapid that we often get in one another's way; therefore patience is required if one is to avoid the destructive effects of friction in human relationships.

Humility of heart is the outgrowth of understanding of man's relationship to his Creator, plus the recognition that the material blessings of life are gifts from the Creator for the common good of all mankind. The man who is on good terms with his own conscience and in harmony with his Creator always is humble at heart, no matter how much material wealth he may have accumulated, no matter what his personal achievements may be.

Appropriateness of attire is important. The best-dressed person usually is the one whose clothes and accessories are so well chosen and whose entire ensemble is so well harmonized that the individual does not attract undue attention.

Effective showmanship, as it constitutes one of the traits of a pleasing personality, consists of a combination of many other traits such as facial expression, control of the tone of voice, effective speech, proper choice of words, mastery of the emotions, courtesy, an appropriate wardrobe, versatility, a positive mental attitude, a keen sense of humor, alertness to the interests of other people, and tactfulness.

Clean sportsmanship is an important trait of an attractive personality because it inspires people to cooperate in a friendly manner, and it connotes sound character. Beyond this it hardly needs further endorsement.

Many people might never think of the habit of handshaking as having anything to do with a pleasing personality, but it has, in fact, a great deal to do with the subject. The person who shakes hands properly coordinates his handshake with his words of greeting, generally emphasizing each word with a firm grip of the hand—not a viselike squeeze, but he does not release the other person's hand until he finishes the spoken greeting.

The term "personal magnetism" is a polite way of describing sex appeal, for that is precisely what it means. Sex emotion is the power behind all creative vision. It is the means by which all living species are perpetuated. It inspires the use of the imagination, enthusiasm, and personal initiative. There has never been a great leader in any calling who was not motivated in part by the creative powers of sex emotion.

A man's personality is his greatest asset or his greatest liability, for it embraces everything that he controls—his mind, body, and soul, A man's personality is the man himself. It shapes the nature of his thoughts, his deeds, his relationships with others, and it establishes the boundaries of the space that he occupies in the world.

Visualize yourself as a loving friend to everyone, radiating warmth, affection, and friendship. You are genuinely interested in them and their welfare. This is the path to achieving a persuasive personality.

A LIVE EXAMPLE

A persuasive personality, to be successful, must be lastingly effective. The remarkable career achieved by Paul Harvey points up the fact that a pleasing personality not only can open many doors, but can attain a high degree of effective communication.

It was while traveling to an airport that Dr. Hill made

the decision to include Harvey in this volume. He had been searching for someone who would be a good example of the effectiveness of a persuasive personality, when Paul Harvey's voice came out to him from the car radio.

The strong, confident voice, with its unmistakable undertones of sensitivity and keen awareness, brought the listener to instant attention and simultaneous decision. Paul Harvey has used, more effectively than most, his talent for a pleasing personality.

Previous associations, during many years of work in the radio broadcast and lecture schedules, had long ago established in the minds of Dr. Hill and his associates the many fine qualities of the man, and it only remained to gain permission to use him in this book as a living example.

Harvey is careful to plan his daily schedules to include plenty of time for thorough, precise checking of the accuracy of every detail. He does not use hearsay or gossip. Although he sometimes projects a lightheaded and humorous attitude, Harvey is extremely serious about his work. He feels that the time he spends with his audience is the most vital part of his day. His voice carries his earnestness, and the audience is instantly aware that here is a man with "something to say." His total personality is in focus at such time.

Paul Harvey, native of Oklahoma and a tireless, dynamic commentator, has, among numerous other honors, received eight honorary doctoral degrees. The Sumter Guards of Charleston, South Carolina, voted Harvey the "man who contributed most toward preserving the American way of life," and presented him with their Award of Honor.

Using imagination, enthusiasm, a pleasing personality, and a keen appreciation for the benefits of masterminding, cooperation, and faith, Harvey has earned himself an enviable record in the field of public information.

His radio career has spanned five decades, and the name Paul Harvey has become synonymous with broadcasting. Over 100 of his broadcasts have been entered in the Congressional Record. He is the author of numerous books and a newspaper column, and has made many records and tapes.

Paul Harvey's vast background and experience in radio stems from his early start in the industry and his profound concentration on the work to which he is devoted. He was in high school when he began announcing at KVOO in Tulsa. He continued announcing while attending Tulsa University.

For a while in his early career he managed a radio station in Salina, Kansas, which in those days meant announcing, selling, and programming. He did news broadcasts in Oklahoma City, then went to KXOK in St. Louis as special events director.

Harvey went to Hawaii for special broadcasts when the Navy concentrated its fleet in the Pacific in 1940. Subsequently, Harvey was Director of News and Information for Michigan and Indiana before his enlistment in the Air Force.

Paul Harvey was named Commentator of the Year in 1962 and in 1975 was named American of the Year by Lions International, the same year he received the Outstanding Broadcast Journalism Award. In 1980, Harvey was awarded the General Omar N. Bradley Spirit of Independence trophy and was also named Man of the Year by the Chicago Broadcast Advertising Club.

In 1982, Harvey was chosen by the Horatio Alger Association of Distinguished Americans to receive the Horatio Alger Award, an honor given to those who embody the highest of American ideals—honor, courage, ethics, perseverance, patriotism, and compassion. That same year, the National Broadcasters Association chose Harvey to receive the Golden Radio award.

Paul Harvey's name is enshrined in the Oklahoma Hall of Fame, the National Association of Broadcasters' Hall of Fame, and he has received dozens of other awards during his career as a journalist and commentator. He has received numerous other awards for his work in behalf of the Humane Society and other causes to which he lends his name and support.

Long before Harvey became a fixture in American broadcasting, Napoleon Hill identified him as an outstanding achiever, one who radiates a positive personality that demonstrates unlimited energy in the effort to render a worthwhile service. Paul Harvey, Dr. Hill said, is a personality who has developed the power of persuasion for the benefit of his fellow Americans.

Chapter Five

POSITIVE DIVIDENDS
THROUGH SERVICE

A remarkable phenomenon which works almost without exception, and has worked since the beginning of mankind, is the law of compensation.

The more we give, the more we get. Bread cast upon the water will return to sustain and to strengthen the person who is rendering more service and better service than he or she is paid or expected to do.

Returns do not always come from the person to whom the gift or service was given. They usually do not, in fact. But returns will come, and in kind. It may be early, it may be late, but it will come. The gift, the word, the attitude, the withholding of the gift, the withholding of the word—what you are will come home.

What is it you seek? Self-satisfaction? Revenge? Help another to experience these things, and they will become your own. Is it wealth, a superior grasp of some secrets of success? Is it more effective efforts toward business expansion?

The entire history of mankind, from the Stone Age to the present, provides indisputable evidence that man's only real limitations are those which he sets up in his own mind, or accepts in the circumstances which surround him.

Fear will make a man miserly of his money, of his time, of his talents, and of his inner resources. Examine this thought. A man may give more time than is called

69

for, out of fear—but the time will be given reluctantly and without real productiveness. His body may be weary, but he is resentfully weary, and sleep will not come easily as it does after physical strain willingly exerted.

But consider the man who goes the extra mile because he is eager to help get the job done well. Willingness to work extra hours, to do the extra bit of "rounding out" that puts the polish on an adequate product, results in a rewarding flood of "well-being" in the innermost consciousness. Even if no one notices at that moment or says "thank you," it is enough to know that one has done a good job, an extra good job, and that the pay is earned. The pure joy of having done more and a better job than was expected is what makes the difference between a worker and a drone. It is the difference between a period and an exclamation mark.

Going the extra mile pays off in prosperity—both in the heart and in the pocketbook. But do not forget that it is a fragile phenomenon. It must be tempered with self-discipline, as a reminder that the gift is not primarily in order to get a gift in return, but is a mile given, an hour overtime expended willingly, with the foremost idea being to "help thy brother's boat to shore." If you can perfect the attitude of helpfulness, for the pure joy of doing a better job for another person, then the delicate balance will become a part of your nature with unexpected dividends being realized in your own life.

One of Dr. Napoleon Hill's favorite real-life stories which illustrates the principle of going the extra mile is the experience of Charles Allen Ward.

A BAD BEGINNING

The story begins in Seattle, where Charles Allen Ward was born. His father was a school teacher who never seemed to be able to make ends meet. Ward's father and mother were divorced, and when he was fourteen, his mother remarried.

From the time he started school, Charlie worked to help support the family. He peddled papers, shined shoes, and hung around saloons, where he picked up spare change running errands for the toughs and hangers-on. His saloon work led to quarrels with his stepfather, and in the arguments between the two, his mother sided with the stepfather. Continued poverty made the home less and less pleasant. Charlie's clothes were always shabby, and he was embarrassed in the presence of other youngsters his own age.

At the age of seventeen, Charlie ran away. He never saw or heard from his parents again. He was strictly on his own, with no background or pleasant memories to help him make a success of his life. He roamed the western part of the country, sleeping in haystacks, riding freight trains, doing odd jobs, panhandling, and begging at back doors. He literally walked the soles off his shoes, and much of the time he was cold and very hungry. From associating with tramps and irresponsible men, he came to share their cynical attitude toward life.

He crossed the Pacific several times, shipping out to China and Japan on various freighters. He went to Alaska and became a saloon flunky in Nome. He drove dog teams, carried mail, and did a bit of prospecting in gold mines. He finally made a little money from his mining and doubled it by playing roulette.

Hearing of the overthrow of President Díaz of Mexico, Charlie worked his way down to that country and joined Pancho Villa's army. Here he struck it rich. Villia's soldiers were driving the ranchers' cattle off and slaughtering them for food, throwing the hides aside to rot. Charlie's keen sense of observation prompted him to ask Villa for permission—which he received—to collect and sell the hides. He had the hides salted down and sent to El Paso, where they piled up a neat little nest egg of $70,000 for him.

Feeling that his financial windfall would carry him through to a better opportunity, he left Villa's army and moved to El Paso. Here he gambled and bought drinks for saloon hangers-on. His associates were the riffraff of the border, soldiers of fortune, fugitives from justice, gamblers, smugglers, and the like.

His lavish spending attracted the attention of federal narcotics agents, who began watching Charlie, believing that his free spending might have been made possible by narcotics peddling.

After a year, Charlie's bank roll was down to a few thousand dollars. He sought to improve his finances by going to Reno and playing the gambling halls, but his assets further dwindled until he was flat. He left Reno and wound up in Denver, where he accepted drinks and handouts from such saloon hangers-on as he could contact. Many of these were small-time dealers in drugs. Narcotics agents were tipped off to his presence in Denver, and after two years of intermittent surveillance, they charged him with peddling narcotics. They had found cocaine and morphine hidden in his lodgings. Charlie claimed they were planted there to justify the time the agents had spent in fruitless efforts to ensnare him.

He was tried and convicted, and at thirty-four he entered Leavenworth prison to begin the long term the judge had meted out.

BEHIND BARS

Charlie had never been in jail before, despite the fact that he had rubbed elbows with criminals and underworld characters most of his life. Conviction for a crime he claimed not to have committed made him bitter. As soon as he arrived at Leavenworth, he vowed to himself that the place was not strong enough to hold him and immediately began to look for some means to make a break. But at this point, something important happened to Charlie Ward. Some silent power within his brain caused him to resolve to adapt himself to the prison rules and to become the most agreeable inmate in the prison. With this resolution, the entire tide of affairs of his life began to reverse. Charlie Ward had finally mastered his greatest enemy, *himself.* He quit hating the federal agents who, he said, had framed him. He quit hating the judge who had, in harsh language, sentenced him. For once in his life, he took a good look at the Charlie Ward he had known in the past, and the picture he saw was not pretty.

The change that came over Charlie by this remarkable reversal of his mental attitude made him feel that his old self had died and a new man had moved in and taken charge. And that was precisely what had happened. As soon as he decided that escape was nothing but an idle dream, he looked about for ways to make his prison stay as pleasant as possible. His first big reward for his change of attitude came when a friendly convict clerk named Peters gave him a tip that one of the "trusties" who worked in the power plant was to be released in three months, leaving an opening for someone who knew electricity.

This happy turn of the wheel of fate gave Charlie an opportunity to move, on his own initiative, in a direction that was destined to bring good fortune. It also gave him an opportunity to learn what a man can do by going the extra mile, giving more than that for which he is paid.

Charlie knew nothing about electricity, but he got technical books from the prison library and began devoting all his spare time to learning. When three months were up, he walked into the deputy warden's office and applied for the job. Something about his manner and his tone of voice impressed the deputy, and he got the job. That "something" was his changed mental attitude from negative to positive.

This job gave Charlie a taste of freedom, since some of the electrical work took him outside the prison walls, such as repairing electrical appliances for the warden's wife and other light jobs. In order that he might do this work, he was given a gate pass good from 8 A.M. to 4 P.M.

In his second year at prison, Charlie, who had continued his night studies, became superintendent of the power plant, supervising one hundred fifty men. From the very first, he showed a kindly attitude toward these men and endeavored to help them to make the best of their situations. By this time, he had gained the confidence both of the prison officials and of his fellow convicts, and he was enjoying privileges not accorded to many of the other trusties.

THE BIG BREAK

Then came the biggest break Charlie had ever known: Herbert Huse Bigelow, sentenced for income tax evasion, arrived at the prison. Mr. Bigelow was the president and major stockholder of the Brown-Bigelow Calendar Company of St. Paul, at that time one of the largest of its kind in the world.

"When I saw Mr. Bigelow," said Charlie, "something within me said, 'Here is the man who can pull you out of the mud.'"

Mr. Bigelow was fifty-three when he entered prison. He walked in with his head high, sporting an overbearing manner. The convicts, who had heard of Mr. Bigelow, did everything in their power to make life miserable for him.

Charlie watched the older man's ordeal with sympathetic interest, and he recognized that Bigelow's spirit was rapidly being broken. One day, he offered the millionaire a cigarette, and as they smoked together, he offered to act as a buffer between the cultured manufacturer and the harshness of prison life. First, he had Mr. Bigelow transferred from the small cell he occupied to his own quarters in the basement, a spacious room without bars adjoining the showers. Next, he got Bigelow an outside job and the daylight pass that went with it. When Bigelow expressed a fear that some of his executives might mismanage his company while he was away, Charlie arranged for him to supervise his office from the penitentiary. He got a typewriter and the services of a convict stenographer to take Mr. Bigelow's dictation after prison working hours. He also managed to get the prison rules relaxed so that Mr. Bigelow could send out seventy-five to a hundred letters a day, instead of only the few that prison rules permitted.

As Mr. Bigelow's term approached its completion, he said to Charlie, "You've been good to me, and I want to show you that I appreciate it. When I leave here I'm going to stop off in Kansas City and deposit $15,000 in your name, so you will have something to go on when you get out."

Charlie thanked him, but declined the offer.

A little later the manufacturer was paroled, and on bidding Charlie good-bye he said, "You'll be out in another month, Charlie. I want you to come to St. Paul and go to work for me. I'll never forget what you did for me."

A FRESH START

Five weeks later, Charlie arrived in St. Paul and was met at the station by Mr. Bigelow, who drove him to his home for luncheon. After luncheon, he drove Ward to a rooming house near the plant, where he had rented a room for his friend.

On Monday morning, Charlie reported for work at the Bigelow plant and was assigned to a job, at $25 a week, feeding raw rubber into a processing machine.

After all that Charlie had done for Mr. Bigelow, his assignment to a dirty job at starvation wages seemed the last word in ingratitude, but instead of quitting in disgust, or complaining to Mr. Bigelow, Charlie did what most men would not have done under the same circumstances. He worked hard and did such a good job that Mr. Bigelow began to think of letting Charlie work where his positive mental attitude would be of the most help to the company.

Within two months, Charlie was a foreman.

Personal initiative and the habit of going the extra mile had paid off for Charlie. Every subsequent job he was assigned was handled so efficiently that the company felt obliged to promote him to a higher one.

Finally, the directors proved that they recognized Charlie's value by creating the job of vice-president and general manager at a salary that was second only to the president's.

Eight months later, Mr. Bigelow died, and the directors appointed Charlie to take his place. From that time, the financial sheet of Brown-Bigelow Calendar Company saw nothing but black ink.

Then came the biggest surprise of Charlie's life. He discovered that Mr. Bigelow had left him a third interest in his estate. Charlie continued to prosper until it became known that his personal net worth was in the millions. He was received by the leading business and political figures of St. Paul. He joined the best clubs and became a thirty-second-degree Mason. President Franklin D. Roosevelt officially restored his civil rights as a citizen as a token of appreciation of his "exemplary life." As one of his close friends said, "When Charlie rises, he invariably pulls many others along with him."

This story proves once again that a man can change his world and his entire life by changing his mental attitude from negative to positive. It proves that the habit of going the extra mile is without equal as a means of lifting oneself to higher levels in life. It also proves that "every adversity carries with it the seed of an equivalent or greater benefit."

It is most significant that the very first time Charlie forgot about himself and began to think about helping someone else, his life began to improve.

There is no mystery about Charlie Ward's rise to fame and fortune. He did it by following principles of success which can make any other person as successful as he became. You have a right to use those same principles. What are you going to do with your right?

A MEETING

It is interesting to note the strange circumstances which brought Charlie Ward and Napoleon Hill together.

Charlie Ward first came to the attention of Napoleon Hill when an autographed copy of *Think and Grow Rich* was presented to President Franklin D. Roosevelt by the author. The President thumbed through the book for a few minutes, read some of the names of the successful men it described, then exclaimed, "I don't see Charlie Ward's name here. If you want a success story running all the way from rags to riches, meet Charlie Ward and you will have it. He is the smartest of all big fellows now living, and a rich man who has not become a slave to money. Charlie's hobby is sharing himself and his blessings with others. You will like Charlie and he will like you."

Napoleon Hill met Charlie Ward for the first time in 1959. Walking into Charlie's office, Napoleon Hill was greeted by Charlie: "I knew the day would come when you would walk through that door and I would be privileged to shake the hand of the man who wrote the greatest book I ever read, *Think and Grow Rich*."

During this visit, they made arrangements for Dr. Hill to write the Charlie Ward story. This was never completed because of Mr. Ward's death. One of Dr. Hill's most treasured gifts is a watch given to him by Mr. Ward during that visit, inscribed, "To my friend, Napoleon Hill," with Charlie Ward's signature. He wore it constantly.

Charlie Ward ranked high with men of success and contributed greatly to the building of the Science of Personal Achievement. In the chapter that follows you will meet others who have achieved great success and mastered the Power of Positive Persuasion.

Chapter Six

PREREQUISITES TO
POWER

It is the opinion of the author that achievement, or lack of it, and the reasons behind each person's degree of success in life, are as different as the individuals who undertake the journey from birth to death.

Circumstances of birth, origin, early or late influences, individuals encountered, physical and geographical situations—all contribute to the difference in the underlying pattern leading to achievement or failure.

Fortunate is the person whose life experiences include the opportunity for encountering individuals or books that help focus the individual's mind on certain basic truths about himself or herself.

When an individual realizes the simple but profoundly vital fact that aiming toward a specific goal is the best insurance of hitting the bull's-eye, then he or she is ready to move toward more complex conclusions. Anyone may climb!

The foundation to Dr. Napoleon Hill's whole philosophy is what he calls the Seventeen Success Principles. Practical application of these, singly or in various combinations, has provided the blueprint for success for countless men and women throughout the world.

1. DEFINITENESS OF PURPOSE

This is the arrow aimed toward the goal. What is it that you want from life? What is your greatest goal? The moment you take hold of this question with your whole attention, you begin to face yourself and to analyze yourself. Who are you, what are you, where are you NOW? Being thoroughly honest with yourself may be your first step toward success. What road are you traveling? What are the road signs you see as you take stock of your present position?

It is well to write a list of the things you want from life—such as health, personal relationships you wish to maintain, the amount of income you desire, the amount you wish to save or invest for retirement, the kind of home, the kind of automobile, the benefits you desire for each member of your family. These are the major purposes you define.

Map a one-year plan, a five-year plan, setting forth goals of achievement for personal improvement, self-discipline, sales goals per day, per week, per month.

Memorize these lists, going over them daily, early in the morning and just before going to sleep at night. Attempt at all times to remember that achievement of these goals will be determined to a large extent by your attitude and constancy of attention to them. Make your definite purposes a daily habit of prayer, conversation, and thought. By this you establish a "success consciousness" in your subconscious mind, and gradually your subconscious mind will aid you in carrying out the actions and reactions which will lead to success.

2. THE MASTERMIND POWER PRINCIPLE

Having clearly defined your goals and purposes in thought and in writing, it is advisable to select an individual or individuals with whom you can share your plan for achievement. The mastermind principle is defined as an alliance of two or more people, working together in a spirit of perfect harmony to accomplish a definite purpose. The value of the "gathering together of those of like mind" is self-evident. Harmony in a home results when a man and woman work toward the establishment of a relationship that is mutually satisfying and productive of comfort and happiness for both.

Your mutual agreement with your employer to work toward high sales is a form of masterminding. If your major purpose in life is an ambitious one that extends beyond the accumulation of the ordinary requirements of subsistence, you will probably need the help of others in achieving it.

The mastermind principle is a means by which you may use the experience, the education, the talent, the influence, and perhaps the finances of other people to aid you in carrying out your major purpose. Your mastermind alliance may begin with your association with one other person. The number of alliances you will require depends entirely on the nature and the extent of the purposes of your alliance. A "meeting of the minds" must be regular, must be mutually beneficial, and must always be harmonious in the basic matters of sincerity and trust.

3. APPLIED FAITH

Deeply embedded in all the processes and the principles leading to achievement and success is the element of faith. Faith is a prerequisite to progress of any kind. A man does not begin a journey across the room to get a drink of water without faith. Faith that his legs will carry him the distance required. Faith that when he turns the faucet, water will pour out. Faith that as he swallows, it will quench his thirst. Is it any less an act of faith to step out toward achievement? The same Creator who gave us faith in our ability to walk to the water fountain can supply faith in our ability to reach goals in business and in personal life.

When the word "faith" is preceded by the word "applied," it means the faith one lives by and acts by—not something one believes in but does not practice, nor the faith in one's instinct to react properly to physical stimuli.

What gives faith its powerful dimension? This is achieved when the individual seizes the truth that faith comes from the infinite God, the same source of power that keeps this world in an orderly continuous movement from day to night, season to season, tide to tide.

There is nothing complicated about the method by which you may draw upon the power of faith for guidance in circumstances and goals you desire from life.

First of all, we must come face to face with our innermost self, honestly face the choice of goals, and evaluate the distance, the work, and the circumstances that stand between us and the attainment of these goals. The thoughtful man will realize then that many things must come to pass, a price must be paid, and help from many sources must be forthcoming, if he is to accomplish all he wants. Therefore, one must put the future, the intangibles, and the yet-to-be determined elements into the hands of the Creator—or else leave all this to luck or happenstance. The thoughtful man, the ambitious man, will then put faith to work, applying it to all those elements over which he can have no control as yet. This "letting go" of certain areas, yet with a belief that all will be well when the time for personal involvement arrives—this is faith. It makes for a relaxed state of mind, sound sleep, and a confidence that attracts positive reactions from every source. Faith is the "rocket fuel" of human endeavor.

4. A PLEASANT PERSONALITY

Your personality reveals the kind of thinking you do, the ethics you observe, your mental and spiritual strengths and standards, the kind of life you lead. What constitutes a pleasing personality? How may we develop a personality which attracts people to us?

There are many kinds of personalities, many kinds of attractiveness. Perhaps the most desired characteristic would be a positive mental attitude. "Smile and the world smiles with you, weep and you weep alone." Everyone has blue days, but the world will not long beat a path to the door of the chronically depressed person, the individual who always looks on the dark side of things. Look for the bright side of the street. Accentuate the positive.

It has been said that if you can make a man laugh,

you can make him like you. If he likes you, he will also listen to what you have to say in a serious vein.

Flexibility, being resilient to the constant changes and strains of life, without losing self-control, is an art, and a worthwhile one. Sincerity is an absolute. Lack of it is as evident as warts on the nose to the perceptive, sensitive, and intelligent observer. Promptness and decisiveness in decision usually denote clarity and directness of thought, self-confidence, and an uncluttered mind. Courtesy, tactfulness, tolerance, frankness, a sense of humor, a pleasant countenance, a ready smile—all help to create and sustain confidence and good relationships.

5. GOING THE EXTRA MILE

This is based on the concept of giving more and better service than is expected or required, with the right mental attitude and with no expectation of immediate reward. The compensations are great, much greater than the investment. Going the extra mile insures an increase in personal courage, self-reliance, personal initiative, and it builds greater enthusiasm. It is conducive to a more positive attitude and a happier, more secure position with one's co-workers and employers.

6. PERSONAL INITIATIVE

Personal initiative is a trait much admired and if carried out with discretion and logic, can very quickly put you ahead of the crowd. Initiative, built on a definite understanding of what must be achieved, puts one in harmony with everyone around him, and with the universe as a whole. If one has a definite goal in mind, then opportunities for personal initiative are easy to find. Initiative is the first step—it is an indication of a good attitude, displayed through action. It is a self-reliant demonstration which seldom goes unnoticed by those in authority. Personal initiative is self-confidence in action, and if you are moving toward a definite goal, it speeds your journey and smooths the way for good work to become easier and more rewarding.

7. SELF-DISCIPLINE

Self-discipline is training which corrects, molds, strengthens, and perfects. Your behavior and your attitudes are expressions of your thoughts. Much of our thinking seems to be uncontrolled, random thinking, or is on a semiconscious level. From time to time we are aware of our "feelings." Feelings may indicate that we have been thinking strongly on certain subjects. When we feel, we become more alert, because we have become aware of power and energy stimulated by thought. We may be stimulated to love, faith, loyalty, or to fear, jealousy, greed, or anger. Self-discipline teaches us to direct the energy generated by our thoughts into feeling—and action—that will be advantageous and strengthening. Self-discipline will help direct our energy into the most useful, successful channels.

8. CONTROLLED ATTENTION

Controlled attention is the act of focusing the mind on a given desire until ways and means for its realization have been worked out and successfully put into operation. Success comes after much concentration. Controlled attention to the power of our thoughts and to the energy we can generate through the mind is a vital tool. Prayer is not only worship. Prayer generates power, energy, unity, strength. Thinking with another person on a certain subject brings new insights, new truths. Attention focused as one individual or several brings power.

9. ENTHUSIASM

Enthusiasm is an emotion, the physical counterpart to our ideas. It begins and ends in our minds. Enthusiasm is harmony, confidence. When you feel yourself taking hold of a definite idea, a definite plan, then you become enthusiastic. Enthusiasm is a feeling of confidence, an awareness of a relationship between oneself and the source of power to achieve. Speak with enthusiasm and positiveness, move with confidence, and observe how enthusiasm grows and spreads to others.

10. IMAGINATION

"The imagination is the workshop of the soul wherein are shaped all plans for individual achievement." Man's greatest gift is his thinking mind. It analyzes, compares, chooses. It creates, visualizes, foresees, and generates ideas. Imagination is your mind's exercise, its challenge, its adventure.

11. LEARNING FROM ADVERSITY

Adversity is a part of life. Every act, situation, or choice of our lives contains cause and effect. In adversities we have situations in which we are made very much aware of the effect. The cause may be known, or it may be elusive or incomprehensible. We experience a very personal, significant reaction, a strong emotion is stirred within us, and we ask, "Why?" Every adversity carries within it the seed of an equivalent or greater benefit. If we can capture this truth, and can accept the fact that this universe is governed by immutable laws which are part of a creative force, no matter how difficult it may be to see the reason—then we can ride out any storm which besets our lives. Your attitude in time of adversity determines much of its eternal effect on your life—for good or ill.

12. BUDGETING TIME AND MONEY

Since your day has the same twenty-four hours in it as everyone else's in the world, you have the same opportunity as anyone for the skillful use of this time. Man has always had to harmonize with the world around him. In every generation, man has had to cope with the changing tides and tempos of the world around him. But as the demands are made, the balance is there, if we seek it out. There is less "time" now, because automation and faster transportation and communication seem to rush us. The art of budgeting time is one of the hardest to master, but most rewarding. The budgeting of money is a critical issue. Our eyes tend to be larger than our pocketbooks. How much time is there to learn to budget our money? All the time there is.

13. A POSITIVE MENTAL ATTITUDE

Our mind is the only thing we can control. Either we control it, or we relinquish control and we drift. We can do something about any situation. We cannot NOT do anything. Being negative is doing something. To govern your life, you must learn to govern your attitudes. How we react is determined by our habits of mind control and our attitudes. Are you looking for positive avenues to success?

14. ACCURATE THINKING

Choose what you want to achieve. Determine how you will set about achieving it. Move toward that goal with definite, positive awareness and with faith. This is accurate thinking. The accuracy of your thinking is affected by the hopes, fears, desires, attitudes you allow to stimulate you. Organize your mind. Be aware of the power of your mind. Keep it controlled, accurate.

15. SOUND PHYSICAL HEALTH

Your thoughts affect your health. Thoughts can make you sick, or thoughts can move you toward good health, good attitudes, sound sleep, good eating habits. Develop a consciousness of good health, well-being. Good thinking generates harmony within our bodies and generates physical manifestations of order and system.

16. COOPERATION

Success within and without is an evidence of cooperation. All achievement is the form of significant and successful cooperation and teamwork between individuals.

Cooperation is the beginning of all organized effort. Our bodies are healthy when there is organization and teamwork of all the organs. Our lives are happy when there is cooperation between us and the world around us.

17. COSMIC "HABITFORCE"

This is perhaps the hardest to define, but it is the principle that supplies the key to the understanding and the utilization of all our inner resources. There are those who would call this the "mystic" element. If you observe and believe that there is order in the universe, the rising of the sun, the regularity of the tides, then you can see an example of a plan being carried out. There are laws by which the equilibrium of the whole universe is maintained. There are physical laws which make our patterns of natural behavior operate in predictable order and regularity. Blending the natural laws of the universe with our own activities helps create that power, that force, that energy which bring harmony, peace of mind, success. You have the power to choose to take hold of the principles of success.

THE SCIENCE OF PERSONAL ACHIEVEMENT

You have just studied an outline that can help you walk in the light of a new success beam to guide you to whatever station in life your hopes may demand. If it's a better-paying position that you need to make you happy, you may find the way to that position through mastery of the seventeen principles of success.

If it is closer harmony and better understanding you need in your present position, the seventeen principles of success can show you the way to attain it.

If the domestic relationship in your home needs improvement, this study can bring you and every member of your family the harmony, peace of mind, and understanding which are so essential for your success in your occupation. The seventeen principles of success will give you a better understanding of yourself and other people so that you may negotiate with others in a friendly spirit which inspires them to cooperate with you at all times.

If you have not been as successful in the past as you wished to be, this philosophy will help you to discover the reason why and show you how to remove the cause.

If you are in business for yourself, you can learn how to convert your customers into friendly workers, who will bring you other customers.

If you are a teacher, the seventeen principles of success can give you that "something" which will increase your earning power and help you promote yourself into wider fields of service in your profession.

A MASTERMIND ALLIANCE

Mr. W. Clement Stone has utilized all the principles described in this chapter for such a long period of time that he has become permanently associated with them. The best example of the lasting effects are embodied in the Napoleon Hill–W. Clement Stone association.

When Napoleon Hill first became associated with Mr. Stone in 1952, Mr. Stone's personal fortune was estimated (by Mr. Stone himself) at $3 million. When the relationship was ended ten years later, Mr. Stone's fortune was estimated at $160 million—an increase of approximately $15 million per year for the ten years of their personal association.

During those ten years Mr. Stone's entire sales and managerial staff was indoctrinated with the Science of Personal Achievement. Many of the salesmen increased their earnings, through the application of this success philosophy, as much as three and four hundred percent.

It is interesting to note that Mr. Stone's personal application of the Napoleon Hill–Andrew Carnegie success philosophy rates next to that of Andrew Carnegie and Thomas A. Edison. Mr. Stone was chosen by Napoleon Hill to receive the award from the Napoleon Hill Foundation as the man who had made the third highest application of the Science of Personal Achievement, following Andrew Carnegie and Thomas A. Edison.

During the Napoleon Hill–W. Clement Stone association, they co-authored a book entitled *Success Through a Positive Mental Attitude* (Prentice-Hall, Inc.) which came a best seller from the very first and remained so for years. The book has been translated into many foreign languages.

Although Napoleon Hill's writings have created wealth in various amounts for millions of people, and he has been called "the kingmaker of millionaires," it was Dr. Hill's belief that W. Clement Stone was one of the most outstanding practitioners of the Napoleon Hill–Andrew Carnegie success philosophy. As will be noted later, another who was singled out by the Napoleon Hill Foundation as an outstanding example is Delford Smith.

It is worthy of note that while Mr. Stone has become fabulously rich through the Napoleon Hill–Andrew Carnegie success philosophy, he also has so generously and effectively indoctrinated his own organization members and countless others with the philosophy that he has enabled all of them to become more successful.

He has probably developed more millionaires from all walks of life than has any other living person.

Mr. Stone knows full well that whatever one has must be used justly and effectively, or it will disappear through the law of diminishing returns.

It is also interesting to note that Mr. Stone has given full and generous credit to the Napoleon Hill–Andrew Carnegie success philosophy for his successful achievements.

The ten years of business association between Napoleon Hill and W. Clement Stone was fabulously beneficial, not only to the thousands of men and women whom they helped through their writings and lectures, but also to both of these men. An example of one very astonishing benefit which Napoleon Hill received from Mr. Stone during this alliance, the following incident is but one of many similar transactions. During this alliance Napoleon Hill invested $37,500 in the Combined Insurance Company of America, the insurance company of which Mr. Stone was chief executive officer. Some ten years later, when the accounts were tallied, the investment had grown until its value (as measured by the market price of the Combined stock) was $640,000. It is safe to say that on precious few occasions could one make such an outstanding return on investment in so short a time.

You have it within you to become as successful as you really want to be. Decide now what you want out of life and then go after it.

Chapter Seven

MANUAL FOR MASTER SALESMANSHIP

Section I

Salesman on Stage

Scientific salesmanship involves principles similar to those on which a successful stage play is based. The psychology of selling an individual is closely akin to actors' strategy in selling an audience. The stage play that succeeds must have the advantage of a strong opening act and a smashing climax, or closing act. If a play does not have these, it will be a flop.

The salesman's approach must be strong enough to establish confidence and arouse interest. If he falls down in his first act, he will find it difficult, if not impossible, to make a sale. The sales presentation may be weak at many places "in the middle" without fatality to the sale, providing the opening and the close are strong and impelling. The act of scientific salesmanship is a three-act drama:

Act I—Interest. It must grip the attention and arouse the interest of the audience. (This is accomplished by neutralizing the mind of the prospective buyer and establishing confidence.)

Act II—Desire. This phase must develop a plot for presentation. Even if it is weak, it may still go over providing the first act has been strong. The audience will be charitable if they have gained sufficient confidence from the first act to arouse expectation of a strong climax. (Desire must be developed through the proper presentation of motive.)

Act III—Action. Here the objective must be realized. This must be a knock-out regardless of the first two acts, or the play will be a flop. In the third, or last, act the sale is closed or lost. (Action or the close can be induced only by the proper presentation of the two preceding acts.)

It is hardly necessary to suggest that the person who successfully presents the three-act drama of selling must possess and use imagination. The imagination is the workshop of the mind where the salesman fashions ideas, plans, and mental pictures with which to create desire in the mind of his prospective buyer. Salespeople whose imaginations are deficient resemble ships without rudders—they go around and around in circles and finish where they began, without making any sort of favorable impression.

Words, alone, will not sell!

Words woven into combinations of thought which create desire *will* sell. Some never learn the difference between rapid-fire conversation which does not end soon enough and carefully painted word pictures which fire the imagination of the prospective buyer.

The sole object of neutralizing the mind of the prospective buyer is, of course, to establish confidence. Where confidence has not first been built in the mind, no sale can be made.

AN OBJECT LESSON IN SALESMAN-CUSTOMER RELATIONSHIPS

This brings us to one of the most effective lessons in salesmanship ever written, Shakespeare's masterpiece, Mark Antony's speech at the funeral of Julius Caesar. It is included here as an object lesson in salesman-customer relationships, for it embraces all the important points in the foregoing chapters.

Perhaps you have read the oration, but we urge you to reread it, carefully and thoughtfully. It is presented here with interpretations in parentheses which may help you to derive a new meaning from it.

The setting for Antony's oration is as follows. Caesar is dead, and Brutus, his slayer, is called on to tell the Roman mob, which has gathered at the Forum, why he put Caesar out of the way. Picture in your imagination a howling mob that believes that Brutus has done a noble deed in murdering Caesar.

Brutus takes the platform and explains his reasons for killing Caesar. Confident that he has won the day, he takes his seat. His whole demeanor is that of a man who believes his word will be accepted without question, one of extreme haughtiness.

Mark Antony then takes the platform, knowing that the mob is antagonistic toward him because he was a friend to Caesar. In a low, humbled tone, Antony begins to speak:

ANTONY: For Brutus' sake, I am beholding to you.

FOURTH CITIZEN: What does he say of Brutus?

THIRD CITIZEN: He says, for Brutus' sake, he finds himself beholding to us all.

FOURTH CITIZEN: 'Twere best he speak no harm of Brutus here.

FIRST CITIZEN: This Caesar was a tyrant.

THIRD CITIZEN: Nay, that's certain; we are blest that Rome is rid of him.

SECOND CITIZEN: Peace! Let us hear what Antony can say.
(Here you will observe, in Antony's opening sentence, his clever method of "neutralizing" the minds of his listeners.)

ANTONY: You gentle Romans—
(About as "gentle" as a gang of rebels in a revolutionary labor meeting.)

ALL: Peace, ho! Let us hear him.
(Had Antony begun his speech by "knocking" Brutus, the history of Rome would have been different.)

ANTONY: Friends, Romans, Countrymen, lend me your
ears; I come to bury Caesar, not to praise him.
*(Allying himself with what he knew to be the state of
mind of his listeners.)*
The evil that men do lives after them;
The good is oft interred with their bones;
So let it be with Caesar. The noble Brutus
Hath told you Caesar was ambitious;
If it were so, it was a grievous fault;
And grievously hath Caesar answered it.
Here, under leave of Brutus and the rest—
For Brutus is an honorable man;
So are they all, all honorable men—
Come I speak at Caesar's funeral.
He was my friend—faithful, and just to me;
But Brutus says he was ambitious.
And Brutus is an honorable man;
He hath brought many captives home to Rome
Whose ransoms did the general coffers fill;
Did this in Caesar seem ambitious;
When the poor have cried, Caesar hath wept;
Ambition should be made of sterner stuff;
Yet Brutus says he was ambitious;
And surely, he is an honorable man.
I speak not to disprove what Brutus spoke.
But here I am to speak what I do know.
You all did love him once, not without cause;
What cause withholds you then to mourn for him?
O judgment! thou art fled to brutish beasts,
And men have lost their reason. Bear with me,
My heart is in the coffin there with Caesar,
And I must pause till it come back to me.

PAUSE AND OBSERVE

*(At this point, Antony paused to give his audience a
chance to discuss hurriedly, among themselves, his
opening statements. His objective was to observe what
effects his words were having, just as a Master Salesman always encourages his prospective customer to
talk so he may know what is in his mind.)*

FIRST CITIZEN: Methinks there is much in his sayings.

SECOND CITIZEN: If thou consider rightly of the matter,
Caesar has had great wrong.

THIRD CITIZEN: Has he, masters? I fear there will be
worse come in his place.

FOURTH CITIZEN: Mark'd ye his words? He would not
take the crown? Therefore 'tis certain he was not
ambitious.

FIRST CITIZEN: If it be found so, someone will dear abide
it.

SECOND CITIZEN: Poor soul! His eyes are red as fire with
weeping.

THIRD CITIZEN: There's not a nobler man in Rome than
Antony.

FOURTH CITIZEN: Now mark him, he begins again to
speak.

ANTONY: But yesterday the word of Caesar might
Have stood against the world; now lies he there
And none so poor to do him reverence.
O masters *(appealing to their vanity)*, if I were dis-
posed to stir
Your hearts and minds to mutiny and rage,
I should do Brutus wrong and Cassius wrong,
Who, you all know, are honorable men.
*(Observe how often Antony has repeated the word
"honorable," how cleverly he makes the first suggestion that, perhaps, Brutus and Cassius may not be as
honorable as the Roman mob believes. This suggestion is carried forth in the words "mutiny" and
"rage," which he here uses for the first time. After
his pause, he observes that the mob is swinging over
to his side of the argument. Observe how carefully
he is "feeling" his way and making his words fit what
he knows to be the frame of mind of his listeners.)*

ANTONY: I will not do them wrong; I rather choose
To wrong the dead, to wrong myself and you,
Than I will wrong such honorable men.
*(Crystallizing his suggestion into hatred of Brutus and
Cassius, he then appeals to the mob's curiosity and
begins to lay the foundation for his climax—a climax
which he knows will win the mob because he is reach-*

ing it so cleverly that they believe it to be their own conclusion.)

ANTONY: But here's a parchment, with the seal of Caesar;

I found it in his closet; 'tis his will;

Let but the commons hear this testament,

Which, pardon me, I do not mean to read—

(He tightens his appeal to their curiosity by making them believe he does not intend to read the will.)

And they would go and kiss dead Caesar's wounds

And dip their napkins in his sacred blood,

Yea, beg a hair of him for memory,

And dying, mention it within their wills,

Bequeathing it as a rich legacy

Unto their issue.

(Human nature always wants what is difficult to get, or something of which it is about to be deprived. Observe how craftily Antony has awakened the interest of the mob and made them want to hear the will with open minds. *This marks his second step in the process of "neutralizing" their minds.)*

ALL: The will, the will! We will hear Caesar's will.

ANTONY: Have patience, gentle friends. I must not read it;

It is not meet you know how Caesar loved you.

You are not wood, you are not stone, but men;

And, being men, hearing the will of Caesar,

It will inflame you; *(exactly what he wishes to do)*

It will make you mad;

'Tis good you know not that you are his heirs,

For if you should, O what will come of it!

FOURTH CITIZEN: Read the will; we'll hear it Antony;

You shall read us the will; Caesar's will.

ANTONY: Will you be patient? Will you stay awhile?

I have o'ershot myself to tell you of it;

I fear I wrong the honorable men

Whose daggers have stabb'd Caesar, I do fear it.

("Daggers" and "stabb'd" suggest cruel murder. Observe how cleverly Antony injects this suggestion into his speech, and observe also how quickly the mob

catches its significance. Antony has carefully prepared their minds to receive this suggestion.)

FOURTH CITIZEN: They were traitors, honorable men!

ALL: The will! The testament!

SECOND CITIZEN: They were villains, murderers; the will!
(Just what Antony would have said in the beginning, but he knew it would have a more desirable effect if he planted the thought in the minds of the mob and permitted them to say it themselves.)

ANTONY: You will compel me then to read the will?
Then make a ring about the corpse of Caesar,
And let me show you him that made the will.
Shall I descend and will you give me leave?
(This was the point at which Brutus should have begun to look for a back door through which to make his escape.)

ALL: Come down.

THIRD CITIZEN: Room for Antony, most noble Antony.

ANTONY: Nay, press not so upon me, stand far off.
(He knew his command would make them want to draw nearer, which is what he wanted them to do.)

ALL: Stand back. Room.

ANTONY: If you have tears, prepare to shed them now.
You all do know this mantle; I remember
The first time ever Caesar put it on;
'Twas on a summer's evening, in his tent,
That day he overcame the Nervii;
Look, in this place ran Cassius' dagger through;
See what a rent the envious Casca made:
Through this the well-beloved Brutus stabb'd;
And as he plucked his cursed steel away,
Mark how the blood of Caesar followed it,
As rushing out of doors, to be resolved
If Brutus so unkindly knock'd or no;
For Brutus, as you know, was Caesar's angel;
Judge, O you gods, how dearly Caesar loved him!
This was the most unkindest cut of all;
For, when the noble Caesar saw him stab,
Ingratitude, more strong than traitor's arms,
Quite vanquish'd him; then burst his mighty heart;
And, in his mantle muffling up his face,

Even at the base of Pompey's statue,
Which all the while ran blood, great Caesar fell.
O, what a fall was there, my countrymen!
Then I, and you, and all of us fell down
While bloody treason flourish'd over us.
O, now you weep, and I perceive you feel
The dint of pity; these are gracious drops.
Kind soul, why weep you when you but behold
Our Caesar's vesture wounded? Look you here;
Here is himself, marr'd, as you see, with traitors.
(Observe how Antony now uses the word "traitors" quite freely, because he knows that it is in harmony with what is in the minds of the Roman mob.)

FIRST CITIZEN: O piteous spectacle!

SECOND CITIZEN: O woeful day!

THIRD CITIZEN: O woeful day!

FIRST CITIZEN: O most bloody sight!

SECOND CITIZEN: We will be avenged.
(Had Brutus been a wise man instead of a braggart, he would have been many miles from the scene by this time.)

ALL: Revenge! About! Seek! Burn! Fire! Kill! Slay! Let not a traitor live!
(Here Antony takes the next step toward crystallizing the frenzy of the mob into action but, clever salesman that he is, does not try to force this action.)

ANTONY: Stay, countrymen.

FIRST CITIZEN: Peace there! Hear the noble Antony.

SECOND CITIZEN: We'll hear him, we'll follow him, we'll die with him.

THE WIND-UP

(From these words Antony knows that the mob is with him. Observe how he takes advantage of this psychological moment—the moment for which all Master Salesmen wait.)

ANTONY: Good friends, sweet friends, let me not stir you up to such a sudden flood of mutiny.
They that have done this deed are honorable.
What private griefs they have, alas, I know not,

That made them do it; they were wise and honorable,
And will, no doubt, with reasons answer you.
I come not, friends, to steal away your hearts;
I am no orator as Brutus is;
But, as you know me all, a plain, blunt man,
That love my friend; and that they know full well
That gave me public leave to speak of him;
For I have neither wit, nor words, nor worth,
Action, nor utterance, nor the power of speech,
To stir men's blood; I only speak right on;
I tell you that which you yourselves do know;
Show you sweet Caesar's wounds, poor, poor dumb
    mouths.
And bid them speak for me; but were I Brutus,
And Brutus Antony, there an Antony
Would ruffle up your spirits, and put a tongue
In every wound of Caesar that would move
The stones of Rome to rise and mutiny.

ALL: We'll mutiny.

FIRST CITIZEN: We'll burn the house of Brutus.

THIRD CITIZEN: Away, then! Come, seek the conspirators.

ANTONY: Yet hear me, countrymen; yet hear me speak!

ALL: Peace, ho! Hear Antony, most noble Antony!

ANTONY: Why friends, you go to do you know not what;
    Wherein hath Caesar thus deserved your love?
    Alas, you know not; I must tell you, then;
    You have forgot the will I told you of.
    *(Antony is now ready to play his trump card; he is
    ready to reach the climax of his sale. Observe how
    well he has marshaled his suggestions, step by step,
    saving until the last his most important statement, the
    one on which he relied for action. In the great field
    of salesmanship and in public speaking, many try to
    reach this point too soon, try to "rush" an audience
    or a prospective purchaser, and thereby lose appeal.)*

ALL: Most true; the will! Let's stay and hear the will.

ANTONY: Here is the will, and under Caesar's seal.
    To every Roman citizen he gives,
    To every several man, seventy-five drachmas.

SECOND CITIZEN: Most noble Caesar! We'll revenge his
    death.

THIRD CITIZEN: O royal Caesar!
ANTONY: Hear me with patience.
ALL: Peace, ho!
ANTONY: Moreover, he hath left you all his walks,
  His private arbors and new planted orchards,
  On this side Tiber; he hath left them you
  And to your heirs forever; common pleasures,
  To walk abroad and recreate yourself.
  Here was a Caesar! When comes such another?
FIRST CITIZEN: Never, never. Come, away, away!
  We'll burn his body in the holy place,
  And with the brands fire the traitors' houses.
  Take up the body.
SECOND CITIZEN: Go fetch fire.
THIRD CITIZEN: Pluck down benches.
FOURTH CITIZEN: Pluck down forms, windows, anything.

(And that was Brutus' finish!) He lost his case because he lacked the personality and the good judgment to present his argument from the viewpoint of the Roman mob, as Mark Antony did. His whole attitude clearly indicated that he thought pretty well of himself, that he was proud of his deed. We all know people who somewhat resemble Brutus in this respect, and if we observe closely, we notice that they do not accomplish very much.

Suppose that Mark Antony had mounted the platform in a "strutting" attitude, and had begun his speech in this way: "Now let me tell you Romans something about this man Brutus—he is a murderer at heart and . . ." He would have gone no further; the mob would have howled him down.

Clever salesman and practical psychologist that he was, Mark Antony presented his case so that it appeared not to be his own idea at all, but that of the mob itself. Observe how Antony emphasized the "you" and not the "I" attitude toward others. And observe, if you will, that this very point is emphasized throughout this book.

Shakespeare was a genius at mapping human psychology. All of his writings are based on unerring knowledge of the human mind. Throughout Antony's speech, you will observe how carefully he assumed the "you" attitude, so carefully that the Roman mob was sure that its decision was of its own making.

We must call your attention, however, to the fact that Mark Antony's appeal to the self-interest of the Roman mob was crafty, and based upon stealth—which dishonest men often use in appealing to the stupidity and avarice of their victims. While Mark Antony displayed great self-control in feigning an attitude toward Brutus that was not real, it is obvious that his entire appeal was based on a knowledge of how to influence the minds of the Roman mob through flattery.

Flattery which is not based upon sincerity can be very dangerous, and is easily detected. Flattery is negative, it kills the truth that one wishes to convey. The positive enthusiasm Mark Antony used is what gave him the power of persuasion.

NEVER FORGET ENTHUSIASM

Study how a friend and graduate student of the Science of Personal Achievement applies and understands a most important principle of the power of persuasion.

"The Importance of Enthusiasm" is the title of an essay written by Robert Swaybill, New York counsellor at law and a successful example of enthusiasm and of definiteness of purpose.

Attorney Swaybill says, "The pinnacle of the legal profession is the art of the trial lawyer. In the pursuit of this art thousands upon thousands of books have been written by legal experts. And wherever lawyers meet, the question is raised, 'What must the trial lawyer possess to reach this pinnacle of success?' The answer is always the same—preparation.

"Well, it's established. You've got to be prepared. Today, even to poach an egg, you must be prepared. But isn't there some other ingredient, other than preparation, necessary for success in this art? Enthusiasm is the answer.

"What exactly is enthusiasm? The dictionary says enthusiasm is 'strong excitement of feeling on behalf of a cause or a subject.' An enthusiastic man is ardent and imaginative, free from fear or doubt; he has an inner power, he is in control of his senses; he electrifies his listeners with his enthusiasm.

"Enthusiasm for one's cause is contagious, it is infectious. Enthusiasm comes from within. Enthusiasm is magnetic.

"From our observations the principles and the laws are the same in all situations. If you are able to convince the jury of the righteousness of your cause, with enthusiasm in this most difficult of situations, how easily it can be applied to other phases of life.

"Enthusiasm—and lack of interest—are equally contagious. The choice is up to you.

"What has been related (here) are universal laws. We do not discover these laws—for they have always been with us. WE DISCOVER OURSELVES. We do not unravel these laws. We unravel ourselves. These universal laws are available to everyone. Develop enthusiasm and set these laws to work. . . ."

No better commentary could be made on the character of a person than what is embodied in these words. They are written by one whose whole career has put these "universal laws" to work in his own life.

Section II

A Guide to Master Salesmanship

Every successful day of your life, regardless of your occupation or profession, you must be a Master Salesman. Master Salesmanship is the key to the attainment of what you desire from life. This applies not only to insurance men, car salesmen, and people who sell professionally, but to housewives, students, and anyone who may desire to reap his share of life's richest blessings.

The major advances in all fields—science, education, industry, technology, religion—have been made, for the most part, by men and women who possessed and utilized the Power of Persuasion. Napoleon Hill stressed the importance of this particular point and emphasized that this section of the book is useful to all who will read it, since it covers the fundamentals of the art of Master Salesmanship.

If you doubt that *everyone* needs to acquire a working knowledge of Master Salesmanship, Dr. Hill recommended the following: Underline in red ink the words "Master Salesman" each time they appear in this chapter. With blue ink, write beside them your own classification, whether it be student, housewife, businessman, artist, or salesman. For best results, do this prior to reading the chapter through carefully.

After having read the chapter thoroughly, observing each underscored word and notation, you will begin to think of yourself as a Master Housewife, a Master Student, a Master Typist—a Master Salesman in whatever field of endeavor you are engaged.

Numerous factors enter into the development program for the successful salesperson. Most of these factors are personal in nature, having a greater bearing on the person than on the product or service he or she offers, or the organization they represent.

By reading the preceding chapters carefully and applying their contents practically, the reader has already taken the first step toward becoming a Master Salesman—he has conducted an honest self-analysis. In addition to the valuable information in the foregoing chapters, there are essential qualities which you *must* possess if you seriously intend to become a successful person.

There follows a list of these very important qualities, qualities which anyone may attain with a bit of serious thought and endeavor. The list is lengthy, and perfection may be attained only through constant effort. But when perfection or near-perfection is finally attained, a Master Salesman is born!

Before entering into a detailed consideration of the complete list of qualities, we would like to define the eight which are *positive musts*.

PREREQUISITES: EIGHT QUALITIES A SUCCESSFUL SALESMAN MUST POSSESS

1. PHYSICAL FITNESS is of tremendous importance for the simple reason that neither mind nor body can function well without it. Fitness is a prerequisite for a positive

mental attitude. Therefore, pay attention to habits of healthful living, including proper diet, sleep, recreation, and exercise.

2. COURAGE must live in every man or woman who succeeds, especially in selling, for it is a high-pressure business that is inherently intensely competitive.

3. IMAGINATION is an absolute requisite for the successful salesman. He must anticipate diverse situations in relation to his prospective customer. He must have an imagination that enables him to place himself in sympathetic understanding of the position, needs, and objectives of his customer. He must "stand in the other person's shoes." This takes real imagination.

4. SPEECH. A salesman's voice must be pleasing. A high-pitched, nasal tone is irritating. Words half swallowed are hard to understand. Speak distinctly and enunciate clearly. A meek voice indicates a weak person. A firm, resonant voice full of assurance and confidence is indicative of a person of enthusiasm and assertiveness.

5. A PLEASING PERSONALITY. The Master Salesman has acquired the art of making himself pleasant to be with. He knows that the prospective buyer must buy the salesman as well as the merchandise he offers.

6. SELF-CONFIDENCE is a simple matter of self-hypnosis. If you dislike the word "hypnosis," call it autosuggestion, or self-suggestion. Self-confidence is the conditioning of the mind to bring desired goals or results.

Dr. Hill has ten invisible guides, or entities, for the sole purpose of keeping his mind positive and conditioned to do whatever he wants done.

Napoleon Hill's philosophy has gone well beyond the status of a classic in the field. It has become recognized as the bedrock on which most motivational theories are based. Elements of his ideas are found in virtually every self-improvement program that has been written about in the almost six decades that have passed since he published his first book on the subject.

Hill noted that all men of affairs, men like W. Clement Stone who built the giant Combined Insurance Company (later Aon Corporation) and Del Smith, chairman and chief executive officer of Evergreen International Aviation—in fact, all successful people—have a system of keeping their minds positive through autosuggestion.

One outstandingly successful man gives full credit for his success to his wife. When they first married, she wrote a creed which he signed and placed over his desk. Read the creed on page 106 and decide if you wish to copy it, sign it, and place it over your own desk. The lady who wrote this creed was a practical psychologist of the first order. Under the influence and guidance of such a woman, any man could achieve noteworthy success. Notice how freely the personal pronoun "I" is used. It begins the affirmation of self-confidence, which is as it should be.

This would be a splendid creed for every salesman to adopt. It will not hurt *your* chances for success if you adopt it. Mere adoption, however, is not enough. You must practice it. Read it over and over until you know it by heart. Then repeat it at least once a day until you have literally transformed it into a part of your mental makeup. Keep a copy of it before you as a daily reminder of your pledge to practice it. By doing so, you will be making efficient use of the principle of auto-suggestion as a means of developing self-confidence. Never mind what anyone says about your procedure. Just remember that it is your business to succeed, and this creed, if mastered and applied, will go a long way toward helping you.

Any idea which you firmly fix in your subconscious mind, by repeated affirmation, automatically becomes a plan or blueprint which an unseen power uses to help you teach your goal.

7. THE MASTERMIND ALLIANCE. No man can accomplish enduring results of a far-reaching nature without the help of others. When two or more persons ally themselves in any undertaking, in a spirit of harmony and understanding, each person in the alliance multiplies his own powers of achievement. Nowhere is this principle more successfully practiced than in an industry or business in which there is perfect teamwork between the employer and the employees. Wherever you find teamwork, you find prosperity and goodwill on both sides.

"Cooperation" is said to be the most important word in the English language. It plays an important part in the affairs of the home, in the relationship of man and wife, parents and children. It plays an important part in affairs of state. So important is this principle of cooperation that no leader can become powerful or last long who does not understand and apply it in his leadership. Lack of cooperation has destroyed more business enterprises than have all other causes combined.

8. WORK, hard work, is the only thing that will turn sales training and ability into money. No amount of good health, courage, or imagination is worth a dime unless it is put to work. A salesman's income is usually fixed by the amount of hard, intelligent work he puts out.

One successful salesman figured out the relationship between work and luck. He explained it to his sales force this way:

"The harder I work and the less I scheme, the better my luck is. Don't look to lady luck for success. Luck is a gamble, and work gives you the safety margin for real success."

Carefully consider these eight qualities. Question yourself repeatedly about those you honestly possess and those in which you are deficient. Work at improving your self-discipline, for self-discipline is the key to the mastery of all eight prerequisites and thus the way to Master Salesmanship.

The following items are also very important to the student of salesmanship. They are the qualities which lend the polish and professional finesse every salesman must possess if he is to become a true Master Salesman.

PROFESSIONAL QUALITIES

1. KNOWLEDGE OF THE MERCHANDISE HE SELLS. The Master Salesman carefully analyzes and is thoroughly familiar with all aspects of the merchandise or service he offers. Knowledge of his product can mean the difference between success and failure.

2. BELIEF IN THE MERCHANDISE OR SERVICE. No salesman can sell successfully something that he himself does not understand and believe in. The Master Salesman never tries to sell anything in which he does not

SELF-CONFIDENCE CREED

I believe in myself. I believe in those who work with me. I believe in my employer. I believe in my friends. I believe in my family. I believe that God will lend me everything I need with which to succeed if I do my best to earn it through faithful and honest service. I believe in prayer and I will never close my eyes to sleep without praying for divine guidance to the end that I will be patient with other people and tolerant with those who do not believe as I do.

I believe that success is the result of intelligent effort and does not depend upon luck or sharp practices, or double-crossing friends, fellowmen, or my employer. I believe I will get out of life exactly what I put into it; therefore, I will be careful to conduct myself toward others as I would want them to act toward me. I will not slander those whom I do not like. I will not slight my work no matter what I may see others doing. I will render the best service of which I am capable because I have pledged myself to succeed in life and I know that success is always the result of conscientious and efficient effort. Finally, I will forgive those who offend me because I realize that I shall sometimes offend others and I will need their forgiveness.

Signed

have implicit confidence, because he knows that his mind will transmit his lack of confidence to the mind of the prospective buyer, regardless of how pleasing his presentation.

3. APPROPRIATENESS OF MERCHANDISE. The Master Salesman analyzes his prospective buyer and the buyer's needs and offers him only what is applicable. He never tries to sell a Rolls Royce to a man who ought to purchase a Dodge, even if the prospective buyer is finan-

cially able to buy the more expensive car. He knows a bad bargain for the buyer is a worse bargain for the seller.

4. VALUE GIVEN. The Master Salesman never tries to get more for his product than it is actually worth, since he realizes that the sustained confidence and goodwill of his prospective buyer are worth more than a "long profit" on a single sale.

5. KNOWLEDGE OF THE PROSPECTIVE BUYER. The Master Salesman is a character analyst. He has the ability to determine which of the basic motives the buyer will respond to most freely, and he bases his sales presentation on these motives. If the prospective buyer has no outstanding motive for buying, then the Master Salesman, knowing that a motive is essential in closing a sale, creates one for him.

6. CATEGORIZING THE PROSPECTIVE BUYER. The Master Salesman never tries to make a sale until he has properly categorized the prospective buyer, informing himself, in advance, on the following points:

(a) The prospective buyer's financial capacity.

(b) His need for the item being offered for sale.

(c) His motives for making a purchase.

Endeavoring to make sales without first categorizing the prospective buyer is a mistake that rates at the head of the list of causes for "no sale."

7. ABILITY TO "NEUTRALIZE" THE MIND OF THE BUYER. The Master Salesman knows that no sale can be made until the mind of the prospective buyer has been neutralized, or made receptive. Armed with this knowledge, he never endeavors to close a sale until he has opened the mind of the buyer and prepared it to receive the seed of desire for the merchandise being offered. Neutralizing the buyer's mind will be discussed in depth in Section V of this chapter.

8. ABILITY TO CLOSE A SALE. The Master Salesman is an artist at reaching and successfully passing the closing point in selling. He trains himself to sense the best psychological moment to terminate his presentation and make his sale. He rarely, if ever, asks the prospective

buyer if he is ready to purchase. Instead, he goes on the assumption that the buyer is ready and conducts his conversation and general demeanor accordingly. This is simply using the power of suggestion effectively. The Master Salesman avoids trying to close a sale until he knows in his own mind that he can close successfully. He conducts his sales presentation (never called "pitch") so that his prospective buyer believes *he* has done the buying. (See "Closing the Sale," Section VI of this chapter.)

PERSONAL QUALITIES

9. SHOWMANSHIP. The Master Salesman is also a super showman. He has the ability to reach the mind of his prospective buyer by dramatizing his presentation honestly and by giving it sufficient "color" to arouse intense interest through an appeal to the prospective buyer's imagination.

10. SELF-CONTROL. The Master Salesman exercises complete control over his head and his heart, at all times. He knows that if he does not control himself, he cannot control his prospective buyer.

11. INITIATIVE. Regardless of what you are now doing, every day brings you face to face with a chance to render some service, outside the course of your regular duties, that will be of value to others. You render this additional service of your own accord and, of course, not with the intention of receiving monetary compensation. You are rendering this service because it provides you with ways and means of exercising, developing, and strengthening the aggressive spirit of initiative which you must possess before you can ever become an outstanding figure in the affairs of your chosen field.

Those who work for money alone, those who receive nothing but money for their work, are always underpaid, no matter how much they receive. Money is necessary, but the big prizes of life cannot be measured in dollars and cents. No amount of money could possibly take the place of happiness and peace of mind.

The Master Salesman understands the value and uses of the principle of initiative. He never has to be told what to do or how to do it. He uses his imagination to create plans which he translates into action through initiative. He needs little supervision, if any.

12. TOLERANCE. The Master Salesman is open-minded and tolerant on all subjects, knowing that open-mindedness is essential for growth.

13. ACCURATE THINKING. The Master Salesman thinks! He takes the time and goes to the trouble of gathering facts as the basis of this thinking. He does not guess when facts are available. He never airs opinions that are not based upon what he knows to be facts.

14. PERSISTENCE. The Master Salesman is never influenced by the word "no" and does not recognize the word "impossible." To him, all things can be achieved. The word "no" to the Master Salesman is nothing more than a signal to begin his sales presentation in earnest. He knows that all buyers take the line of least resistance by resorting to the "no" alibi. Because he possesses this knowledge, he is rarely susceptible to the negative influence of sales resistance.

The story which follows is a lucid example of how one salesman learned to hear only what he wanted to hear—a "yes"!

THE EAR TRUMPET STORY

While conducting a school of salesmanship in New York City, Dr. Hill received a call from the New York Life Insurance Company asking him to come to talk with them about a salesman who had gone bad. He had been one of their top salesmen until, suddenly, he just stopped producing. They wanted to find the trouble.

Dr. Hill met Mr. James C. Spring, and talked with him for a few moments.

Spring selected ten prospects and the two men started out. Before they had reached the office of the first prospect, Dr. Hill was hearing "no" before Mr. Spring even talked to the prospect! As they went in, Mr. Spring said, "Well, we'll go in here, but I've been here several times before, and I know it's useless."

Dr. Hill says, telling the story, "Well, of course, I

INITIATIVE PLEDGE

Having chosen—————as my life work, I now understand that it is my duty to transform this purpose into reality.

Therefore, I will form the habit of taking some definite action each day that will carry me one step nearer the attainment of a Master Salesman.

I know that procrastination is a deadly enemy of all who would become leaders in any undertaking, and I will eliminate this habit by:

1. Doing some definite and useful thing each day, without anyone telling me to do it.

2. Searching until I find at least one thing that I can do each day that I have not been in the habit of doing, and that will be of value to others.

3. Telling at least one other person, each day, of the value of practicing this habit of doing something that ought to be done without being told to do it.

I can see that the muscles of the body become strong in proportion to the extent to which they are used; therefore, I understand that the habit of initiative also becomes fixed in proportion to the extent that it is practiced. I realize that the place to begin the habit of initiative is in the small, commonplace things connected with my daily work; therefore, I will go at my work each day as if I were doing it solely for the purpose of developing this necessary habit of initiative.

I understand that by practicing this habit of taking the initiative in connection with my daily work, not only will I be developing that habit, but I will also be attracting the attention of those who will place greater value on my services as a result of this practice.

———————
Signed

knew that with that kind of attitude, it was useless. We went on to the next call. Again he said, 'This one is doubtful. I've been here only once, but he impresses me as being a man who is not going to buy.'

"That sort of thing went on for half a day. Finally, I said to Mr. Spring, 'Let's go back to the office now, and I'll tell you what the trouble is and how to find the answer to your problem.'

"Mr. Spring was sixty-five but someone had called him 'the old man' long before that. He had gotten the impression that he was too old to sell insurance. He had very good hearing, however—so good, in fact, that he thought he could hear the word 'no' before he even saw his prospect."

Dr. Hill explained the situation, and the superintendent of agents asked what to do about it. Dr. Hill answered, "Well, I want Mr. Spring to go out and find one of those old-fashioned ear trumpets. I want a really old one that has been in use for a long time. Then when someone starts to tell Mr. Spring 'no,' I want him to put that ear trumpet to his ear, pretend he didn't hear, and go right on talking."

Mr. Spring was listening to all of this. Amazed, he said, "And what do you want me to do that for?"

"Mr. Spring, I want you to do that in order to get your confidence back."

Mr. Spring went out that day and found an old-fashioned ear trumpet. It had been knocked around quite a bit and was perfect for the job. It had a string around it, and Mr. Spring tied it so that it would swing around his neck. Then the two men started out again.

The first man they visited took a look at the ear trumpet and said: "Mr. Spring, I didn't know you were hard of hearing."

Spring took the trumpet, put it up to his ear and shouted, "Eh?"

The man repeated the comment.

Spring grinned and said, "Yes, I guess I am," and began his presentation. The sale was successful.

By the end of the week, he had made five more sales, the biggest record he had ever had.

Mr. Spring learned not to consider himself a man too old to sell insurance. He learned not to hear the word "no" even after it had been said, and certainly not *before* it had been said.

When a salesman goes in to talk to a prospective buyer, the buyer picks up his mental attitude, whether he realizes it or not. If the salesman is doubtful, it is unlikely that he will be successful.

That is the way the human mind works. A Master Salesman never lets the prospective buyer take the initiative. He takes it from the very beginning and holds it right through to the end. If the prospective buyer raises objections, the Master Salesman has a stock of rebuttals to offset every objection, and he has everything organized in his mind before he goes in to talk.

Note: Dr. Hill emphasizes that he did this in order to dramatize to Mr. Spring the reason for his lagging sales. Mr. Spring got Dr. Hill's point in a short time, set the ear trumpet aside, and returned to successful selling. The ear trumpet had taught him not to look for, hear, or expect the "no can do" part of the sales presentation.

15. FAITH. The Master Salesman has the capacity for "super faith" in:
   (a) Himself
   (b) What he is selling
   (c) His prospective buyer
   (d) Closing the sale

He never tries to make a sale without the aid of faith. He knows faith is contagious and that it is transmitted to the "receiving station" of the prospective buyer's mind, positively influencing his decision to buy. Without faith, there can be no Master Salesmanship. Faith is a state of mind which may be described as an intensified form of self-reliance. It is said that "faith moves mountains." It also makes sales.

16. THE HABIT OF OBSERVATION. The Master Salesman is an astute observer of small details. Every word uttered by the prospective buyer, every change of facial expression, every movement, is observed and its significance weighed.

17. THE HABIT OF RENDERING MORE SERVICE THAN IS EXPECTED. The Master Salesman follows the habit of rendering service which is greater in quantity and finer in quality than what is expected, thereby profiting by the law of increasing returns, as well as by the law of contrast.

18. PROFITING BY FAILURES AND MISTAKES. The Master Salesman experiences no such contingent as "lost effort." He profits by all his mistakes and, through observation, by the mistakes of others. He knows that every failure and mistake, if analyzed, may be found to contain the seed of an equivalent success.

19. THE MASTERMIND. The Master Salesman understands and applies the mastermind principle, through which he greatly multiplies his power to achieve. This principle is simply the coordination of two or more individual minds, working in perfect harmony for a definite purpose.

20. A DEFINITE MAJOR AIM. The Master Salesman works always with a definite sales quota, or goal, in mind. He never goes to his work merely with the aim of selling all he can. Not only does he work with a definite goal in mind, but he sets a definite time in which to attain the object of that goal.

21. THE GOLDEN RULE APPLIED. The Master Salesman uses the Golden Rule as the foundation of all his business transactions, putting himself in the other person's shoes, and seeing the situation from his or her viewpoint.

THE GOLDEN RULE APPLIED

The best illustration of the Golden Rule applied is a story which took place around the turn of the century. One rainy afternoon, those many years ago, an old lady walked into a Pittsburgh department store. She wandered around aimlessly, very much in the manner of a person who is just "browsing." Most of the sales personnel gave her the "once over" and busied themselves with stock to avoid being troubled with her.

However, one young man saw her and made it his business to inquire politely if he might serve her. She informed him that she was only waiting for the rain to stop and that she did not wish to make a purchase. The young man assured her that she was welcome and, by engaging her in conversation, made her feel that he meant what he said. When she was ready to go, he accompanied her to the street and raised her umbrella for her. She asked for his card and went on her way.

The incident had been forgotten by the young man when, one day, he was called into the office by the head of the firm and shown a letter from a lady who wanted a salesman to go into her mansion in Scotland and take an order for its furnishings.

That lady was Andrew Carnegie's mother. She was also the same lady whom the young man had treated courteously many months before. In the letter Mrs. Carnegie specified that this young man was the one whom she desired to be sent to take her order. The order amounted to an enormous sum, and the incident brought the young man an opportunity for advancement that he might never have had except for his courtesy to an old lady who did not look like a "ready sale."

Just as the great fundamental laws of life are embodied in the most common everyday experiences, so are the real opportunities often hidden in the seemingly unimportant transactions of life. Never suspecting that a fabulous opportunity would result from his courtesy, the young man was simply applying what he understood about the principle of the Golden Rule.

22. ENTHUSIASM. The Master Salesman has an abundance of enthusiasm which he can draw on at will. He knows the vibrations of thought which he releases through enthusiasm will be picked up by the prospective buyer in the same manner as faith and, like faith, will positively influence the buyer's decision. Enthusiasm is an intangible but readily recognized quality. Everyone likes the enthusiastic person. He has high spirits and radiates a positive attitude, good fellowship, and faith. Perhaps enthusiasm is born of one's own deep faith in himself and in the purpose of the work in which he is involved. Enthusiasm may be compared to the light of a flashing diamond on a jeweler's tray. Its spontaneous,

many-faceted brilliance compels admiration and demonstrates its value. Every salesman should heed this bit of sage advice: "With all thy getting get enthusiasm."

23. GOOD MEMORY. The principles by which an accurate, unfaltering memory may be trained are few and comparatively simple:

(a) *Retention*. The receiving of an impression through one or more of the five senses, and the recording of this impression in a logical fashion. This process may be compared to the recording of a picture on the sensitized plate of a camera.

(b) *Recall*. The reviving or recalling into the conscious mind those sense impressions that have been recorded in the subconscious mind. This process may be compared to the act of going through a card index and pulling out a card on which information has been previously recorded.

(c) *Recognition*. The ability to recognize a sense impression when it is called into the conscious mind, to identify it as being a duplicate of the original impression, and to associate it with its original source. This process enables us to distinguish between "memory" and "imagination."

IMPROVE YOUR MEMORY

These are the three principles which enter into the act of remembering. Now let us make application of these principles and determine how to use them effectively.

(a) When you wish to be sure of your ability to recall a sense impression, such as a name, date, or place, make the impression vivid by concentrating your attention upon it in fine detail. An effective way to do this is to repeat, several times, the item you wish to remember. Just as a photographer must give the proper exposure time to the sensitized plate of a camera, so must we give the subconscious mind time to record properly and clearly any sense impression that we wish to be able to recall with readiness.

(b) Associate what you wish to remember with some

other object, name, place, or date with which you are quite familiar, and which you can easily recall when you wish. For example, you might use the name of your home town, a close friend, the date of your birth, and so on. Your mind will then take the sense impression that you wish to be able to recall and file it away with the one that you can easily recall, so that bringing one into the conscious mind also brings the other.

(c) Repeat what you wish to remember a number of times, concentrating upon it. The common failing of not being able to remember names results largely from not having properly recorded the name in the first place. When you are introduced to a person whose name you wish to be able to recall at will, repeat that name four or five times, first making sure that you clearly understand the name. If the name is similar to that of some person whom you know well, associate the two, thinking of both as you record the new name.

If someone gives you a letter to be mailed, look at the letter, increase its size in your imagination, and see it hanging over a letter box. Fix in your mind a letter approximately the size of a door, associating it with a mailbox of equal proportion. You will observe that the first letter box you pass on the street will cause you to recall that big, odd-looking letter which you have in your pocket.

Suppose that you were introduced to a lady whose name was Elizabeth Shearer, and you wished to be able to recall her name at will. As you repeat her name, associate it with Queen Elizabeth and a large pair of scissors, perhaps ten feet in length. You will observe that the thought of either the large pair of shears or the name of the Queen will help you to recall the name Elizabeth Shearer.

The law of association is the most important feature of a well-trained memory, yet it is a very simple law. All you have to do to make use of it is link something familiar or similar with the thing that you would like to recall in the future.

Many years ago a friend gave Dr. Hill his home telephone number in Milwaukee, Wisconsin. Although he did not write it down, Dr. Hill remembers it today as well as he did the day he received it. This is the way it was recorded.

The number and exchange were Lakeview 2651. At the time his friend gave him the number, they were standing in sight of Lake Michigan. Dr. Hill used the lake as an associated object with which to file the name of the exchange. It so happened that the telephone number was made up of the age of his brother, who was 26, and that of his father, who was 51. He associated their names with the number, and to recall the exchange and number, he had only to think of Lake Michigan, his brother, and his father!

24. HUMILITY. Many people think of humility as a negative virtue. It isn't. It is a powerfully positive one. Humility is a force that man can put into action and operation for his own good. All of his greatest advances—spiritual, cultural, technical—have been based on it. It is the prime requisite of true Christianity. With its help, Gandhi set India free. Dr. Albert Schweitzer created a better world for thousands of Africans in the jungles, and for all of us.

Humility is absolutely essential for the type of personality you need to achieve personal success, no matter what your goal. You will find it even more essential after you have reached the top.

Without humility you will never gain wisdom, for one of the most important traits of a wise man is the ability to say, "I could be wrong."

Without humility you will never be able to find the "seed of an equivalent or greater benefit" in adversity and defeat.

Humility is a positive force that knows no limitations. It's quite a small thing, but don't overlook it. Humility is a vital ingredient of greatness.

25. BELIEF IN SUCCESS. Success is achieved by those who are thoroughly imbued with the belief that they can attain it. They are convinced of one fact: *Whatever my mind can conceive and believe, my mind can achieve.* They are consciously working to develop belief in them-

THE BARNES CREED
(Business Partner to Thomas A. Edison)

1. I will channel my mind toward prosperity and success by keeping my thoughts as much as possible on the major goal I have set for myself.
2. I will free my mind of self-made limitations by drawing on the power of the Creator through unlimited faith.
3. I will keep my mind free of greed and covetousness by sharing my blessings with those who are worthy to receive them.
4. I will substitute a positive type of discontent for indolent self-satisfaction so that I may continue to learn and grow both physically and spiritually.
5. I will keep an open mind on all subjects and toward all people so that I may rise above intolerance.
6. I will look for good in others and school myself to deal gently with their faults.
7. I will avoid self-pity. Under all circumstances I will seek stimulation to greater effort.
8. I will recognize and respect the difference between the material things I need and desire, and my rights to receive them.
9. I will cultivate the habit of "going the extra mile" and always rendering more and better service than is expected of me.
10. I will turn adversity and defeat into assets by remembering that they always carry with them the seed of equivalent benefits.
11. I will always conduct myself toward others in such manner that I may never be ashamed to face the man I greet at the mirror each morning.
12. Finally, my daily prayer will be for wisdom to recognize and live my life in harmony with the overall purpose of the Creator.

selves and in their capability to realize any goal they set for themselves.

If you have unfulfilled desires, repeating this creed to yourself at least once a day will help you to realize your greatest wishes, too.

26. DECISION. Any well-informed salesman will tell you that indecision is the outstanding weakness of the majority. Every salesman is familiar with that time-worn alibi, "I will think it over," which is the last defense of the prospect who simply does not have the courage to say yes or no.

The great leaders of the world were men and women of quick decision. General Grant certainly was no paragon of virtue, but he was an able general because he had the quality of firm decision, and this was sufficient to offset his weaknesses. The whole story of his military success may be gathered from his reply to critics: "We will fight it out along these lines if it takes all summer."

DECIDE—AND ACT!

When Napoleon reached a decision to move his armies in a given direction, he permitted nothing to change that decision. If his line of march brought his soldiers to a ditch dug by his opponents to stop him, he would give the order to charge the ditch until it had been filled with dead men sufficient to bridge it.

The suspense of indecision drives millions of people to failure. A condemned man once said that his approaching execution was not so terrifying once he had reached the decision to accept the inevitable.

Andrew Carnegie's vision of a great steel industry would never have materialized had he not reached a decision to transform his vision into reality.

Wallace Johnson and Kemmons Wilson of Memphis, Tennessee, dreamed of being the nation's innkeepers—and the chain of Holiday Inns is a testimonial to the vision of the founders. Holiday Inns adopted innovative marketing techniques and established franchise quality requirements that became a standard in the industry. Among the most widely publicized was the slogan: "Our sign stands for quality or it doesn't stand at all." If a franchise didn't meet Holiday Inns' quality standards, Johnson and Wilson sent in a crane to remove the big green sign. Procrastination certainly had no part in this phenomenal success story.

Imagination alone is not enough to insure success. Millions of people have imagination and build plans that would easily bring them both fame and fortune, but those plans never reach the decision stage. It takes a DEFINITE DECISION! The man of decision gets what he goes after, no matter how long it takes, no matter how difficult the task. The man of decision cannot be stopped. The man of indecision cannot be started. Take your own choice.

> Behind him lay the gray Azores,
> Behind the gates of Hercules;
> Before him not the ghosts of shores;
> Before him only shoreless seas.

> The good mate said: "Now must we pray,
> For lo! the very stars are gone,
> Brave Adm'r'l, speak; what shall I say?"
> "Why, say, Sail on and on!"

When Columbus began his famous voyage, he made one of the most far-reaching decisions in the history of mankind. Had he not remained firm in that decision, the freedom of America would never have become a reality.

HIS INCOME DOUBLED

The late Earl Nightingale, whose radio program "Our Changing World" was heard daily on hundreds of radio stations, made a decision and took the time to learn the secrets of success. You will note that he learned a very valuable lesson in one week and doubled his income. His efforts brought him great financial security and recognition on a national basis. Besides his radio program, he was a well-known public lecturer and made many best-selling personal albums and audio tapes.

Earl Nightingale was the voice and personality behind

the "Think and Grow Rich" recording, taken from Dr. Hill's most popular book, *Think and Grow Rich*.

Earl Nightingale has said, "In over twenty years spent searching for a formula with which a person could utilize every possible element in his favor, it was not until I read Napoleon Hill that I found all the answers.

"Using Dr. Hill's formula for achievement, I was able to double my income in one week. This was quite a feat, because my income previous to this time was rather considerable. I then figured that if it would work once, I could double it again and at the same time remove all doubts as to the efficacy of the procedure. I repeated the process.

"Any person who carefully studies and diligently practices Dr. Hill's proved methods cannot fail to achieve that which he has set his heart on.

"Dr. Hill's work changed my life, and I wholeheartedly recommend it to anyone who is interested in a better life."

Take notice of those about you and observe this significant fact—*the successful men and women are those who reach decisions quickly and then stand firmly by those decisions after they are made.*

If you are in the habit of making up your mind today and changing it tomorrow, you are doomed to failure. If you are not sure which way to move, it is better to shut your eyes and move in the dark than to remain still and make no move at all.

The world will forgive you if you make mistakes, but it will never forgive you if you make no decisions, because it will never hear of you outside of the community in which you live.

You are using time. It is always your next move. Move with quick decision, and time will favor you. Stand still and time can wipe you out. You cannot always make the right move, but if you make enough moves, you will learn about the special inner power that can keep you working for and with success.

Mastery of these qualities entitles those who sell to rate as Master Salesmen. Study the list carefully. You may acquire every quality listed.

YOU TOO CAN LEARN

A very good example of the fallacy of the notion that "salesmen are born and not made," and a proof that salesmanship is an art which may be mastered by those with the will to learn it, is the story of Clarence Walker of Atlanta, Georgia.

Clarence N. Walker, retired executive staff representative of the Coca-Cola Company, Atlanta, Georgia, built a highly successful career in the art of salesmanship. Mr. Walker's remarkable ability to capture and to hold the attention of an audience not only won him the distinction of being one of his company's most outstanding public relations men, but also afforded him the greater reward of a wealth of friends. His wit and humor are a sparkling showcase for a more serious message—the value of thoughtful, responsible citizenship in whatever field of endeavor one chooses to work.

Salesmanship is an art which may be mastered by anyone with a will to learn. Clarence Walker certainly demonstrated this in his life. He dealt most often with the salesman, and he lived by what he preached—the value of the power of persuasion. He did not demonstrate persuasion through calls on merchants or by selling commodities to individuals, but he demonstrated how to represent his company well in public relations through service to others. His life is a good example of how salesmanship is vital and necessary in every walk of life.

In a talk made to the New York Rotary Club, Mr. Walker said, "Make your vision big. Your success and happiness will never be any purer or brighter or finer than the vision you have or the picture you paint for yourself. . . . Have faith in your vision. Have faith in your plans, faith in your business, faith in the government, faith in your city, faith in God, faith in prayer, faith in things that are fine and fundamental . . . and not the least of these—have faith in yourself. Have courage. This is sometimes the hardest part. But have the courage to be willing to go out and do the work necessary to carry out the vision and the faith which you claim. I think that Shakespeare must have been right when he said, 'If to do were as easy as to know what were good to do, chapels had been churches and poor men's cottages princes' palaces,' but it is not that easy, is it? It is sometimes harder to live and work for the right than it is to fight and die for it.

"But never forget the value of these things . . . and the value of an investment in friendship. . . . And as for me—'Let me live in my house by the side of the road/ Where the race of men go by./ Men that are good, men that are bad,/ As good and as bad as I./ I would not sit in the scorner's seat/ Or hurl the cynic's ban./ Let me live in my house by the side of the road/ And be a friend to man.' "

Born in Ellijay, Georgia, Mr. Walker was graduated from the Berry Schools, Mt. Berry, Georgia. He received his LL.B. degree from the University of Georgia in Athens. During World War I he served as an officer and personnel executive of aircraft production, and in World War II he was regional director of the National Housing Agency, supervising eight southeastern states.

He practiced law in Georgia and North Carolina for six years. He was later in the banking, real estate, and investment business and was business manager of the Berry Schools. He was for fourteen years a member of the Coca-Cola Company staff.

Active in church, civic, community, and fraternal organizations, Mr. Walker has been a Rotarian for more than forty years. He is a member of the board of deacons of Atlanta's First Baptist Church and teaches a men's Bible class there.

Mr. Walker is a salesman every day of his life. In whatever pursuit he is engaged, he thinks and acts as a salesman. It is an art he has practiced and made to produce a full and satisfying career. You can match his story if you will.

Section III

Major Weaknesses in the Personality and Habits of Salesmen

Just as there are positive qualities essential to becoming a Master Salesman, there are negative qualities which the student salesman should avoid. These are weak points in personality and professional ability.

Read this list of weaknesses carefully. Check off each of the weaknesses you know you have already overcome. Where you feel you need improvement, place an "X."

REVIEW UNTIL IMPROVEMENT COMES

If you sincerely desire success, come back to this section and study it until you can give yourself a grade of one hundred per cent. Once you have done this, get a close friend, someone who knows you well, to give you his honest opinion and grading. If your associate or friend grades you by past performance, and you have made improvements in your personality or habits, mark "Improved" by the items listed. Be sure to take a positive stand, telling your friend how and when you changed. Give specific examples. By committing yourself to others on your improvement program, you will have an added source of inspiration and encouragement.

1. THE HABIT OF PROCRASTINATION. There is no substitute for prompt and persistent action.

2. ONE OR MORE OF THE SIX BASIC FEARS. The man whose mind is filled with any form of fear cannot sell successfully. The six basic fears are:

(a) The fear of poverty
(b) The fear of criticism
(c) The fear of ill health
(d) The fear of loss of love of someone
(e) The fear of old age
(f) The fear of death

To this list of basic fears should, perhaps, be added the fear that the prospective buyer will not buy.

3. SPENDING TOO MUCH TIME MAKING "CALLS" INSTEAD OF SALES. A "call" is not an interview. An interview is not a sale. Some who call themselves salesmen have not learned this truth. You must see the person who can say yes or no!

4. SHIFTING RESPONSIBILITY TO THE SALES MANAGER. The sales manager is not obligated to go with the salesman to make calls. He hasn't enough hours or legs to do this. His business is to tell the salesman what to do, not to do it for him.

5. PERFECTION IN CREATING ALIBIS. Explanations do not explain. Orders do! Nothing else does! Don't forget that.

6. SPENDING TOO MUCH TIME IN HOTEL LOBBIES OR COFFEE SHOPS. A hotel lobby or coffee shop is a fine place to "park," but the salesman who parks there too long is bound to get walking papers sooner or later.

7. BUYING "HARD LUCK" STORIES INSTEAD OF SELLING MERCHANDISE. Current business trends and the market are a common topic of discussion, but don't let the prospective buyer use it to switch your mind from your own story.

8. IMBIBING TOO FREELY "THE NIGHT BEFORE." Parties are exciting, but they do not add to the next day's business.

9. DEPENDING ON THE SALES MANAGER FOR PROSPECTS. Order takers expect prospective buyers to be hogtied and held down until they arrive. Master Salesmen catch their own prospects "on the fly." This is one of the chief reasons they are Master Salesmen.

10. WAITING FOR BUSINESS CONDITIONS TO PICK UP. Business is always good with the robins. They do not wait for someone to dig the worms out of the ground. Be at least as clever as a robin. Orders are not being slipped under the salesman's door this year.

11. HEARING THE WORD "NO." This word, to a real salesman, is only a signal to begin fighting. If every buyer said yes, salesmen would have no jobs, for they would not be needed.

12. FEARING COMPETITION. Henry Ford had plenty of competition, but he apparently did not fear it, because he had the courage and ability to turn out an eight-cylinder car at an amazingly low price during a period in which many motor manufacturers were retrenching.

PLANNING, EQUIPMENT, MANNERS

13. FAILURE TO PLAN YOUR DAY IN ADVANCE. The man who plans his day in advance goes about his work logically and efficiently, accomplishing what he has planned to do that day. When there is no organization of schedule, a salesman literally "does not know where to begin."

14. KEEPING POOR RECORDS AND DATES ON CALLS. Prospects and established customers soon weary of the salesman who habitually "forgets" to call on specified days. When a customer needs merchandise, he needs it then!

15. TARDINESS. The salesman who is habitually late for sales meetings, business appointments, and to the office soon finds himself looking for new customers and, often, a new job.

16. USING WRINKLED OR OUT-OF-DATE MATERIAL. Crumpled, untidy, and out-of-date material denote disorganization and a lack of interest on the part of the salesman.

17. BEING UNEQUIPPED WITH A PEN. A writing instrument is a vital factor to the salesman's efficiency. The Master Salesman invests in a good pen or pencil which will adequately meet his requirements. He knows that prospects quickly tire of the salesman who always has to borrow something to write with in order to take an order. The customer tires even more quickly of the salesman who borrows a pen and never gets around to returning it.

18. USING GLASSES OR PERSONAL ADORNMENT AS A "PROP." Fidgeting with your wristwatch, twirling a ring, biting the rim of your glasses, or using them as a toothpick, as if it helps you to think better, are sure-fire ways

to set a customer's nerves on edge and consequently lose a sale.

19. A TIRED SALES PRESENTATION. Running through your sales presentation as if you were tired of hearing it—singing it out in a monotone and appearing bored with the whole thing—makes your customer or prospect bored with *you and your presentation*.

20. RELATING PERSONAL PROBLEMS TO ASSOCIATES AND CUSTOMERS. Your personal problems are important to you and only you. Everyone has his share and doesn't want to hear yours.

21. FAILURE TO READ AND COMPLY WITH PERTINENT MATERIAL. Your organization does not produce bulletins or contribute to trade papers to have them made into paper airplanes, or thrust into the wastepaper basket unread. They are produced to tell you something. Read them and keep well informed.

22. DISCOURTESY IN PARKING YOUR CAR. The customer who finds a salesman's car parked in his own allotted parking space is not overly encouraged to buy. Creating a traffic jam by blocking a business driveway is a first-class way to incur the wrath of any prospect and lose the possibility of sales with him in the future. It's just not that difficult to take the trouble to walk an extra block out of your way.

23. PROMISING WHAT YOUR COMPANY CANNOT DELIVER. What the salesman promises the customer expects to receive. Inability to fulfill a promise is not only embarrassing for the customer and your company, but is plain bad business.

24. NOT BEING PREPARED FOR RAIN. The rain-soaked and soggy salesman, who neglected to prepare for an inevitable rainy day, is a sorry sight to the prospect. A light raincoat and umbrella are always invaluable when needed.

25. RUNNING OUT OF SUPPLIES. The salesman who is not well stocked with contracts, brochures, order blanks, and so on often finds himself running as low on sales as on his supplies.

26. PLAIN PESSIMISM. The habit of expecting that the prospective buyer will give you the gate is likely to result

in your getting it. Life has a queer way of trying to please. It usually gives what is expected.

This is not a complete list of salesman's "don't's," but it is a fair sample. Perhaps some may interpret the list to be a little too personal. Others may see in it a touch of sarcasm. Remember, as you read, that it was intended only for those who need it. Others will not be offended.

This list is not original with Napoleon Hill. It was compiled from observation of thousands of salespeople Dr. Hill trained or managed during his long and distinguished career.

Need we suggest that not one of these "don't's" is an attribute of a pleasing personality?

Section IV

Major Factors on
Which Confidence Is Built

By careful observation of thousands of sales people from whom Napoleon Hill modestly said he gained much of his knowledge about selling, he discovered that numerous factors contribute to the development of confidence. A list of the most important of these follows.

1. Following the habit of rendering more service and better service than you are paid to render.

2. Entering into no transaction which does not benefit, as nearly equally as possible, everyone it affects.

3. Making no statement which you do not believe to be true, no matter what temporary advantages a falsehood might seem to offer.

4. Having a sincere desire in your heart to be of the greatest possible service to the largest number.

5. Cultivating a wholesome admiration for people; liking them better than you like money.

6. Doing your best to live, as well as you sell, your own philosophy of business. Actions speak louder than words.

7. Accepting no favors, large or small, without giving favors in return.

8. Asking nothing of any person without believing that you have a right to what you ask.

9. Entering into no arguments with any person over trivial or non-essential details.

10. Spreading the sunshine of good cheer wherever and whenever you can. Be a happy person!

11. Servicing what we sell may be an overused phrase, but when it is true, it's the salesman's best guarantee for repeated business.

12. Remembering, if you are successful, that someone helped you to become successful.

This list is well worth memorizing. It is also worth following.

SALESMAN—NOT CON MAN

A Master Salesman can sell a man anything he needs if the purchaser has confidence in the salesman. He can also sell a man many things he does not need, but he doesn't. Remember, a Master Salesman plays the double role of buyer and seller. He therefore does not try to sell any person anything that he himself would not buy if he were actually in the position of the prospective buyer.

There is a well-known type of crook who calls himself a Master Salesman. He is known as a confidence man. His sole asset is his ability to build confidence in the minds of his victims. His stealings run into the millions, and his victims may be found among the shrewdest businesspeople, professionals, and laymen.

These crooks often "stalk" their victims for months, or even years, in order to build a relationship of perfect confidence. When this foundation has been properly laid, the smartest people may be "taken in." We are all without defense against those in whom we have perfect confidence.

If confidence can be used successfully as the sole tool of operation for the crook, surely it can be used with greater effect for legitimate business and professional purposes. The salesman who knows how to build a bridge of confidence between himself and his prospective purchasers may write his own income ticket, as all such salesmen do.

High-pressure methods, exaggerated statements of fact, willful misrepresentation, whether by direct statement or by implication or innuendo, destroy confidence.

Every successful business firm must have the confidence of its patrons. The salesman is the intermediary through which this confidence is acquired—or he may be the medium through which it is lost. The Master Salesman, knowing as he does the importance of acquiring and holding the confidence of his buyers, bargains with them as if he were the owner of the business he represents. He deals with his customers exactly as he would want them treated if he were, in fact, the owner of the business.

Confidence is the basis of all harmonious relationships. The salesman who overlooks this fact is unfortunate. He can never acquire the Master Power of Persuasion. This means that he limits his earning capacity and circumscribes his possibilities of advancement.

There are two forces that cause men and women to talk, and thus to advertise a business favorably or unfavorably. They talk when they think they have been cheated, and when they have received a fairer treatment than expected.

All people are like this. They are impressed by the law of contrast. Anything unusual or unexpected, whether it impresses favorably or unfavorably, makes a lasting impression.

THE TEN BASIC MOTIVES

Motive is a force which operates on the human will, causing it to act. In terms of salesmanship, we might say simply that when a salesman makes his presentation to a prospective buyer, he bases his appeal on whatever will cause the customer to buy.

Three basic appeals to motive are:

1. Appeal to instinct.
2. Appeal to emotion.
3. Appeal to reason.

The appeals which cause most people to buy food, clothing, and shelter fall primarily into the first group, though in lesser degree they may find expression in the other two.

All beautiful things in the world that are desirable because of their beauty may be sold through appeals made under the second heading—emotion.

Love, marriage, and religion deal largely in appeals that are emotional.

Many goods and services are sold on emotional appeal. Education, books, the theater, music and art, life insurance, advertising, cosmetics, luxuries, toys are among the many things that are all sold on emotional appeal.

Investments, savings, mechanical appliances, business machines, and scientific works often change hands by appeals to reason.

There are ten basic motives to which people respond, and which—singly or in combinations—influence practically every human thought and deed. When the Master Salesman categorizes his prospective buyer, he looks first for the most logical motive with which he may influence the buyer's mind, and bases his appeal on this knowledge.

The ten basic motives are:

1. The desire for self-preservation.
2. The desire for financial gain.
3. The desire for love.
4. The desire for sex.
5. The desire for power and fame.
6. The desire to overcome fear.
7. The desire for revenge.
8. The desire for freedom (of body and mind).
9. The desire to build and create in thought and material.
10. Pity for the unfortunate.

These motives are listed in the approximate order of their importance and greatest usefulness.

SELLING THROUGH MOTIVES

The Master Salesman checks his sales presentation against these ten motives to make sure that it embraces an appeal through as many of them as possible. He knows that a sales presentation is more effective when based upon more than one motive.

No salesman has the right to try to sell anything to anyone unless his sales presentation can offer a logical motive for the purchaser to buy—and without a motive, no Master Salesman will try to make a sale. Master Salesmanship involves the rendering of useful service to the buyer. High-pressure methods do not come within the category of Master Salesmanship, mainly because such methods presuppose the lack of a logical motive for buying. High-pressure methods would not be necessary if the person doing the selling could show the prospective purchaser a logical motive for buying.

High-pressure salesmen usually depend on superlatives to take the place of motives for buying. This is a form of hijacking to which Master Salesmen never resort.

SIX MOST COMMON WEAKNESSES

If your sales presentation plan does not emphasize one or more of the ten basic motives, it is weak and should be revised. Careful analysis of sales people showed the fact that the outstanding weaknesses of approximately 98 per cent of them were found among the following:

1. Failure to present a motive for buying.
2. Lack of persistence in sales and in closing.
3. Failure to categorize prospective buyers.
4. Failure to neutralize the minds of prospective buyers.
5. Lack of imagination.
6. Absence of enthusiasm.

These deficiencies are common among the majority of sales people in all fields of selling. Any one of these weaknesses is sufficient to destroy the chance of a sale.

You will observe that *failure to present a motive for buying* heads the list of the six most common weaknesses of sales people. Nothing but indifference or lack of knowledge of scientific selling could explain this weakness.

Section V

Neutralizing the Buyer's Mind

Armed with a knowledge of himself, of his abilities and desires, the student salesman is ready to advance to a study of the customer. An understanding of the psychology of the salesman-customer relationship is the difference between success and failure in selling.

THE FIRST STEPS

The salesman-customer relationship is dependent on two conditions, both of which are controlled by the salesman:

1. The salesman must believe in himself and in his product.
2. The salesman must neutralize the mind of his customer. It must be cultivated and prepared before the seed of desire can be successfully planted in it.

To neutralize the mind of the buyer, the salesman must first establish three things:

1. *Confidence.* The buyer must have confidence in the salesman and in his product.
2. *Interest.* The buyer must be reached through an appeal to his imagination. The commodity offered for sale must arouse his interest.
3. *Motive.* The buyer must have a logical motive for buying.

Failure to neutralize the mind of the prospective buyer is one of the five major weaknesses of the majority of unsuccessful salesmen. There is no fixed rule to follow in neutralizing the minds of prospective buyers; each individual case must be handled on its own merits. The salesman with imagination will not be slow to recognize the most appropriate methods of approach for his particular customers.

Some of the methods that have been used successfully for sales preparation or neutralization purposes are the following:

1. SOCIAL CONTACTS THROUGH CLUBS. It has been said that more business is done on the golf courses of America than in all business offices. Certainly every Master Salesman knows the value of club contacts.

2. CHURCH AFFILIATIONS. Here one may make acquaintances without the usual formalities, under circumstances which tend to establish confidence if it is deserved.

3. LODGE AND OTHER AFFILIATIONS. In many lines of selling, the salesman will find it helpful to establish contacts through lodges and luncheon clubs, where it is natural to let down the barriers of formality.

4. PERSONAL COURTESIES. Dinner engagements offer favorable opportunity to break down the resistance of formalities and to establish confidence, a condition that leads to neutrality of mind.

5. MUTUAL INTEREST IN HOBBIES. Nearly everyone has a hobby or some interest outside of his or her business or calling. When discussing or pursuing hobbies, everyone is inclined to relax defense barriers that are upheld in the course of the business routine.

PLAY A ROLE IN THE COMMUNITY

6. PUBLIC SERVICE. You can display your talent to its highest degree by assisting local drives that benefit your community. No one will criticize hard work and a job well done for the United Way, the Heart Fund, Girl or Boy Scouts, or any other civic organization that needs

an enthusiastic worker. If you have not been asked, you can get a job simply by volunteering. Once they find that you will work, there will be no limit to the assignments you will get. This can be a very important stepping stone to success for any young man or woman.

7. LETTER WRITING. Brief letters of appreciation to people who have contributed a vital service to the community or who have assisted you in resolving a problem are a good idea. Special services deserve written thanks. This should not be a form letter, but a brief, personal note based on truth and sincerity, with no exaggeration. It is most important that you have the proper name, title (if appropriate), address, and zip code.

8. PUBLIC SPEAKING. Perhaps you would like to deliver free lectures for the P.T.A., civic clubs, or other nonprofit organizations on material such as *Succeed and Grow Rich Through Persuasion* or other motivation books. If you do this as a civic service, it is not deemed professional. Although most authors and publishers allow short quotations for press reviews and public lectures on copyrighted material, most copyright attorneys strongly recommend that any person or persons using copyrighted material for the purpose of lecturing should first secure written permission from the owners of the copyrighted material.

Once you have neutralized the mind of the buyer and established confidence, the next step in making a sale is to turn that confidence into interest in your product. Here the salesman must build his entire sales presentation around a central motive suited to the business and financial status of his prospective buyer. When the three requisites—confidence, interest, and motive—have been met, the salesman has reached the point at which the sale may be closed.

Section VI

Closing the Sale

It is not true that the closing of a sale is the most difficult part of the entire transaction; it is not difficult if the preparatory groundwork has been effectively laid. In fact, when the sale has been properly planned and executed, the climax of a sale becomes a mere detail.

Knowing how to close a sale makes the difference between success and failure. Whether you are selling stocks and bonds, furniture, cosmetics, insurance, advertising, a new home, or a vacation trip on the twelve-month credit plan, you must have a closing before you have a sale.

Many sales have been lost before any effort was made to secure a favorable decision for the product or service being sold. This occurs when the salesman fails to see the person who can give him a definite yes or no.

Once he is inside the prospective buyer's office to make a sale, the salesman must first obtain the prospect's attention. (Study "Neutralizing the Buyer's Mind," Section V.) Many salesmen try the joke routine, using the infamous "Have you heard the one about . . ." If you must tell a joke, it should be after the buyer has set the tempo and has told a few himself, or has created an atmosphere conducive to humor. Never take a serious statement and try to laugh it off with "That reminds me of the story . . ." This is a close, all right—a closed door!

It is the sadly informed salesman who thinks that sex is a sure shot and whose concept of sex usually consists of the latest filthy tale that neither stimulates nor amuses.

TO SMOKE OR NOT TO SMOKE?

Many a sale has been lost on the second puff of a cigarette. It is never proper to smoke when making a sale. Some think it proper to smoke if they have asked permission. This is rather ridiculous, because very few people will actually refuse to let you smoke. Others think it proper to smoke only when a cigarette is offered by the client.

One sales executive watched a sale "go up in smoke" in less than thirty seconds when the prospect offered the salesman a cigarette, and the salesman glibly replied, "No, thank you, I prefer to have one of these." Lighting his own brand, he puffed the sale away by chain-smoking for the remainder of the presentation.

Three months later, the prospect asked the sales manager the name of the man who accompanied him when he was offering a particular sales promotion. He remembered the program name, but not the salesman's. He made several pointed remarks indicating why an affirmative answer on the sale was never given.

"I have often wondered," said the disgruntled prospect, "what he thought I was smoking—marijuana, or 'roll your own.' "

Although the executive understood why the sale had turned from positive to negative with the cigarette incident, it seemed a little extreme that smoking should have killed the sale in the prospect's mind so quickly. Almost fifteen years later, it was disclosed that this gentleman's wife had inherited a fortune in a tobacco company, and that at that time, all their dreams of the future were linked to the success of that particular brand.

The simple and safe rule is to say, "No, thank you," when offered a cigarette by a prospect. Also, be assured that the prospect is never interested in how you stopped smoking or how you managed to evade the habit.

THE SIMPLE, DIRECT WAY

What does the prospect want to hear? Simply this: What you can do for him.

Clearly and concisely, tell him why you are there and what you know about what you are selling. Check off for him the benefits. Spell out the advantages, the services, the quality, and the value available to him.

After (1) seeing the person who can say yes or no, and (2) telling him or her what you have to offer and why he or she needs your product or service, you are ready to move toward the last step in closing.

The Master Salesman never begins to repeat or rehash what he has already said. A salesman who does not know how to close finds himself attached to a verbal merry-go-round, with no stopping place.

There are many stock closings recommended and endorsed by sales organizations throughout the country. At one time or another you will encounter salesmen who use some or all of them. However, it is our belief that a closing can be as simple as "leading the way to buy." Using an honest and sincere approach to secure an affirmative decision has proved the most successful of all closings.

The basic sales presentation and closing are so simple and direct that many salesmen are inclined to make them difficult and risky by resorting to trickery or trying to outwit the prospect with gimmicks. A former foundation executive experienced a presentation by a "pro" selling a special service for company employees, complete to a weekly supplement for the salesmen's spouses. After twenty minutes of a well-prepared and well-executed presentation, the salesman, handsomely dressed in a silk suit and custom-made shirt, began what he called his "close."

First, he reached into his pocket and pulled out a mousetrap, set it, and tripped it with a gold pen, saying that with his service, the employer would never get caught in the trap of always training new employees. Then he shuffled a deck of cards and arranged a full house, saying that his service covered every employee and that the buyer had a full house with this winner. At that point, he took his order book out of his briefcase and laid it confidently on the desk. Finally, he laid two parched peanuts (in the shell) on the prospect's desk and said his service cost only "peanuts a day."

Being a salesman himself, the executive never forgot the experience. Needless to say, his reply was "No, thank you." However, he felt that his time was well spent, for he had observed an unfortunate—but perfect—example of the best way to blow a sale, demonstrated by a competent salesman who could have made the sale in no time had he been honest and given the facts. The potential buyer had liked the premium of the service and had given serious consideration to buying, but "peanuts a day" was the only reference made to price, contract, or financial arrangement. It was not only insufficient, but it was an insult to the intelligence of the prospect.

Selling is great fun. It is a fascinating business, with unlimited potential. When you see the man who can say yes or no, tell him what you know about your product, and lead him to buy, you are practicing the art of real salesmanship. When you see that your prospect is buying, give him the facts he needs to close the sale with you. Inform him of future price increases, emphasizing special sales seasons, and describe special franchises. Always tell your prospect the facts, the facts that will be of value to him or to the company he represents.

YOUR EXIT

No sale is made until a definite agreement is reached. Do not be afraid to show him how it works. If your company requires you to make out an order blank or to get a purchase order, check, or cash advance, make your request in a businesslike and confident manner. It is most important that you gently show him how your company does business. If it is a new order, you must discuss the procedure. If it is a repeat order, discuss it if necessary. Just go into action and move authoritatively, handling it efficiently and saving his time. Let it be known that you are accepting this as the completion of the sale.

Once the sale is closed, start leaving. Express a brief, sincere word of appreciation and thank him for his business. On some occasions, an invitation for a future luncheon or dinner is excellent. A personal word while you are picking up your briefcase is acceptable, depending upon the length and nature of your association with the prospect.

Leave the office with the same friendliness that you had when you walked in. A polite thank you and a good-day to the secretary are sufficient. Some salesmen walk into an office with shoulders back and head up, speaking to everyone at the water fountain, having practiced on the elevator boy on the way up. Once they make the sale and close the prospect's door, they deflate and lose all their zest. Keep a balance going and coming. It paves the way for the next appointment and the next sale.

In summing up, remember that closing a sale is simple, having three basic steps:

1. See the people who can give you a definite answer.
2. Tell them what you have to sell and why you think it will be of benefit to their interests.
3. Lead them to buy.

To illustrate the lesson on closing a sale, we would like to present an amazing story of an occasion when Dr. Hill found it absolutely necessary to make a sale. It was not so much the account he wanted. He needed to demonstrate to one of his students that the principles of good salesmanship work. Dr. Hill realized that if he failed, many, many sales would be missed by his student and sales manager, young Jack Randall. This is a good example of what a Master Salesman can do and will do, completely within the framework of honesty, when he is motivated by a real reason to make a sale. This is a case history of a sale in progress, told by Dr. Hill himself.

THE NEWARK LAUNDRY COMPANY SALE

One morning in my New York headquarters, I received a telephone call from the president of the Newark Laundry Company. He asked me to come and talk with him about training his salesmen. Until then, I had never known that a laundry employed salesmen. Later, I learned that all his drivers operated independently and that they had to procure their own accounts and hold them. In order to do that, they had to know something about selling. It was a new field for me, and I made up my mind that I was going to get the account, come what may.

I decided to condition my mind before I went to Newark so that it would be impossible for me to come back without the sale. "Can you do that?" people have asked. I had done it before and knew that I could do it again.

Instructing my telephone operator not to ring my phone until I came out, I went into my office and closed the door. I sat down at my desk and began to condition my mind. I said, "Napoleon, you are going to see this laundryman and you are not coming back until you make a sale." I repeated that five hundred times, at least, until the psychological moment arrived when I knew that I was going to make the sale, even before I saw the man. But to make sure of it, I called in my sales manager, Jack Randall, and I said, "Jack, you and I are going over to Newark to make a sale for the Newark Laundry Company and we are not coming back until we have it."

He said, "Now, where do you get this 'not coming back' stuff? I have a family and I've got to come back."

"I have a family too, and I am coming back, but I'm not coming back until we make a sale," I answered. I had even packed my overnight bag, to be prepared if I had to stay overnight.

When we were introduced to the president, he said, "Gentlemen, you have arrived just about the right time. It's a quarter to twelve. Let's go over to the Athletic Club for lunch, and afterwards we will go out into the library, sit down, and have no disturbance while we talk." I looked at Jack Randall and he winked at me as much as if to say, "Boss, it's all in the bag." That's what he thought—and that's what I thought too.

During the luncheon, the laundryman began telling me his troubles. Someone had circulated the report among his customers that his work was not sanitary. It had reached the drivers, and they were losing one account after another. By the time I had heard his story, I knew what had to be done.

I told him what I thought was wrong, how it could be corrected, how long it would take, and how much it would cost. All the time that I was talking, I could see from the expression on his face that he was buying. Any Master Salesman knows you have to watch a man's maneuvers to know whether your story is getting across or not. This man's face indicated that he was receiving my presentation favorably, and I knew that I was making a sale.

After I got my story across, I slowed down a bit. The laundryman said, "Mr. Hill, I like your plan. I like it wonderfully well. I like you and I like your manager, but . . ."

THE OBSTACLE

That was the moment which generally comes in most sales, that unexpected moment when something crops up to keep a man from going ahead.

"But," he said, "when I telephoned your office, I telephoned two other gentlemen who were also in the business of training salesmen and I made appointments with them. They are coming here tomorrow. I am sure that you are going to get the contract, so after I interview them, I will telephone your office."

That would have been a good place for me to get up and say, "Thank you for your luncheon and your courtesy, and when you hear what the story is, telephone me," and most salesmen would have done that. I would have too, if I had not conditioned my mind before going not to come back until I made the sale.

What would you have done if you had been in my place at that point?

This is what I did. I ignored what he said and went into the second phase of my sales talk. A good salesman always has two or three or four different approaches, but he doesn't spring them all at one time.

I had been talking for about five or six minutes when I slowed down again.

Finally, Mr. Laundryman asked, "Mr. Hill, if you were in my place, what would you do?" That was just the point I was waiting for!

I said, "I'll tell you what I would do. I would telephone those other two gentlemen and tell them you have already employed Napoleon Hill, thank them for their consideration, and save them a trip over to your place."

He replied, "By gosh, that's exactly what I'll do." We shook hands, and that was it!

RESULTS ARE SURE TO COME

Successful industrial and financial enterprises are managed by leaders who either consciously or unconsciously apply the principles described in this manual. You can become a great leader in any undertaking by applying these principles and surrounding yourself with other minds which can be allied in a spirit of cooperation.

Whether you are on top, or on your way up, the manual will help you to build and hold your best qualities in focus.

Try it for yourself. Adopt the policies and desired principles and traits as your own. It has been tested. We know of the practicality and soundness of the material in these pages. They will bring business success, financial wealth, and peace of mind to those who have a desire to project and use them. The Master Power of Persuasion will help you to look for the better qualities in members of your family and your business associates, and it will serve as a mirror or reflector for self-analysis.

Will Rogers once said, "Every human being has at least one good quality." He said that he looked for it when he met a man and then tried to compliment him on it.

One of Napoleon Hill's students once said of a client who owed him a great sum of money: "I will embody the best of him, and in doing so, my character will be improved." At this point, according to Dr. Hill, the pupil had found the true meaning of the principle that "every adversity carries with it the seed of an equivalent benefit." Although he was not pleased with the client's attitude and the slow method of payment, the student rendered very satisfactory service to his other clients and increased his business while dealing with a most unpleasant situation. In this way he was able to make the most of his own experience during many years in the front line of selling, and to combine it with the fruits of Dr. Hill's lifetime of experience as a teacher of salesmen.

In the last section of this book, you will learn specific ways and means to get productive power. You will learn of a man who never violates the rights of others, yet

built a personal fortune and maintains peace of mind
and happiness by following the principles outlined in this
book. You will learn of his humble beginnings, how he
learned of this philosophy in an orphanage and began
applying it with great success at an early age. You will
learn why this exceptional person was selected by the
Napoleon Hill Foundation to be included in *Succeed and
Grow Rich Through Persuasion*.

After you study the next chapter on power, you will
be ready to meet Mr. Delford Smith of Evergreen International Aviation, Inc., McMinnville, Oregon. Do not
skip over the next chapters on power. They are necessary
to help you receive the full benefit of this amazing story.

Chapter Eight

MASTERING YOUR
MIND POWER

WHEN YOU THINK YOU CAN, YOU AWAKEN IN YOUR
MIND THE POWER THAT CAN

Do you want and need more power—power to work and achieve, power to study and learn, power for the right ideas, power for greater love, power for unselfish service to mankind?

Do you need additional power and strength to face the changes that confront you every day of your life?

Do you need more power to get what you desire from life without violating the rights of others?

Do you utilize the Master Power of Persuasion which lies within your "other self"?

Do you realize the power your subconscious mind contains—a power which you can tap and utilize even as you sleep? Do you recognize the source of power for achievement and success that can be gained by pooling your mind's resources with the resources of others for mutual benefit?

The power for all achievement, the power that you need in order to understand and apply the philosophy of success is readily available. The power you need for a productive life is in the storehouse of your own mind.

The major objective of this chapter is to describe some of the most important of the powers available to you and to help you to take possession of your mind, directing it to the ends of your own choice.

THE POWER OF ACCURATE THINKING

We now approach the analysis of the "mystery of all mysteries"—the power of the human mind. Let us approach this subject in a spirit of awe, for it is the most profound subject of this book. It holds the secret of all successes and all failures. It is one principle which is of necessity on the "must" list of all who would attain the Master Power of Persuasion. It is the most important subject known to mankind—yet, paradoxically, it is the least understood of all subjects—*accurate thinking*.

The power of thought may be likened to a rich garden spot. The soil may be converted, by organized effort, into necessary products of food, or by neglect it may be allowed to produce useless weeds. The mind is eternally at work, building up or tearing down, bringing misery, unhappiness, and poverty, or joy, pleasure, and riches. It is never idle. It is the greatest of all the assets available to mankind; yet it is the least used and the most abused of all assets. Its abuse consists mainly in its non-use.

Science has revealed many of nature's most profound secrets, but not the secret of man's great source of riches—the power of his own thoughts. This is one secret which has never been revealed to mankind, perhaps because mankind has shown such unpardonable indifference toward this divine gift.

The power of thought is the most dangerous, or the most beneficial, power available to man, depending of course on how it is used. Through the power of thought, man builds great empires of civilization. Through that same power, other men trample down empires as if they were so much helpless clay.

Every creation of man, whether it be good or bad, is created first in a thought pattern. All ideas are conceived through thought. All plans, purposes, and desires are created in thought. And thought is the only thing over which man has been given the complete privilege of control.

Thought is the master of all other forms of energy, because it is a form of energy which is mixed with intelligence. Thought holds the solution to every human problem. When it is properly used, thought is the greatest known remedy for all physical ailments. Its therapeutic powers are unlimited. Thought is the source of all riches, whether they be material, physical, or spiritual, for it is the means by which the Twelve Great Riches of Life may be appropriated by all who desire them. Men search all their lives for worldly riches, not recognizing that the source of all riches is already within their reach and under their control, only awaiting recognition and use.

The accurate thinker recognizes all the facts of life, both the good and the bad, and assumes the responsibility of separating and organizing the two, choosing those which serve his needs and rejecting all the others. He is not impressed by hearsay evidence. He is not the slave, but the master, of his own emotions. He lives among men without giving them the privilege of encroaching upon his inner thoughts or his methods of thinking. His opinions are the result of sober analysis and careful study of facts or dependable evidence of facts. He avails himself of the counsel of others but reserves to himself the right to accept it or reject it without apologies. When his plans fail, he promptly builds other plans to take their place, but he is never deflected from his purpose by temporary defeat. He is a philosopher who determines causes by the analysis of their effects. He gets most of his clues by observing the laws of nature and adapting himself to them. When he prays, his first request is for more wisdom. But he never offers insult to Deity by asking for the circumvention of any natural law, or by demanding something for nothing. Thus his prayers are usually answered in full, for he has thrown himself on the side of his Creator. He does not covet the material possessions of other men; he has a better way of acquiring all of his needs by first earning them. He does not envy other men, because he knows that he is richer, in the values which count most in life, than most other men are. He gives aid to others freely and accepts it only when its acceptance has been fully justified.

A SMALL MINORITY

These are the traits of an accurate thinker. Study them carefully if you would become one of that small minority who think accurately. The traits are simple and easily understood but not so easily cultivated, for cultivation requires more self-discipline than the majority of men are willing to exercise. But the reward for accurate thinking is worth the effort required to obtain that reward. It consists of many values, among them peace of mind, freedom of mind, freedom of body, wisdom and understanding of the laws of nature, the material necessities of life and, above all, harmony with the great scheme of the universe, as it is established and maintained by the Creator. No one can deny that the accurate thinker has established a working relationship with his Creator. Accurate thinking is a priceless asset which cannot be purchased with money, or borrowed from others. It must be self-attained through the strictest habits of self-discipline as they have been defined by successful men and women in many walks of life.

It is the rarest sort of experience to find a person anywhere, at any time, who lives his own life, thinks his own thoughts, develops his own habits, and makes even the slightest attempt to be himself. Most people are imitators of others, and many are neurotics who would rather "keep up with the Joneses" than be themselves. Observe those whom you know best, study their habits carefully, and you will realize that most of them are merely synthetic imitations of other people, without a thought they can truthfully call their own. Most people trail along, accepting and acting upon the thoughts and habits of others, very much as sheep tag along after one another over established paths. Once in a great while some individual with a tendency toward accurate thinking will pull away from the crowd, think his own thoughts, and dare to be himself. When you find such a person, take note—you are face to face with a thinker.

THE POWER OF DESIRE AND MOTIVE

All success is achieved through the application of power. Keeping in mind the definition of success (the power to get whatever one desires from life without violating the rights of others), we realize that the starting point for success is a burning desire for the achievement of some specifically defined objective.

Just as the oak tree, as an embryo, sleeps within the acorn, success begins in the form of an intense desire. Out of strong desire grow the motivating forces which cause us to cherish hopes, build plans, develop courage, and stimulate our minds to action in pursuit of a definite plan or purpose. There is nothing behind desire except the stimuli through which it may be turned into action.

It has been said, and not without reason, that one may have anything one wants, within reasonable limitations, providing one wants it intensely enough! Anyone who is capable of stimulating his own mind to produce intense desire is capable also of the achievement of that desire. It must be remembered, however, that wishing for a thing is not the same as desiring it with such intensity that out of this desire grow impelling forces for constructive action.

The ten basic motives to which man responds in acting to achieve a goal are all prefaced by the desire for a specific thing. Desire defines objective, and motive is the starting point for action.

Men of ordinary ability become supermen when aroused by desire which stimulates one or more of the basic motives for action. Bring a man face to face with the possibility of death in a sudden emergency, and he can develop physical strength and imaginative strategy of which he would not be capable under the influence of a less urgent motive for action.

When driven by the natural desire for sexual contact, men will build plans, develop imagination, and engage in action which would seem impossible without the urge of this desire.

The desire for financial gain often lifts men of mediocre ability into positions of great power. The desire for fame and for personal power is easily discernible as the chief motivating force of leaders in every walk of life.

The animalistic desire for revenge often drives ordinarily unimaginative people to create the most intricate and ingenious plans for carrying out their objectives.

The desire for life after death is such a strong motivating force that it drives men to both constructive and destructive extremes in their search for eternal perpetuation. It also develops highly effective leadership ability, evidence of which may be found in the life work of practically all the founders of religion.

If you would achieve great success, plant a strong motive in your mind!

Millions of people struggle all the days of their lives with no stronger motive than that of acquiring the necessities of life, such as food, shelter, and clothing. Now and then a man will step out of the masses and demand of himself and of the world more than a mere living, He motivates himself with desire and achieves fulfillment through action.

Elbert Hubbard once said: "Tell me what you desire most and I will tell you who can do most to help you get it."

When asked who that person was, Hubbard replied, "Look in a mirror and you will see him."

When the average person desires something that is out of his reach, he begins to think how he can get someone to help him to acquire it. If he recognizes that there is always something he can do on his own personal initiative that will give him a start toward his objective, he will learn to utilize his own resourcefulness, making it unnecessary for him to depend on others. Once a man discovers the powers of his own mind and self-reliance, he is well on his way toward the attainment of whatever he desires most from life.

THE POWER OF APPLIED FAITH

Nothing great has ever been achieved without the aid of a positive mental attitude which begins with a definite purpose, activated by a burning desire for the attainment of that purpose, and intensified until the desire becomes applied faith.

Wishes are not a burning desire, because everyone has a flock of them. Idle curiosity often inspires one to action, but it generally leads to a dead-end street without benefiting anyone. Hopes are helpful, but most people live out their lives on hopes which never materialize, because hope is not enough to inspire action based on definiteness of purpose. Burning desire is a combination of wishes, idle curiosity, and hopes. No one ever succeeds in the upper brackets of achievement without the urge of this action-impelling state of mind.

Applied faith is a state of mind which can exist only when the mental attitude is positive. It is the power that opens the door to successful living. Applied faith is a concentration of all of one's wishes, hopes, and desires, so intensified that they inspire one to begin the pursuit of his aims and purposes in the belief that they will be attained.

Applied faith permits us to look into the future and justify our belief in the attainment of our desires even before we begin to acquire them. When our purpose is founded upon this positive mental attitude, our every desire becomes a prayer.

Look about you and you will see that the world's most successful people are those who recognize and use their capacity for faith. However, this power is not to be flicked on and off like an electric current. It must be nurtured and strengthened through everyday use.

FEARS THAT CAN PARALYZE US

What strange fears invade the minds of men and short-circuit their approach to that master power which can lift them to great heights of achievement? How and why do the vast majority of people become the victims of a negative hypnotic rhythm which destroys their capacity for the use of the power of their own minds?

Too often, people let fear, the negative power, rule all their decisions and actions. Their every yearning is for a sort of overall protection summed up in the catch-all cliché of "security."

The truly successful person doesn't think in these terms. His reasoning is based on creativeness and productivity. As former President Eisenhower said, "One can attain a high degree of security in a prison cell if that's all he wants out of life."

The successful person is one who is willing to take risks when sound logic shows they are necessary to reach the desired goal.

All of us suffer from fear. What is it? Fear is an emotion intended to help preserve our lives by warning us of danger. Hence, fear can be a blessing when it raises its flag of caution so that we pause and study a situation before making a decision or taking action.

We must control fear rather than permit it to control us. Once it has served its emotional purpose as a warning signal, we must not permit it to intrude in the logical reasoning by which we decide upon a course of action.

The famous statement from FDR's first inaugural address, "We have nothing to fear but fear itself," is as applicable now as when he spoke it during the Depression.

How can you overcome your fears? One of the best ways is to ask yourself bluntly: "What am I afraid of?" Often it turns out that we are shying at mere shadows.

Let's examine some of the most common worries and see how this system works.

SICKNESS. The human body is endowed with an ingenious system for automatic self-maintenance and repair. Why worry that it might get out of order? It is better to marvel at how it stays in proper working order, in spite of the demands we place on it.

OLD AGE. The Golden Years are something to look forward to, not to fear. We exchange youth for wisdom. Remember, nothing is ever taken away from us without an equal or greater benefit being made available.

FAILURE. Momentary failure is a blessing in disguise, carrying with it the seed of an equivalent benefit if we but seek to learn its cause and use our knowledge to better our effort on the next attempt.

DEATH. Recognize that it is a necessary part of the

overall plan of the universe, provided by the Creator as a means of giving man a passageway to the higher plane of eternity.

CRITICISM. You should, after all, be your own most severe critic. What then, can you fear in the criticism of others? Such criticism may include constructive suggestions that will help you better yourself.

HOW TO DEAL WITH FEAR

Fear results mainly from ignorance.

It also helps to consider every facet of what you fear. What are the risks? Is the expected reward worth taking them? What are the other possible courses of action? What unexpected problems are likely to be encountered? Do you have all the necessary data, statistics and facts at hand? What have others done in similar situations, and what were the results?

Once you have completed your study, take action—immediately. Procrastination leads only to more doubt and fear. A noted psychologist once said that a frightened person, alone at night and imagining noises, can settle his or her fears quickly. All that is necessary is to put one foot on the floor. In doing so, one has taken the first step on a positive course of action toward overcoming fear.

The person seeking success must force himself, in the same way, to control his fear with absolute faith by taking the first step toward his goal.

Fear, the negative power of the mind, can be overcome if one will learn to draw strength and courage from the positive power which lies within each of us.

How may one tap that power that comes from within? The answer is faith—faith backed by action. Faith, rightly understood, is always active, never passive. Passive faith has no more power than an idle dynamo. To generate power, the machine must be set in motion. Active faith knows no fear, no self-imposed limitations. Reinforced with faith, the weakest mortal is mightier than disaster, stronger than failure, more powerful than fear.

The emergencies of life often bring men to a crossroads where they are forced to choose between avenues marked Faith and Fear. What is it that causes many to stumble down the road of fear? The choice hinges upon one's mental attitude, and the Creator has so arranged man's powers that each individual controls his own.

The man with faith is a man who has conditioned his mind to believe. He has conditioned it a little at a time by prompt and courageous decisions and action in the details of his daily work. Conversely, the man who lives in fear does so because he has neglected to condition his mind to a positive attitude.

THE NEED FOR CHANGE

The real test of a man's belief in a positive mental attitude and of his faith is in the challenge of change which he must meet every day of his life. One of the first requirements for enduring faith and success is a capacity to accept and profit by change.

It has been said that the only permanent thing known to man is change. In order to preserve the faith which will give you power for the attainment of success, you must make yourself flexible enough to adjust to all types of change. If you are flexible, you will ride with the tide of change instead of going down under it.

Consider the following suggestions and determine which, if utilized, would strengthen the power of faith you need each day.

Change from the habit of thinking about and fearing the things you do not desire, to the habit of believing you can and will make life pay off on your own terms.

Change from the habit of thinking and talking of the physical ailments you may have or fear you will acquire, to the habit of speaking and thinking of the perfect health you desire, until you develop a "health consciousness." Remember that imaginary ailments can do you as much harm as if they were real, if you accept them and encourage them by fear.

Change from the habit of desiring more material things than you need and can use, to the habit of sharing your riches so that they will serve others and thereby multiply themselves in your behalf.

Change from the habit of self-satisfaction to the habit of positive discontentment sufficient to keep you searching for more knowledge and wisdom to make your life richer both spiritually and materially.

Change from the habit of intolerance to the habit of open-mindedness on all subjects, toward all people, remembering that a closed mind doesn't grow, but atrophies and becomes powerless.

Change from the habit of fault-finding to the habit of looking for the good in other people and letting them know that you have discovered it. It is true that people will see in you whatever you see in them, be it good or bad.

Change from the habit of self-pity to the habit of facing facts about yourself and the real causes of your fears and worries. Remember that the looking glass will be helpful in making this change.

Change from the habit of speaking disparagingly of others to the habit of praising them, for this is also a habit which will inspire reciprocation.

While you are considering these suggestions, be sure to recognize the difference between your needs and your right to receive. We need many things which we have not earned the right to receive. The one sure way to obtain the right to receive is by going the extra mile, putting others under obligation to you by rendering more service and better service than that for which you are paid.

The great German philosopher Goethe set forth the following principles for having a well-balanced life:

> Health enough to make work a pleasure.
> Wealth enough to support your needs.
> Strength enough to battle difficulties and overcome them.
> Patience enough to toil until some good has been accomplished.
> Grace enough to confess your sins and forsake them.
> Charity enough to see the good in your neighbors.

Love enough to move you to be useful and helpful to others.
Faith enough to make real the things of God.
Hope enough to remove all fears concerning the future.

Everyone needs a blueprint by which to build his life. Goethe's creed may give you the basis of one you can form for yourself which will help you to make life pay off on your terms, without violating the rights of others. A daily creed helps one to keep before him a clear picture of the person he desires to become. It helps to give him the power of faith to meet and overcome obstacles along the way.

If you sincerely desire success, then you must enthusiastically search until you find the point of approach to that master power within you. When you find it, you will have discovered your true self, that "other self" which makes use of every experience of life. Success will be yours, no matter who you are or what may have been the nature and scope of your past failures. You must apply your faith. You must master your mind power, and direct it toward your desired goal with enthusiasm.

Emerson, the great American man of letters, well stated, "Nothing great is ever achieved without enthusiasm." Enthusiasm is an important trait of a pleasing personality. It is a necessary component of the success-desiring individual living in today's fast-paced world. The great men of yesterday and the successful men of today are men who defined their desires in terms of definite goals and applied and directed their powers of faith toward the achievement of those goals.

Enthusiasm is not a patented or copyrighted trait of personality, but it can become a priceless asset to all who learn how to apply it and follow the habit in their daily relationship with others. To be enthusiastic, act enthusiastically. Realize that enthusiasm possesses its own unique power, for it is a combination of mental and physical energy. Enthusiasm is simply faith in action. It is this faith, your ability to believe, which is the greatest power within your mind, and which can be released and directed toward the achievement of your desired goal. The successful people of today and those who will become the successful people of tomorrow are those who have mastered and utilized the vast powers residing within their own minds.

THE POWER OF THE SUBCONSCIOUS MIND

The subconscious mind is the source of man's greatest power. It can be influenced to work toward desired goals even while one sleeps, as well as during the waking hours.

Although man has not yet learned to use the total power of the subconscious, he has learned to utilize what he does understand as a guide to the attainment of his goals.

In a lifetime of research into patterns of success, we have studied the case histories of hundreds of leaders in many fields of achievement. One thing has impressed us during these studies—the way many of these highly successful persons used the power of their subconscious minds, especially in moments of extreme stress or of great decision.

Woodrow Wilson, for example, followed the habit of writing out a clear statement, just before retiring, of what he wished to accomplish the following day. He would read it aloud several times and, in his nightly prayer, ask guidance for its fulfillment.

Often, he would awaken during the night with the complete solution in his mind. At other times, the desired answer never came.

In discussing it in an interview with Dr. Hill, Wilson stated: "The state of mind in which I ask help from my subconscious seems to have much to do with the results. In times of great emergency, under the stress of intense emotion, the guidance I need comes quickly. If there is any doubt in my mind, I also find the result is generally negative. But when my belief is so intense that I almost feel myself in possession of the answer to my problems, then the result is always positive."

Wilson was convinced that the subconscious mind is

the gateway to the infinite intelligence of our Creator and can be used effectively only through that mental attitude of complete belief known as faith. When you harmonize your mind with that of the Creator, you gain guidance, power, and revelation not available to you by any other means. In this way, your subconscious mind can help you achieve both material and spiritual security.

However, you must give it a chance to operate for you. One way to do this is to set aside a definite portion of each day for meditation. Concentrate your mind on prayerful reverie.

You'll find that this time of meditation is well spent. You will come away from each session spiritually replenished and bubbling with ideas to enhance your welfare.

Through our five physical senses we can detect, and protect ourselves against, many dangers, such as cuts and burns. But we are subject to greater dangers than those we detect through the physical senses. These greater dangers slip through to our subconscious minds by way of auto-suggestion, clothed in daily experiences which we accept as inevitable, such as physical ailments, fear, worry, failure, and defeat.

A positive mental attitude cannot cure every human ill, but it can cure many if we understand how it works and keep it screened from the acceptance of circumstances we do not desire.

Man is just beginning to learn that the power of self-suggestion is a silent worker that can bring success or failure, sound health or illness, peace of mind or misery.

There is something about the subconscious which influences it to accept as real any impression that reaches it, whether it be negative or positive, constructive or destructive, reliable or unreliable. That is why we must condition our minds to feed upon the circumstances and things we desire, and protect it against the influences of suggestion related to what we do not desire.

Imagination can kill a man. Or it can aid him in rising to heights of achievement that border upon the miraculous, if he keeps his mind busily engaged in the direction of the things he desires most. For example, the hypochondriac's continuous belief that illness is his lot and that nothing can be done about it usually results in his ill health. Because the subconscious accepts any thought or impression fed to it, its power can be as destructive as it can be marvelously constructive. This is the reason for the necessity of a continuing positive mental attitude.

STEPS TOWARD HARNESSING THE MIND'S POTENTIAL

The human mind is the nearest thing to perpetual motion known, for it works while we sleep, just as when we are awake. If we take fear and worry to bed with us, the subconscious accepts them as something we desire and goes right on working out ways and means of clothing them in their physical equivalent.

On the other hand, the subconscious mind will just as readily accept and help us plan to get the things we desire if we give it specific orders and believe they will be carried out.

There are important facts regarding the use of the mind which one must recognize and respect:

1. The mind can be controlled, guided, and directed to ends of one's own choice. In fact, there are definite penalties if one fails to do so.
2. The mind can attract unpleasant and undesired circumstances, and will do so unless it is kept busily engaged in the attainment of what one desires.
3. All of man's constructive achievements are the result of organized thought directed to definite ends in a positive mental attitude backed by belief.
4. The majority of thoughts that voluntarily enter the mind are not accurate; therefore, all thinking needs careful analysis before any of it is accepted and acted upon as sound.
5. Whatever the mind of man can conceive and believe, it can achieve. It may do so by the application of natural laws and the established principles accepted by man as workable.

Not one of these five facts regarding the use of the mind calls for extensive formal education. Each of them

can be verified for its soundness by anyone who is interested in knowing the potential powers of his own mind.

To aid you in learning to tap the unlimited powers
of your own subconscious, we present the following
suggestions.

1. Write a clear statement of the most important objective you wish to accomplish within the next thirty days.
Be careful to let it be something to which you are entitled, or to which you will become entitled within the
thirty-day limit. For example, a promotion to a better
position, an increase in business patronage, improvement
in your health, or constructive changes in your personality might be desirable goals.

2. Have a talk with your subconscious several times
during the day, including in the evening just before you
retire. Tell it what you have written out as your objective, including the reasons you believe you are entitled
to get what you seek. State your case enthusiastically.

3. Write out a clear statement of all the reasons you
believe you are entitled to the achievement of your objective. Do not be too modest in this description, but do
not include anything that you do not believe or that is
untrue. Be sure to include in your list a clear statement
of what you intend to give in return for the fulfillment
of your goal. This is important. The subconscious mind
will not violate natural laws, and a request for something
for nothing would end in defeat. If you are seeking success in a business venture, for example, be sure that your
part of the transaction is clean and fully justified, for
there will always be a silent partner in all of your associations with others whom you will not see. He is a score-
keeper who jots down your every deed and intention,
keeping a record which may bless or curse you at some
later time. He never makes a mistake in either charging
or crediting your account. Emerson called this invisible
partner the law of compensation.

4. Commit your two written statements to memory,
the one describing what you are seeking during the next
thirty days (or within some other specific time), and the
other describing why you believe you are entitled to re-

ceive it and what you intend to give in return. Repeat these statements daily, and end by expressing your gratitude for having received fulfillment.

5. If you are married, enter into a mastermind alliance with your spouse so that you will jointly carry out this program just as it has been described. If you are not married, form a mastermind alliance with your closest friend or business associate and follow the same instructions. However, do not disclose your program to any other outsider who might ridicule your procedure because of lack of understanding of the power of the subconscious mind.

6. Your subconscious mind embraces and acts upon desires and requests which are presented under extreme emotion much more quickly than those submitted in a calm frame of mind. Therefore, do a good job of selling yourself with unwavering faith in your ultimate success. Put enthusiasm into your words and thoughts. Move on the assumption that you are talking to another person who can say yes or no, and do your best to persuade him or her in your favor.

THE POWER OF AN OPEN MIND

An open mind is a free mind.

The person who closes his mind to new ideas, concepts, and experiences enslaves his own personality.

Intolerance, the product of a closed mind, is a two-edged sword which cuts off new opportunities and lines of communication on the backswing.

When you open your mind, you give your imagination freedom to act for you. You utilize the gift of vision.

It's hard to realize now that seemingly intelligent people laughed at the Wright brothers' experiments with flight, and aviation icon Charles Lindbergh could scarcely find backers for his trans-Atlantic flight.

Today, men and women of vision have put man on the moon, and photos of other planets in our solar system are regularly transmitted back to earth by space-exploration vehicles, while we now dream of space stations, hotels, and recreation facilities. The goal of NASA is to develop and demonstrate the capability of interplanetary travel. Where are the early scoffers at moon flight?

A closed mind is a sign of a static personality. It lets progress pass it by and never takes advantage of the opportunities progress offers.

Only if you have an open mind can you grasp the full impact of the first rule which leads man to any form of success: *Whatever the mind of man can conceive and believe, it can achieve.*

The person blessed with an open mind can perform miracles in business, industry, and the professions while those with closed minds are still shouting "impossible."

Take stock of yourself. Are you among those who say "I can" and "It will be done," or do you fall into the "No one can" group at the very moment someone else is accomplishing it?

An open mind requires faith—in yourself, your fellowman, and the Creator, who laid out a pattern of progress for man and his universe.

The days of superstition are gone, or at least they should be. But the shadow of prejudice is as dark as ever. You can come out into the light by closely examining your own personality. Do you make decisions based on reason and logic rather than on emotion and preconceived ideas? Do you listen closely, attentively, and thoughtfully to the others' arguments? Do you seek facts rather than hearsay and rumor?

The human mentality withers unless it is stimulated by fresh thought. The dictator, in brainwashing, knows that the quickest way to break a man's will is to isolate his mind, cutting him off from other people, from books, newspapers, radio, television, and other normal channels of intellectual communication.

Under such circumstances, the intellect dies for lack of nourishment. Only the strongest will and the purest faith can save it.

Is it possible that you have imprisoned your mind in a social and cultural concentration camp? Have you subjected yourself to a brainwashing of your own making?

If so, it is time to sweep aside the bars of prejudice that imprison your intellect. Open your mind and set it

free. Discover for yourself the added power of a mind
which knows no barriers.

THE POWER OF YOUR THOUGHTS

Thomas Paine was one of the great minds of the American Revolutionary period. To him, perhaps more than
to any other one person, we owe both the beginning and
the happy ending of the American Revolution. It was his
keen mind that helped in drawing up the Declaration
of Independence and in persuading the signers of that
document to translate it into terms of reality.

In speaking of the source of his great storehouse of
knowledge, Paine stated: "Any person who has made
observations on the state of progress of the human mind
by observing his own, cannot but have observed that
there are two distinct classes of what are called thoughts:
those that we produce in ourselves by reflection and the
act of thinking, and those that bolt into the mind of their
own accord.

"I have always made it a rule to treat those voluntary
visitors with civility, taking care to examine, as well as I
was able, if they were worth entertaining, and it is from
them I have acquired almost all the knowledge that I
have. As to the learning that any person gains from
school education, it serves only like a small capital, to
put him in the way of beginning learning for himself
afterwards. Every person of learning is finally his own
teacher, the reason for which is, that principles being of
a distinct quality to circumstances, cannot be impressed
upon the memory; their place of mental residence is the
understanding, and they are never so lasting as when
they begin by conception."

In the foregoing paragraphs, Paine, a great American
patriot and philosopher, described a phenomenon which,
at one time or another, is the experience of every person.
Who is so unfortunate as not to have received positive
evidence that thoughts and even complete ideas will
"pop" into the mind from outside sources?

What means of conveyance is there for such visitors
except the ether? Ether fills the boundless space of the

universe. It is the medium of conveyance for all known forms of vibration such as sound, light, and heat. Why would it not also be the medium of conveyance of the vibration of thought?

Every mind, or brain, is directly connected with every other brain by means of the ether. Every thought released by any brain may be instantly picked up and interpreted by all other brains that are in rapport (vibrating at the same rate) with the sending brain. Napoleon Hill was as sure of this fact as he was that the formula H_2O would produce water.

Nor is the ether's property as a conveyer of thought from mind to mind the most astounding of its performances. There is convincing evidence that every thought vibration released by any brain is picked up by the ether and kept in motion in circuitous wave lengths corresponding in length to the intensity of the energy used in its release, that these vibrations remain in motion forever, and that they are one of the two sources from which thoughts which "pop" into one's mind emanate— the other source being direct and immediate contact through the ether with the brain releasing the thought vibration.

Thus, it will be seen that if this theory is a fact, the boundless space of the whole universe is now and will continue to become literally a library wherein may be found all the thoughts released by mankind.

One of the most marvelous discoveries yet made by man is the radio principle, which operates through the aid of ether, important in the laws of nature. Imagine the ether picking up the ordinary vibration of sound, and transforming (stepping up the rate of vibration) that vibration from the audio frequency into radio frequency, carrying it to a properly attuned receiving station and there transforming it back into its original form of audio frequency, all in the flash of a second. It should surprise no one that such a force could gather up the vibration of thought and keep that vibration in motion forever.

The established and known fact of instantaneous transmission of sound through the agency of the ether, by means of the modern radio apparatus, means that the theory of transmission of thought vibrations from mind to mind is not merely possible, but also probable.

In the chapter that follows, you will learn about how to accelerate the capacity of your mind to receive and transmit thought vibrations. Be sure the communication system stays positive for this important study.

Chapter Nine

THE POWER OF THE
MASTERMIND

At this point in the study of this book, take three minutes for meditation, concentrating upon what you have learned about the power of your own mind. Write it down for later reference, and review it after you conclude this chapter. The three moments of meditation can well be three of the most important minutes you will spend during the study of the Master Power of Persuasion. The value of this time will depend on your ability to concentrate seriously and quietly.

It is vital that you understand the material in Chapter Eight before you undertake to study in depth the mastermind alliance and the chemistry of the mind. The three minutes of meditation will make your mind active and alert, linking your subconscious and conscious minds together for greater comprehension.

MINDS DEMONSTRATE ATTRACTION—AND REPULSION

It is a fact, as well known to the layman as to the man of scientific investigation, that some minds clash the moment they come in contact with each other. Between the two extremes of natural antagonism and natural affinity growing out of the meeting or contacting of minds, there is a wide range of possibility for varying reactions of mind with mind.

Some minds are so naturally adapted to each other

166

that "love at first sight" is the inevitable outcome of the contact. Who has not known such an experience? In other cases, minds are so antagonistic that violent mutual dislike shows itself at first meeting. These results occur without a word being spoken, and without the slightest sign of any of the usual causes for love and hate acting as a stimulus.

It is quite probable that the mind is made up of a substance or energy, similar to the ether (if not, in fact, the same substance). When two minds come close enough to form a contact, the mixing of the units of this "mind stuff" (let us call it the electrons of the ether) sets up a chemical reaction and starts vibrations which affect the two individuals pleasantly or unpleasantly.

The effect of the meeting of two minds is obvious to even the most casual observer. Every effect must have a cause. What could be more reasonable than to suspect that the cause of the change in mental attitude of the two minds, which have just come into contact, is in fact the disturbance of the electrons or units of each mind as they rearrange themselves in the new field created by the contact?

For the purpose of establishing this philosophy upon a sound foundation, we have gone a long way toward success by admitting that the meeting or coming in close contact of two minds sets up in each of those minds a certain noticeable "effect" or state of mind quite different from the one existing immediately prior to the contact. While it is desirable, it is not essential to know the "cause" of this reaction of mind upon mind. That the reaction takes place in every instance is a known fact, which gives us a starting point from which we may show what is meant by the term "mastermind."

A mastermind may be created through the bringing together or blending of two or more minds in a spirit of perfect harmony toward a specific objective. Out of this harmonious blending, the chemistry of the mind creates a third mind which may be appropriated and used by one or all of the individual minds. This mastermind will remain available as long as the friendly, harmonious alliance between the individual minds exists. It will disintegrate and all evidence of its existence disappear the moment the friendly alliance is broken.

YOU WON'T FIND IT IN TEXTBOOKS

The term "mastermind" is abstract, and has no counterpart in the field of known fact, except to a small number of people who have made a careful study of the effect of one mind upon other minds.

Throughout his life Napoleon Hill searched in vain through available textbooks and essays on the subject of the human mind, but could find no reference to the principle described here as the mastermind.

The term first came to the attention of Dr. Hill in an interview with Andrew Carnegie. Mr. Carnegie attributed the accumulation of his great fortune in the steel industry to the utilization of the mastermind principle. He explained that his mastermind alliance was made up of about twenty men and that they had given of their experience, their education, and their background for one definite objective, and that was the manufacturing and marketing of steel.

This group held the assembled knowledge of everything known relating to the steel industry at that time. Mr. Carnegie's primary job was to keep this alliance moving in a spirit of perfect harmony for the common objective.

Any adult knows that the first two or three years of marriage are often marked by much disagreement of a more or less petty nature. These are the years of "adjustment." If the marriage survives them, it has a good chance of becoming a permanent alliance. No experienced married person will deny these facts. Again, we see the effect without understanding the cause.

While there are other contributing causes, in the main, lack of harmony during these early years results from the slowness of the chemistry of the minds in blending harmoniously. Stated differently, the electrons or units of the energy called the mind are often neither extremely friendly nor antagonistic upon first contact, but through constant association, they gradually adapt themselves in harmony, except in cases where association has the opposite effect and leads eventually to open hostility.

It is a well-known fact that after a man and woman have lived together for ten to fifteen years, they become practically indispensable to each other, even though there might be no evidence of the state of mind called love. Moreover, this association not only develops a natural affinity between the two minds, but actually causes the two people to take on similar facial expressions and to closely resemble each other in many other marked ways.

Any competent analyst of human nature can go into a crowd of strange people and easily pick out the wife after having been introduced to her husband. The expression of the eyes, the contour of the faces, and the tone of the voices of two people who have been long associated in marriage become similar to a remarkable degree.

APPLIED MIND CHEMISTRY

So pronounced is the effect of the chemistry of the human mind that any experienced public speaker can quickly interpret the manner in which his statements are accepted by his audience. Antagonism in the mind of just one person in an audience of one thousand can be detected by the speaker who has learned how to "feel" and register the effects of antagonism. Because of this fact, an audience may cause a speaker to rise to great heights of oratory or heckle him into failure, without making a sound or forming a single facial expression denoting satisfaction or dissatisfaction.

All Master Salesmen know the moment the psychological time for closing has arrived, not by what the prospective buyer says, but from the effect of the chemistry of his mind as interpreted or "felt" by the salesman. Words often belie the intentions of the person speaking them, but a correct interpretation of the chemistry of the mind leaves no loophole for such a possibility. Every able salesman knows that the majority of buyers have a habit of affecting a negative attitude almost until the very climax of a sale.

Every able lawyer has developed a sixth sense with which he "feels" his way through the most artfully selected words of the clever witness who is lying, and correctly interprets them. Many lawyers have developed this ability without knowing the real source of it. They possess the technique without the scientific understanding upon which it is based. Many salesmen have done the same thing.

A person who is gifted in the art of correctly interpreting the chemistry of the minds of others may, figuratively speaking, walk in the front door of the mansion of a given mind and leisurely explore the entire building, noting all its detail, and then walk out again with a complete picture of the interior, the owner never having realized that he has entertained a visitor.

Enough has been stated to introduce the principle of mind chemistry, and to prove, with the aid of the reader's own everyday experiences and casual observations, that the moment two minds come within close range of each other, a noticeable mental change takes place in both, sometimes registering in an antagonistic manner and at other times in a friendly manner. Every mind has what might be termed an electric field. The nature of this field varies, depending upon the mood of the individual mind behind it and upon the nature of the chemistry of the mind creating the field.

It is believed that the normal or natural condition of an individual's mind is the result of physical heredity, plus the nature of thoughts which have dominated his mind. Every mind is continuously changing to the extent that the individual's philosophy and general habits of thought change the chemistry of his mind.

These principles Napoleon Hill believed to be true. It is a known fact that any individual may voluntarily change the chemistry of his mind so that it will either attract or repel all with whom it comes in contact. In other words, any person may assume a mental attitude which will attract and please others, or one which will repel and antagonize them, and this without the aid of words, facial expression, or other forms of bodily movement or demeanor.

ESPRIT DE CORPS AT WORK

Go back now to the definition of a "mastermind," a mind which grows out of the blending and coordination of two or more minds, in a spirit of perfect harmony, and you will catch the full significance of the word "harmony" as it is used here. Two minds will not blend, nor can they be coordinated, unless the element of perfect harmony is present—the element that holds the secret of success or failure of practically all business and social partnerships.

Every sales manager, military commander, and leader understands the necessity of esprit de corps, a spirit of common understanding and cooperation for the attainment of a common goal. This mass spirit of harmony of purpose is obtained through discipline, voluntary or forced, of such a nature that the individual minds are blended into a mastermind. This occurs when the chemistries of the individual minds blend and they function as one.

The methods through which this blending process takes place are as numerous as the individuals engaged in the various forms of leadership. Every leader has his own method of coordinating the minds of his followers. One will use force. Another uses persuasion. One will play upon the fear of penalties, while another plays upon rewards. We do not have to search deeply into the history of statesmanship, politics, business, or finance to discover the technique employed by the leaders in these fields.

The really great leaders of the world, however, have been provided by nature with a combination of mind chemistry that is favorable as a nucleus of attraction for other minds.

No group of minds can be blended into a mastermind if one of the individuals of that group possesses an extremely negative, repellent mind. The negative and positive minds will not blend in the sense here described as a mastermind. Ignorance of this fact has brought many an otherwise able leader to defeat.

Any leader who understands this principle of mind

chemistry can temporarily blend the minds of practically any group of people so that it will represent a mass mind, but the composition will disintegrate almost the very moment the leader's presence is removed from the group. The most successful life insurance sales organizations and other sales forces meet once a week, or more often, for the purpose of merging the individual minds into a mastermind which will, for a limited number of days, serve as a stimulus to the individual minds.

It may be, and generally is, true that the leaders of these groups do not understand what actually takes place in these meetings, which are usually devoted to talks by the leader and other members of the group. Meanwhile, the minds of the individuals are contacting and recharging one another.

The brain of a human being may be compared to an electric battery in that it will become exhausted or run down, causing the owner to feel despondent, discouraged, and lacking in pep. Who is so fortunate as never to have had such a feeling? When the human brain is in this depleted condition, it must be recharged. This is done through contact with a more vital mind or minds. The great leaders understand the necessity of this recharging process. This knowledge is the main feature that distinguishes a leader from a follower.

Fortunate is the person who sufficiently understands this principle to keep his brain vitalized or recharged by periodically bringing it in contact with a more vital mind. Seldom do we feel more invigorated than when we share an intellectually stimulating experience with someone of equal or greater intelligence. Such interaction keeps us mentally alert. Likewise, nothing is more depressing and counterproductive than constant association with negative people.

What, then, may be the future possibilities in the field of mind chemistry?

Through the principle of harmonious blending of minds, perfect health may be enjoyed. With the aid of this same principle, sufficient power may be developed to solve the problems of economic necessity which constantly press upon every individual.

We may judge the future possibilities of mind chemistry by taking inventory of its past achievements, remembering that these achievements have been largely the result of accidental discovery and of chance groupings of minds. We are approaching the time when university professors will teach mind chemistry as a part of the required curriculum. Meanwhile, study and experimentation in connection with this subject open up impressive possibilities for mental development.

STRENGTH COMES FROM UNITY

It is a demonstrable fact that mind chemistry may be appropriately applied to the workaday affairs of the economic and commercial world.

Through the principle of mind chemistry, two or more minds may be blended in a spirit of perfect harmony, and may develop sufficient power to enable the individuals to perform seemingly superhuman feats. Power is the force with which men achieve success in any undertaking. Power in unlimited quantities may be enjoyed by any group of men, or men and women, who possess the wisdom with which to submerge their own personalities and their own immediate individual interests in the union of their minds.

Observe the frequency of the appearances of the word "harmony." There can be no development of a mastermind where this element of perfect harmony does not exist. The individual units of one mind will not blend with the units of another mind until the two minds have been aroused and warmed, in a spirit of perfect harmony of purpose. The moment two minds begin to take divergent roads of interest, the individual units of each mind separate, and the third element, the mastermind, will disintegrate.

When two or more people harmonize their minds to produce a mastermind, each person in the group becomes vested with the power to contact and gather knowledge from the subconscious minds of all the other members of the group. This power becomes immediately noticeable, having the effect of stimulating the mind to a higher rate of vibration, which takes the form of a more vivid imagination and the consciousness of what appears to be a sixth sense.

It is through this sixth sense that new ideas will flash into the mind. These ideas take on the nature and form of the subject dominating the mind of the individual. If the entire group has met for the purpose of discussing a given subject, ideas concerning that subject will come pouring into the minds of all present, as if an outside influence were dictating them. The minds of those participating in the mastermind become magnets, attracting ideas and thought stimuli of the most highly organized and practical nature—from no one knows where.

The process of mind blending may be likened to the act of connecting many electric batteries to a single transmission wire, thereby stepping up the power passing over that line by the amount of energy the batteries carry. This applies to the blending of individual minds into a mastermind. Each mind stimulates all the other minds in the group until the mind energy becomes so great that it connects with and penetrates the universal energy known as ether, which in turn touches every atom of matter in the universe.

We have mentioned the influence of mind chemistry on an experienced public speaker and have seen how the speaker can often rise to gratifying heights of oratory if he feels the individual minds of an audience in rapport with him.

The first five or ten minutes of the average speech are devoted to what is known as "warming up." This is the process by which the minds of the speaker and his audience are becoming blended in a spirit of perfect harmony.

Every speaker knows what happens when this state of perfect harmony fails to materialize.

It is a known fact that any individual may explore the store of knowledge in another's mind, through this principle of mind chemistry. It seems reasonable to suppose that this power may be extended to include contact with whatever vibrations are available in the ether.

The theory that all the higher and more refined vibrations (such as thought) are preserved in the ether, stems from the known fact that matter and energy may be neither created nor destroyed. It is reasonable to suppose that all vibrations, which have been amplified sufficiently to be picked up and absorbed in the ether, will go on forever. The lower vibrations, which do not blend with or otherwise contact the ether, probably live a natural life and then die.

All the so-called geniuses probably gained their reputations because they formed alliances with other minds which enabled them to amplify their own mind vibrations until they were able to contact the vast temple of knowledge recorded and filed in the ether of the universe. All of the great geniuses, as far as Napoleon Hill was able to gather the facts, were highly sexed people. The fact that sexual contact is the greatest known mind stimulant would seem to support the theory.

THE BIG SIX

Let us inquire further into the source of economic power, as manifested by the achievements of men in the field of business, and study the case of the Chicago group known as the Big Six. The group consisted of William Wrigley, Jr., who owned the chewing gum business bearing his name, and whose individual income was said to have been more than $15 million a year; John R. Thompson, who operated the chain of lunchrooms bearing his name; Mr. A. D. Lasker, who owned the Lord and Thomas Advertising Agency; Mr. McCullough, who owned the Parmalee Express Company, once the largest transfer business in America; and Mr. Ritchie and Mr. Hertz, who owned the Yellow Taxicab business.

The yearly income of these six men was estimated at upward of $25 million, or an average of more than $4 million a year per man, at a time when an income of a few thousand dollars a year was considered relative affluence.

Napoleon Hill's analysis of the group revealed that not one of them had had special educational advantages, that all had begun without capital or extensive credit, and that their financial achievement was due to their own individual plans and not to any fortunate turn of the wheel of chance.

These six men formed a friendly alliance, meeting at stated periods for the purpose of assisting one another, with ideas and suggestions, in their various and sundry lines of business endeavor.

With the exception of Hertz and Ritchie, none of the six men were in any manner associated in a legal partnership. These meetings were strictly for the purpose of sharing ideas. Each of the individuals belonging to the Big Six was a millionaire many times over. As a rule there is nothing worthy of special comment about a man who has done nothing but accumulate a few million dollars.

However, there is something about the financial success of this particular group of men that is well worth comment, study, analysis, and even emulation. That "something" is the fact that they learned how to coordinate their individual minds by blending them in a spirit of perfect harmony, creating a mastermind that unlocked, for each individual of the group, doors which are closed to most persons.

Whenever you find an outstanding success in business, finance, industry, or any of the professions, you may be sure that behind the success is some individual who has applied the principle of mind chemistry to create a mastermind. These outstanding successes may often appear to be the handiwork of just one person, but on closer examination, the other individuals whose minds have been coordinated with his own may be found.

Power is organized knowledge, expressed through intelligent action. No effort can be said to be organized unless the participating individuals coordinate their knowledge and energy in a spirit of perfect harmony. Lack of such harmonious coordination of effort is the main cause of practically every business failure.

WHAT WERE HENRY FORD'S ASSETS?

An interesting experiment was conducted by Napoleon Hill in collaboration with the students of a well-known college. Each student was requested to write an essay on "How and Why Henry Ford Became Wealthy."

Each student was required to describe what he believed to be the nature of Ford's real assets and what these assets consisted of. The majority of the students gathered financial statements of Ford's wealth.

Included in these sources of Ford's wealth were such items as cash in banks, raw and finished materials in stock, real estate and buildings, goodwill, estimated at ten to twenty-five per cent of the value of the material assets.

One student out of the entire group of several hundred wrote:

"Henry Ford's assets consist, in the main, of two items:

"1. Working capital and raw and finished materials.

"2. The knowledge gained from experience and the cooperation of a well-trained organization which understands how to apply this knowledge to best advantage from the Ford viewpoint. It is impossible to estimate with anything approximating correctness, the actual dollars and cents value of either of these two groups of assets, but it is my opinion that their relative values are:

"The organized knowledge of the Ford Organization——75%

"The value of cash and physical assets of every nature including raw and finished materials——25%."

Dr. Hill was of the opinion that this statement was not compiled by the young man whose name was signed to it without the assistance of some very analytical and experienced mind or minds.

Unquestionably Henry Ford's most valuable asset was his own brain. Next came the brains of his immediate circle of associates, for it was through coordination of these that the physical assets that he controlled were accumulated.

If every plant the Ford Motor Company owned had been destroyed, including every piece of machinery, every ton of raw or finished material, every finished automobile, and every dollar on deposit, Ford would still have been one of the most economically powerful men in America. The brains which built the Ford business could have duplicated it again in short order. Capital is always available in unlimited quantities to such brains as Ford's.

Despite Ford's great power and financial success, he may often have blundered in the application of the principles through which he accumulated this power. There is little doubt that Ford's methods of mind coordination were often crude. They must certainly have been crude in the earlier days of his experience, before he gained the wisdom of application that would naturally go with maturity of years.

Nor can there be any doubt that Ford's application of the principle of mind chemistry was the result of an alliance with other minds, particularly Edison. It is more than probable that Mr. Ford's remarkable insight into the law of nature was first utilized as the result of his friendly alliance with his own wife long before he ever met either Mr. Edison or Mr. Firestone.

Many a man is made (and some unmade) by his wife, through application of the mastermind principle. Mrs. Ford was a remarkably intelligent woman, and we have reason to believe that it was her mind, blended with Mr. Ford's, which gave him his first real start toward power.

It may be mentioned, without in any way depriving Ford of any honor or glory, that in his earlier days he had to combat the powerful enemies of illiteracy and ignorance to a greater extent than did either Edison or Firestone, both of whom were gifted with an aptitude for acquiring and applying knowledge. Ford had to hew his talent out of the rough, raw timbers of his none too favorable hereditary estate.

Within a short period of time, Ford mastered three of the most stubborn enemies of mankind and transformed them into assets. These enemies were ignorance, illiteracy, and poverty.

Any man who can stay the hand of these three savage forces—and, what is more, harness and use them to good account—is well worth close study.

The source of all power is organized effort. Knowledge, when general in nature and unorganized, is not power. It is only potential power, the material out of which real power may be developed. Any modern library contains a record of all the valuable knowledge the present civilization has inherited, but this knowledge is not power because it is not organized. Every form of energy and every species of animal or plant life, to survive, must be organized. The oversized animals whose bones fill nature's boneyard left mute but certain evidence that nonorganization means annihilation. One of nature's first laws is that of organization. Fortunate is the individual who recognizes the importance of this law and makes it his business to familiarize himself with the various ways the law may be applied to advantage.

NO POWER WITHOUT ORGANIZATION

The astute businessman not only has recognized the importance of the law of organized effort, but has made this law the basis of his power.

Without any knowledge of the principle of mind chemistry, many men have accumulated great power by merely organizing the knowledge they possessed. The majority of those who have discovered the principle of mind chemistry and developed that principle into a mastermind have stumbled upon this knowledge by accident, often failing to recognize the real nature of their discovery or understanding the source of its power.

It is a well-known fact that one of the most difficult tasks that any businessman must perform is to induce those who are associated with him to coordinate their efforts in a spirit of harmony. To induce continuous cooperation among a group of workers in any undertaking is next to impossible. Once in a great while, however, such a man will rise in the field of industry, business, or finance, and then the world heralds a new leader.

"Power" and "success" are synonymous terms. One grows out of the other; therefore, any person who has the knowledge and the ability to develop power may be successful in any reasonable undertaking that permits successful termination.

The human brain and nervous system constitute a piece of intricate machinery which very few men, if any, fully understand. When controlled and properly directed, this piece of machinery can be made to perform wonders of achievement, and if not controlled, it will perform wonders fantastic and phantom-like in nature, as may be seen by observing the inmates of any mental institution.

The human brain has direct connection with a continuous influx of energy from which man derives his power to think. The brain receives this energy, mixes it with the energy created by the food taken into the body, and distributes it to every part of the body, with the assistance of the blood and the nervous system. It produces what we call life. From what source this outside energy comes no one knows. What we do know is that we must have it or die. It seems reasonable to assume that this energy is none other than what we call ether, and that it flows into the body along with the oxygen from the air as we breathe.

Every normal human body possesses a first-class chemical laboratory which carries on the business of breaking up, assimilating, and properly mixing and compounding the food we take into the body, preparatory to distributing it wherever it is needed as a body builder.

Tests have been made, on both man and beast, to prove that the energy known as the mind plays an important part in the chemical operation of compounding and transforming food into the substances required to build and keep the body in repair.

It is known that worry, excitement, and fear interfere with the digestive process, and in extreme cases, stop this process altogether, resulting in illness or death. It is obvious, then, that the mind enters into the process of food digestion and distribution.

It is believed by many, although it may never have been scientifically proved, that the energy known as thought may become contaminated with negative or "unsociable" units to such an extent that the whole nervous system is thrown out of working order, digestion is disrupted, and disease manifests itself. Financial difficulties and unrequited love affairs lead the list of causes of such mind disturbances.

A negative environment, such as that existing where some member of the family is constantly "nagging," will interfere with the chemistry of the mind to such an extent that the individual will lose ambition and gradually sink into oblivion. This fact is the basis for the old saying that your spouse can either make you or break you.

Any high-school student knows that certain food combinations will, if taken into the stomach, result in indigestion, violent pain, and even death. Good health depends, in part at least, on a food combination that "harmonizes." But harmony of diet is not sufficient to insure good health. There must also be harmony between the units of mind energy.

HARMONY, THE ABSOLUTE "MUST"

Harmony is one of nature's laws, and without it there could be no such thing as organized energy, for life in any form. The health of the body, as well as of the mind, is literally built upon the principle of harmony. The life energy begins to disintegrate and death approaches when the organs of the body stop working in harmony. The moment harmony ceases at the source of any form of organized energy, the units of that energy are thrown into a chaotic state of disorder and the power is rendered neutral or passive.

This truth has been stated and restated, for unless one grasps this principle and learns to apply it, this chapter on the mastermind is useless.

Success in life—no matter what one may call success—is largely a matter of adaptation to environment in such a manner to produce harmony between the individual and his environment. The palace of a king becomes less than the hovel of a peasant if harmony does not abound within its walls. Conversely stated, the hut of a peasant may be made to yield great happiness if harmony reigns there.

Without perfect harmony the science of astronomy

would be as useless as the "bones of a saint," because the stars and planets would crash with one another, and everything would be in a state of chaos and disorder.

Without the law of harmony, there can be no organization of knowledge, for what is organized knowledge except the harmony of facts, truths, and natural laws?

The moment discord begins to creep in by the front door, harmony does not abound within its walls. Conversely stated, the application is made to a business partnership, or to the orderly movement of the planets in the heavens.

If the reader feels that this philosophy places undue stress on the importance of harmony, let him remember that lack of harmony is the first, and often the last and only cause of failure.

There can be no poetry or music or oratory worthy of notice without the presence of harmony.

Good architecture is largely a matter of harmony. Without harmony a house is nothing but a mass of building materials, more or less a monstrosity.

Sound business management builds upon the foundation of harmony. Every well-dressed man or woman is a living picture and a moving example of harmony.

With all these workaday illustrations of the important part that harmony plays in the affairs of the world and in the operation of the entire universe, how could any intelligent person leave harmony out of his definite major purpose in life?

The human body is a complex organization of organs, glands, blood vessels, nerves, brain cells, muscles, and so on. The mind energy which stimulates to action and coordinates the efforts of the component parts of the body is also a plurality of ever-varying energies. From birth until death there is a continuous struggle, often assuming the nature of open combat, between the forces of the mind. An example is the lifelong struggle between the motivating forces and desires of the human mind, which takes place between the impulses of right and wrong.

Every human being possesses at least two distinct personalities. As many as six distinct powers may be discovered in one human being. One of man's most delicate tasks is that of harmonizing these mind forces so that they may be organized and directed toward the orderly attainment of a given objective. Without this element of harmony, no individual can become an accurate thinker.

WHAT IS LEADERSHIP?

It is no wonder that leaders find it so difficult to organize groups of people to function without friction for the attainment of a given objective. Each individual human being possesses forces within himself which are hard to harmonize, even when he is placed in the environment most favorable to harmony. If the chemistry of the individual's mind is such that his mental units cannot be harmonized easily, think how much more difficult it must be to harmonize a group of minds so they will function as one!

The leader who successfully develops and directs the energies of a mastermind group must possess tact, patience, persistence, self-confidence, intimate knowledge of mind chemistry, and the ability to adapt himself (in a state of perfect poise and harmony) to quickly changing circumstances without showing the least sign of annoyance.

How many are there who can measure up to this requirement?

The successful leader must possess the ability to change the color of his mind, chameleon-like, to fit every circumstance that arises in connection with the object of his leadership. Moreover, he must possess the ability to change from one mood to another without showing the slightest signs of anger or lack of self-control. The successful leader must understand the seventeen principles of the Science of Personal Achievement and be able to put into practice any combination of these laws whenever occasion demands.

Without this ability, no leader can be powerful, and without power, no leader can long endure.

There has long been a general misconception of the meaning of the word "educate." The dictionaries have not aided in the elimination of this misunderstanding because they have defined the word "educate" as "an act of imparting knowledge."

The word "educate" has its roots in the Latin word *educo,* which means to develop from within, to educe, to draw out, to grow through use.

Nature hates idleness in all its forms. She gives continuous life only to those elements which are in use. Tie up an arm, or any other member of the body, taking it out of use, and it will soon atrophy and become lifeless. Reverse the order, give an arm more than normal use, such as that engaged in by the blacksmith who wields a heavy hammer all day long, and that arm (developed from within) grows strong.

Power grows out of organized knowledge. It grows out of it through application and use.

A person may become a walking encyclopedia without possessing any power of value. This knowledge becomes power only to the extent that it is organized, classified, and put into action. Some of the best-educated men in the world possess much less general knowledge than some who are known as fools, the difference between the two being that the former put what knowledge they possess to use, while the latter make no such application.

THE TRUE MEANING OF EDUCATION

An educated person is one who knows how to acquire everything he needs in the attainment of his main purpose in life, without violating the rights of his fellowmen.

The successful lawyer is not necessarily the one who best memorizes the principles of law. On the contrary, the successful lawyer is the one who knows where to find a principle of law, plus a variety of opinions supporting that principle which fit the immediate need of a given case.

In other words, the successful lawyer knows where to find the law he wants when he needs it. This principle applies, with equal force, to the affairs of industry and business.

Henry Ford had very little elementary schooling, yet

he was a highly educated man because he acquired the ability to combine natural and economic laws and the minds of men to achieve the power to get anything of a material nature he wanted.

During World War I, Mr. Ford brought suit against the *Chicago Tribune,* charging that newspaper with libelous publication of statements concerning him, one of which was the statement that Ford was "an ignoramus, an ignorant pacifist," and so on.

When the suit came to trial, the attorneys for the *Tribune* undertook to prove that their statements were true, that he was ignorant, and with this objective in mind, they catechized and cross-examined him on many subjects.

One question they asked was: "How many soldiers did the British send over to subdue the rebellion in the Colonies in 1776?"

With a dry grin on his face, Ford nonchalantly replied: "I do not know just how many, but I have heard that it was a lot more than ever went back."

Of course, this brought loud laughter from court, jury, courtroom spectators, and even from the frustrated lawyer who had asked the question.

This line of interrogation was continued for an hour or more, with Ford remaining perfectly calm. Finally, however, he tired of it and in reply to a question which was particularly obnoxious and insulting, Ford straightened himself up, pointed his finger at the questioning lawyer and replied:

"If I should really wish to answer the foolish questions you have just asked, or any of the others you have been asking, let me remind you that I have a row of electric push buttons hanging over my desk and, by placing my finger on the right button, I could call in men who could give me the correct answer to all the questions you have asked and to many that you have not the intelligence either to ask or to answer. Now, will you kindly tell me why I should bother about filling my head with a lot of useless details in order to answer every fool question that anyone may ask, when I have able men all about me who can supply me with all the facts I want when I call for them?"

This answer is quoted from memory by Dr. Hill, but it substantially relates Ford's answer.

There was silence in the courtroom. The questioning attorney's jaw dropped and his eyes opened wide. The judge leaned forward from the bench and gazed in Mr. Ford's direction. Many of the jury awoke and looked around as if they had heard an explosion, which they actually had.

Henry Ford's answer proved to all who had the intelligence to accept the proof that true education means mind development, not merely the gathering and classifying of knowledge.

Ford could not, in all probability, have named the capitals of all the states of the United States, but he could have, and in fact had, gathered the capital with which to turn many wheels within every state in the Union.

Ford probably could not have gone into his chemical laboratory and separated water into its component atoms of hydrogen and oxygen and then recombined these atoms in their former order, but he knew how to surround himself with chemists who could do this for him. The man who can intelligently use the knowledge possessed by another is as much or more an educated man as the person who merely has the knowledge, but does not know what to do with it.

HOW TO FORM THE MASTERMIND ALLIANCE

Before condensing into one sentence the key to the stupendous power you will have by mastering your mind power, let us summarize the principles of the mastermind alliance and enumerate the steps for forming one.

The mastermind consists of an alliance of two or more minds working in perfect harmony for the attainment of a definite objective.

To form a mastermind group you must:

1. Write out a list of qualifications you want in the members.
2. Whom to elect? Think of qualities of a good employee or friend:

    (a) Dependability
    (b) Loyalty
    (c) Ability
    (d) A positive mental attitude
    (e) Going the extra mile
    (f) Applied faith

3. Be sure that you are in complete harmony with the second person, and then the two of you agree on number three, and the three of you on number four, and so on. This is important. You must take all members into your complete confidence. Each member should accept the others at "face value," without reservation.

4. Choose and *eliminate* if necessary until you have the right group working in perfect harmony.

5. Be sure you set up a motive strong enough to assure getting the job done. If you make a profit, be willing to share it with those who help you, in proportion to their contribution. Go the extra mile.

6. Be sure you have a definite time and place to meet to discuss plans and action to be taken. Neglect here spells failure.

7. Keep perfect harmony. This is your job as a leader. It will help here to remember Carnegie's major purpose: "To make men."

8. *Get on good terms with yourself.* Do some masterminding with your "other self," who recognizes no such thing as defeat, until you are thoroughly acquainted. This is an alliance you cannot do without. The place to start for success is you. When you use the mastermind principle to avail yourself of the minds of others, be sure you begin by taking complete charge of your own mind.

An excellent summary of the principle of mastering your mind power and the power of the mastermind is the repetition of a phrase which illustrates the source from which the Master Mind derives its potential for power:

WHATEVER THE MIND OF MAN CAN CONCEIVE AND BELIEVE, IT CAN ACHIEVE.

The "mind of man" as here stated consists of the sum total of knowledge which has been recognized, organized, and recorded by mankind since the dawn of civilization. It is available to all who have the desire and intelligence to appropriate and use it, to all who have taken possession of their own minds and who seek success through the Master Power of Persuasion.

Chapter Ten

SEARCH FOR A SYMBOL

The Napoleon Hill Foundation chose Del Smith an example of an individual who successfully uses the seventeen principles to achieve success and to enjoy the true riches of life. In Chapter 6 we described each of the seventeen principles. As you read this chapter, see how many of the principles you can identify that Del Smith used in his life and his experiences.

When the shooting stopped and the war with Iraq ended, the first commercial airplane to land in Kuwait City was a Gulfstream II, an executive jet owned by the chairman of Evergreen International Aviation, Inc. The smoke was so thick from the oil field fires set by the retreating Iraqi army that Noel Fletcher, the thirty-year-old pilot of the craft, was unable to see the airfield.

There were no navigational aids. The radar, instrument-landing system, and other electronic equipment had been destroyed by the fleeing Iraqis. Fletcher announced his position on a prearranged frequency so that other aircraft in the area could stay out of his way. This primitive system was the only way air-traffic control could be regulated in the war-ravaged city.

As the Gulfstream II eased through the oily smoke, the picture of a country destroyed by war gradually came into view. The countryside surrounding the once bustling Kuwait City airport was covered with refuse of the war.

189

Burnt-out hulks of tanks, trucks, and other vehicles, spent ammunition casings and the corpses of fallen soldiers and animals unfortunate enough to be caught in the cross-fire littered the landscape.

On board the jet was Evergreen's sixty-year-old chairman, Delford M. Smith. He was there because his company had for months ferried troops and supplies to the Middle East as the U.S. and its allies readied for war. A cornerstone of his philosophy of service is physical presence. "First, you have to sell yourself," he says. "Second, sell the need, third, sell the solution, and have it close at hand. We sell real solutions to real problems."

He fervently believes that if Evergreen is serving its customers properly, its people—including the chairman—have to be where they are needed. The rule applies whether the company is flying mail for the government, spraying crops, fighting forest fires, flying oil field supplies to remote locations in Alaska, or ferrying troops to a war zone.

Soon after the Gulfstream II touched down in Kuwait City, Smith and his crew were at work figuring out what was most needed and where they could help. The city was desperately short of drinking water, medical supplies, and electric power. Without hesitation, Smith removed the seats from his executive jet and began flying in bottled water, medical supplies, and generators. For weeks he and his crew, aircraft commander Fletcher, copilot Steve Lilley, twenty-three, and Smith's personal assistant Mary Simmons, twenty-four, made four trips a day from pickup points in Saudi Arabia to Kuwait City, bringing in desperately needed supplies.

It was one of the many ironies of war that it was far easier to fly supplies to Kuwait City than to truck them. Access at the borders was still controlled by the troops while at the airport, the entire infrastructure—including customs and passport control—was out of operation. The best and safest route to the city was by air.

It was no accident that Smith was on hand when the services of his company were needed. He's made a career out of being where his customers have needed him. Evergreen has fought river blindness in Africa, famine in Ethiopia, and helped explore for oil in every oil patch in the free world.

With just six hours' notice from Washington, Evergreen flew the Shah of Iran from Panama to Cairo, and while aiding the El Salvador government in repairing power lines downed by guerillas, flew the daughter of former Salvadorian President Jose Napoleon Duarte to safety when she was released by leftist rebels. For days after the last U.S. military plane left Vietnam in 1975, Evergreen remained in the country to ferry out Royal Dutch Shell employees and their families stranded there.

Evergreen's willingness to tackle tough assignments for the government has led to some media speculation that the company is a front for the CIA, a rumor that has dogged the company for years. Smith doesn't talk about any of his customers; he just quietly goes about taking care of their needs in the most efficient, cost-effective manner possible. His leadership encourages employees to do the same. It is an accepted fact throughout the company that he never asks anyone to do anything that he wouldn't do or hasn't already done himself.

Tim Walhberg, a twenty-two-year veteran with the company who is now president of Evergreen International Airlines, says that most of the risks the company has taken over the years have been Smith's risks. "He believes in himself and in his organization; he knows we can do anything. Once we commit, we do it no matter what.

"Over the past few years we have been involved in some important projects like spraying heroin and marijuana crops in Mexico. Occasionally we ran into some shooting and we had some equipment burned by the drug lords who didn't like us destroying their crops, but to us, a job is a job. We do what has to be done. We are a no-nonsense company that performs. That attitude starts with Del, works its way through management and to every employee," Wahlberg said.

"Del gives us an opportunity to prove ourselves and we would never let him down. He interviewed me for a job because I had some army helicopter experience and that's what he needed when he was just starting the company. It was a perfect match: I was looking for adventure, and he was looking for crews. He asked me if I wanted to go somewhere or if I wanted to stay here and kick dirt clods.

"I've since been around the world and back again. I've worked in Alaska, Australia, Africa, the Amazon jungle, and a lot of places in between. Del teaches us to believe in ourselves and to act and respond quickly. If he said, 'We're going to Pakistan,' we'd collect our pots and pans and go. From the beginning, we always delivered quality, on-time service.

"There was no room for complacency or bureaucracy. We were a company with a strong work ethic and a commitment to profitability. We knew that if we were to grow and prosper, we had to sell a quality product at a quality price. Del used to say, 'If you think quality is expensive, try the alternative—paying for it twice.' The customer always came first and foremost whatever the job might be."

Smith's fearlessness in tackling assignments that would terrify others may be rooted in his early life. He had none of the security that is normally a staple of childhood. Orphaned as an infant when his natural parents were killed in an accident, Smith was adopted when he was little more than a year old, but the little family was soon deserted by the adoptive father.

Mabel Smith fought poverty and poor health as she struggled to raise young Del alone. When she was unable to care for him, Mabel returned Smith to the orphanage and later to her sister's family until her health improved. She was family, though, and Smith visited her daily until she was well enough for him to come home. When times were so tough that they couldn't even afford coal for heat, young Smith would throw cow chips at the trainmen as the freights passed through to entice them to throw coal at him. He picked up the coal and took it home.

As a child he carried burdens that would have staggered many adults. He can't recall not working, and managed three newspaper routes to help keep body and soul together. By the time he had reached age ten, he had saved enough to make the down payment on a small cottage in Centralia, Washington, where he lived with "Mother Smith."

It was at the orphanage that Smith found a copy of

Napoleon Hill's *Think and Grow Rich,* the book that was to have a profound influence in his development. As he studied the book, he realized that Hill had put into words his own feelings. The book clarified his desires and helped him focus his goals. For the first time he understood what he wanted to accomplish with his life and how to accomplish it. The formula was spelled out for him in the pages of the book.

One success inspired another as Smith applied the principles of success that Napoleon Hill wrote about. He realized that a college education was essential if he was to achieve the goals he had set for himself, and he developed a burning desire to earn his degree. He worked nights and summers at a logging camp to support himself and pay college tuition, attending school by day. Smith proudly accepted his diploma from the University of Washington in 1953.

As a teenager he developed a love of flying that has remained with him throughout his life. He earned his fixed-wing flying license in 1949 at age eighteen and his rotary-wing license in 1957, the early days of the whirly-bird. He got a job as a helicopter pilot with Dean Johnson, a local helicopter-flying service operator, in the hope of parlaying his love of flying into a living.

He quickly learned the business, and despite the risks during the pioneering days of the helicopter and the long hours, he loved it. He flew transport jobs and fire-fighting missions for the forestry service in the Pacific Northwest and ferried parts, supplies, and oilfield workers on Alaska's North Slope and in the Middle East.

By 1960, he was itching to get out on his own, to build a company that would allow him to incorporate in his own business his devotion to quality and intense desire to succeed. He bought two helicopters with no money down; his track record and his penchant for hard work were his primary collateral. Evergreen Helicopters, Inc., was incorporated in McMinnville, Oregon, on July 1, 1960.

The motto of the fledgling company was "Quality Without Compromise." Smith had a basic vision for Evergreen that was shared by his crew:

1. Performance was the only thing that counted!
2. Looking after the customer properly was the reason for being.
3. What they did should be beneficial for mankind.

His determination and dedication quickly paid off. His customers appreciated his fanatical attention to detail and to meeting their needs and requirements. His word was more than his bond; it was a sacred vow. If Del Smith told you he would do something by a certain time, you could put it in the bank. Regardless of the personal sacrifice or difficulties encountered along the way, he got the job done.

During those early days it was standard practice for Smith and his crew to drive most of the night in a caravan of flatbed trucks hauling the helicopters, tank trucks with fuel and chemicals, and the other supporting equipment following along behind. Park and snooze for a couple of hours, and it was up with first light to begin the day's work. Those habits have stuck with Smith; after thirty years in business, he still maintains a schedule that exhausts men half his age.

By the end of his first year in business, Evergreen Helicopters had grown to a fleet of seven. Of necessity during the early, undercapitalized years, Smith developed management and accounting controls for his tiny company and hired Phoebe Hocken to run accounting and administration. The team spirit and the management controls Smith installed during those early days continue today. The systems are more sophisticated, but the rudiments are the same.

Essentially, each aircraft is treated as a separate profit center. Revenues and costs are charged against the craft, and its utilization and cost per hour of operation are carefully monitored. A helicopter is a working machine, Smith believes—a sort of airborne tractor, an angel of mercy—and should be kept busy. An idle helicopter is a cash drain. Though his fleet now numbers 165, he has a surprising grasp of the details of the business. He can recite operational statistics in minute detail, and drives himself relentlessly in a tireless quest to improve performance.

John Carnemolla, Senior Vice President of Evergreen Aircraft Sales & Leasing, a trading company that buys and sells everything from spare helicopter parts to Boeing 747s, joined Evergreen in 1975. He recalled: "Del always had his hand in everything that goes on in the company. When I started here, we had something like thirteen helicopter bases and 130 helicopters. He could stand up at a meeting and recite operating statistics by ID number and tell you how every aircraft was doing—how many hours it was working and what kind of revenue it was generating. We've grown a lot since then, but I would bet that he can do just about the same thing today. He has an incredible grasp of the business."

Mike Clark, president of Evergreen Helicopters, says Smith has an amazing intellect, the kind of mind that allows him to focus on several things at once. "I once brought my wife's cousin, an attorney, to work with me. We have a management meeting every Monday morning at seven o'clock and we often invite guests to our meetings, so I brought him along.

"As is our custom, the holding company did its reports and each of the operating companies went through their priorities for the week. Later on in the day, we had a couple of sessions in which Mr. Smith was involved, so the attorney had a fair amount of exposure to him and could see how he operates.

"As we were driving home, I asked him what impressed him most about Del Smith. He said, 'Well, he is as bright as anyone I have ever met. I have known some pretty intelligent people, but I was surprised at his ability to focus on so many issues at once. I was amazed at his in-depth knowledge of every aspect of such a diversified business.'

"Del stays involved," Carnemolla said. "That's his method. The system he has developed brings successes and failures to the top so they can be analyzed or fixed, if necessary, so he can give the credit to those who deserve it or take corrective action if it is required."

The majority of Evergreen's business during the 1960s was concentrated in forestry and agriculture. Smith's contracts were mostly for tree seeding and spraying, firefighting, and logging. In his first year in business, he landed a contract with the U.S. Bureau of Land Management to reseed thirty thousand acres of forest land devastated by forest fires. The bureau concluded that Del Smith and his crew could do the work by helicopter for a third of the cost of replanting the burnt-out areas manually, and could reach remote, mountainous areas that were inaccessible on foot.

Word of Smith's achievements spread, and along with it his reputation. In its first few years of operation, Evergreen was engaged to perform such diverse missions as counting Ruby River moose, transporting blood for open-heart surgery, and planting utility poles.

The rugged terrain in which Evergreen operated produced rugged men unafraid to tackle the difficult jobs. But they did so with due prudence. Every precaution was taken to minimize risk, and Smith never wavered from his commitment to safety first. Equipment was kept in peak condition, regardless of the cost.

Risks were taken only when lives were at stake. In 1966, Smith received several honors for his daring December 27, 1965, rescue of a young girl who was trapped on a tiny island in the middle of a raging river.

Rains over the previous few days had swollen the Yamhill River near McMinnville until it overflowed its banks and flooded nearby farms. During the afternoon a young couple, David Hughes, then nineteen, and Mary Lou Boyers, eighteen, went out on the river in an inflatable raft to check out the flood damage. Their boat capsized, stranding them on a small island that before the flood had been part of a farm.

When the duo couldn't attract any attention with their cries for help, they decided that Hughes would attempt to swim to shore and get help. He made the half mile in the raging river and ran to the nearest farmhouse for help, cold, wet, exhausted, and nearly incoherent.

According to newspaper accounts at the time, Smith was home with the flu and Evergreen's eight helicopters were grounded because of bad weather when he received a call from local law-enforcement officials asking for help. "We couldn't put men in boats out in the river at night," Sheriff W. L. "Bud" Mekkers told the McMinnville *News-Register*. "It was too swift, full of swirling currents and fast-moving logs, and many barbed-wire fences were hidden just below the water level.

"As a pilot myself," Mekkers said, "I knew what I was asking Del to do. He did it without question, knowing it had to be done or that girl might have washed into the currents or died of exposure." According to the sheriff's account, Smith didn't even stop for a life jacket for himself as he raced to his helicopter. He removed the doors from his bubble helicopter and took off.

Flying sideways for better visibility, Smith performed numerous letdowns and vertical climbs as he searched among the islands for the young girl. When he located her, he was required to land on "a tree-shrouded site no wider than the helicopter's rotor diameter—about thirty-five feet—while gusts up to sixty miles per hour threatened the three-place helicopter."

When the rescue was finally completed, the tiny island was within a foot of submergence. Characteristically reticent about his own accomplishments, Smith told the *News-Register* simply, "It was a little scratchy."

For selfless disregard for his own safety in performing the rescue, Smith was nominated for the Helicopter Association of America's Pilot of the Year Award and summoned to Washington, D.C., to receive the Frederick L. Feinberg Award. That same year, Evergreen was cited for its outstanding safety by the Federal Aviation Agency.

The story of Smith's life and the commercial history of rotary wing aircraft are inextricably linked. He invented the helicopter spray system for agricultural applications and pioneered uses for the whirlybird that had never before been conceived. Evergreen pilots restrung power lines in remote areas and were the first to use helicopters to place heavy air-conditioning systems atop skyscrapers.

Never satisfied with the status quo, during the mid-sixties, Smith invested heavily in research and development searching for even more commercial applications for rotary-wing aircraft. By 1966, the company was marketing its patented aerial-dispensing system throughout the country.

The late sixties brought Smith recognition in other ways as well. Evergreen's precision flying during the worst July flying weather on record as the company battled an invasion of the Hemlock Looper in Washington brought wide acclaim for the largest insect-spraying operation ever undertaken in the U.S. It brought Smith wide acclaim—and more business.

In 1968, the company purchased Bell's first commercial turbine powered helicopter, and Smith again expanded the company's horizons. The Bell 205 became a workhorse for construction and heavy-lift operations. Smith caught the attention of *Men of Action* magazine, which profiled his globe-trotting escapades: spraying bananas in Central America, working with an Antarctic whaling expedition, and flying for mining operations in Alaska.

To make sure he had the right people in the right jobs, Smith stayed involved in recruiting, despite the fact that the company had grown substantially and had earned quite a reputation in commercial aviation circles. Wade Green, now head of flight operations for the helicopter company, recalled his first meeting with Smith.

"I was just out of the army where I was a helicopter pilot in Vietnam, and had put out several feelers for a job. One of them was with Evergreen. As agreed, I met this guy at a motel in Fort Worth, Texas, to talk about going to work as a pilot for Evergreen.

"I was pretty blunt with him. I had other opportunities, and I didn't have to take the first thing that came along, so I asked all about the company, its benefits, problems, and anything else I could think of. I didn't pull any punches. I thought I was talking to one of the pilots, so I asked him everything I wanted to know.

"We talked about going to Alaska, and I told him that I was interested in what was in it for me. I would be away from home for long periods of time, and we both knew it would be very hard work. He was truthful with me, never tried to paint it gray. It was either black or it was white.

"After the interview, I walked out to his car with him,

still talking, and I realized that I had been talking to Del Smith, the owner of the company. He impressed me not only in that he was very down-to-earth, but he also seemed to have a very good sense of where the industry was going.

"As I thought about the interview later, I figured I had probably blown it with my bluntness. I hadn't really been trying to impress him because I thought he was just one of the guys. But I decided that he seemed like a pretty straight shooter, and if he wanted me, I would join Evergreen and go to Alaska.

"I guess Del likes plain talk, because he called three days later and offered me a job. I accepted on the spot, and the next day I was in Prudhoe Bay, Alaska, working on the pipeline. Those were exciting days. We were in on the ground floor, at the very beginning of trying anything we could imagine with a helicopter. We fertilized forests, used the first big machines for spraying, went into logging and construction, worked on buildings and power lines.

"From the beginning, Del practiced the principles of success—definiteness of purpose, in particular. He knew where he was going and how he was going to get there. He knew we were building something worthwhile, something that would be good for a whole lot of people someday. He is so intent on achieving his goals that he doesn't allow anything to get in his way. He doesn't know the meaning of the word *stop*. In those early days, we would work all day, then drive all night to get to the next job. He no longer has to drive all night to get to the next job, but he still works at the same pace as he did when we were starting out.

"Del is also a great believer in teamwork. We are in the kind of business that requires cooperation; everyone must do his job well or the whole operation fails, but Del goes beyond what would normally be expected."

It's part of the company lore that Green was the beneficiary of Smith's dedication to his people and his commitment to teamwork. When Green and Walhberg were part of the Evergreen's crew working on the Alaska pipeline, a combination of bad weather and navigational problems left them and their helicopter stranded on an iceberg and out of fuel. Green slept and Walhberg worried, but they both knew that Smith would find them eventually.

They activated the on-board emergency transmitter that would give patrolling aircraft a fix on their location. Despite their confidence that Smith and the others would find them, they knew it would be dicey. They were way off course on a moving iceberg. Even if their emergency signal were picked up and the weather cooperated, by the time someone could be sent to pick them up, their location would have changed.

They had been on the ice twenty-four hours when they were spotted by a patrol plane and several more hours elapsed before an Evergreen airplane could reach them. They were taken back to base camp, where they were fed, supplied with fuel, and flown back to get their helicopter. It was soon back to business as usual. Once again Smith and his Evergreen team had performed admirably—with little fanfare.

Smith's willingness to go the extra mile with his customers and employees earned him a reputation as the leader of a quality organization, but he wanted more. He wanted a world-class company, a respected leader in the field. As he worked tirelessly to keep the company moving forward, he continued to plan ahead.

Much of Evergreen's growth can be attributed to Smith's long-range vision. He is an extraordinarily accurate thinker who is able to control his attention and focus on the business at hand while keeping an eye on the future. "Del is a visionary," said Richard Nelson, a director of human resources for Evergreen International Aviation. "He really believes the Napoleon Hill philosophy and that 'what the mind can conceive and believe, it can achieve.' He is very goal-oriented. He sets high goals for himself and for the company, and he achieves them through persistent practice. He teaches the principles to the young people in the organization and to everyone else. His concept of goal-attainment permeates the organization."

An R.O.T.C. graduate of Oregon State University, Nelson joined the army in 1965 as a second lieutenant and served two tours of duty in Vietnam, the second as an aviator. He retired twenty years later and joined Evergreen as Director of Human Resources.

"Del is an outstanding leader in the military leadership model," Nelson believes. "Performance is the name of the game. Nothing else matters. He rewards those that perform; others don't survive, but even they have improved themselves through their association with Evergreen.

"Some people are not suited for our style of working," he says. "They are just not Evergreen people. Whether they do well or not, Del never pulls any punches with his associates. He is a man of honesty and integrity, and he is totally straightforward. He has no hidden agenda. What you see is what you get.

"*Can't* is not in Del's vocabulary. He has an uncanny ability to size up a job and tell immediately if it is going to be profitable. If it is, we're there. We like to make money. It's important to our lenders, our vendors, our employees, and our growth. We believe that if we perform as we should, every job should be profitable.

"Over the years Del has learned what works and what doesn't. He and we learn from our mistakes. We audit every job after it's completed to determine what we might have done more efficiently. We recently found in a job in Africa, for example, that the turbine blades lasted only half as long as they should because of the dust and sand. We'll allow for that in the next contract there.

"We have very high standards and we maintain them. Del is always there to make sure they don't erode. We apply the same principles to our contracts. Our model contract is one that we think is the best it can be, because we assume that through the negotiation process, everyone is required to give a little. We start with high standards so we can maintain our quality commitment.

"I would say that Del Smith is a natural leader with ability equal to an Eisenhower or MacArthur," Nelson says. "The principles he learned from studying the writings of Napoleon Hill have stayed with him throughout his career, and he has taught them to others in key positions in Evergreen. He inspires people because he has faith in them. His way is the humanitarian way. First and foremost in his thought process is that through the performance of our contracts we will in some way better life on earth. If he doesn't believe it, we don't accept the contract."

Always looking to the future, as the helicopter business prospered, Smith began to anticipate the time when Evergreen would be required to add large fixed-wing aircraft to its fleet to continue expanding. Not everyone in the company agreed. Tim Wahlberg recalled, "As an old helicopter jock, I didn't see the point. I didn't believe we should be in the airline business, but Del saw it for what it was worth."

To get into the business in the days before deregulation of the airline industry involved miles of governmental red tape and approval of the Civil Aeronautics Board, something akin to a minor miracle. Nevertheless, Smith set the wheels in motion to buy Missoula, Montana-based Johnson Flying Service, an early certificate, subject to the approval of the CAB. Its acquisition would give Evergreen operating authority throughout the U.S.

Friends and customers he had helped over the years lent a hand. According to a profile of Smith in the December 10, 1990, issue of *Forbes*, George Doole, who had started the CIA's Air America took a personal interest in the hearings. "Earlier, the CAB had turned down applications, first by U.S. Steel and later by General Curtis LeMay and film actor/partner Jimmy Stewart to buy Johnson," *Forbes* continued. "At about the same time, the CIA came under pressure from Congress to get rid of CIA-owned airlines like Air America and Intermountain Airlines, and sold the lease to its big air base at Marana, Arizona, to Evergreen."

Forbes writer Richard L. Stern goes on to speculate about Smith's government connections, but concludes: "While there are plenty of people who will claim that Smith got a big boost from 'certain government agencies,' there are few who would deny that Evergreen is superb at what it does."

After eighteen months of hearings and courtroom battles, the CAB did eventually affirm the law judge's initial decision that found that the acquisition of Johnson Flying Service would benefit Johnson, its employees, and the public.

Evergreen Helicopters would pay $5 million for Johnson's FAA certificate and operations. A pioneering aviation company, Johnson Flying Service had been in business since 1924, literally the earliest days of flight in the U.S. Bob Johnson's logbook was endorsed by Orville Wright. In a historic gesture, in 1975 President Gerald Ford awarded Johnson's operating authority, Supplemental Certificate No. 1, to Evergreen, citing the company's "proven" track record in aviation. The award with "grandfather rights" gave the company a five-year edge over the competition that would appear with deregulation of the industry. It was the big boost that allowed Smith and Evergreen to expand into the airline business and recorded in the company's history as the birthdate of Evergreen International Airlines, Inc.

Evergreen Airlines quickly assumed residence at the newly acquired Marana, Arizona, base, now renamed Evergreen Air Center, and Smith, having learned from painful experience about the intricacies of doing business in Washington, D.C., opened a government liaison office there. Its mission would be to pursue additional operating authority for Evergreen.

The year 1975 brought other successes to Evergreen as well. The roof of the Detroit Lions stadium was installed by a Sikorsky S64 helicopter, cutting the installation time by ninety percent, according to construction officials. The company also made national news for rescuing country singer Hank Williams, Jr., after he was injured in a fall in the mountains in Montana.

The company began to seriously expand in September of the following year with the acquisition of DC-9 aircraft that Evergreen contracted to the U.S. Air Force for its Logistics Air Command program. The contract provided for domestic freight hauling, an operation that is still maintained. It is a source of pride to Smith and the company that this program is one of Evergreen's longest-running operations.

Evergreen joined the jet age in 1976 with the purchase of two DC-8s, and the company expanded into international charter flights as it exercised its rapidly expanding operating authority. Smith liked what he called "quick-change" aircraft that would allow rapid conversion from freight to passenger traffic to accommodate customers' needs.

Evergreen Airlines flew charter flights and filled in for major airlines when maintenance or labor problems grounded flights. The airline numbered among its customers Emery, United Parcel Service, tour operators, freight forwarders, and the U.S. government. The airline was chosen to fly Frank Sinatra's entourage to Las Vegas for his birthday celebration in 1981.

The maintenance facility at the base in Marana, Arizona, established a reputation for excellence and reliability that spread throughout the industry. Other airlines and owners of private aircraft—including the pop music group, the Bee Gees—liked the quality of service Marana provided and flew their planes to the Evergreen Center for maintenance as NASA does now with the shuttle aircraft carriers.

Ever alert for an opportunity, when Smith didn't like the cargo handling and ground service he received at some major U.S. airports, he started his own ground-handling company. Named E.A.G.L.E. (Evergreen Aviation Ground Logistics Enterprises), the new operating unit gave the company the edge in ground operations. It was soon operating at major airports throughout the country.

When it comes to facilities' maintenance, Smith is a fanatic. Hangar floors are painted and polished, tools are neatly stowed, and all equipment is spotless and organized. Hangars have more in common with hospital operating rooms than they do with an oily maintenance and storage facility.

Ground equipment is similarly handled. Trucks are freshly painted, washed regularly, and parked in neat rows. If Smith observes anything out of order when he flies over the operation, the facilities manager can expect a call from the chairman asking him to get down to the hangar and straighten things out, whether the infraction occurs during the workday, in the evening, or on a weekend. With an aircraft taking off every eight minutes somewhere in the world, Evergreen is in operation twenty-four hours a day.

Evergreen employees are expected to conduct themselves with professionalism Monday morning at seven o'clock and on Sunday afternoons when Smith takes a rare day off to watch son Mark, twenty-four (who was recently named rookie of the year in the American Racing Series), drive his Evergreen-sponsored racing car.

Smith has made it a top priority to attend the races since Mark and his older brother, Mike, twenty-five, now an Air National Guard F-15 pilot, raced go-carts as boys. "We didn't realize how much of an effort Dad made to get to the races," Mike recalled. "When we were kids we thought it was normal for fathers to fly home from Alaska or South America where they had been working to watch us race. He was almost always there."

Smith travels to the races these days in his Gulfstream II, taking along various guests, visiting dignitaries, employees, and their children on a space-available basis. It is a prized Evergreen perk to be invited to go to the races with the chairman. Everyone aboard is given the same VIP treatment by the crew, and those that are on duty are expected to adhere to highest company standards whether they are at the race or providing food service for guests.

On one occasion, the driver of the Evergreen bus responsible for ferrying Smith and his guests from the airport to the racetrack committed a definite faux pas by not knowing the route, an unacceptable error in the company's culture. He was expected to have made the drive at least once before the actual event to make sure he knew the best way to the track. Everyone knew he would be severely reprimanded.

When the group had been delivered to the track, the Evergreen driver pulled Smith aside to apologize. "I volunteered for this assignment because I wanted to meet you," he told Smith. "Since I worked all week I didn't have time to check out the route. I realize now that I should have made time."

"Did you learn something from the experience?" Smith asked.

"Yes, I did," the driver replied. "I'll never make a mistake like that again."

"That's the spirit," Smith said. "You are doing a good job. A mistake isn't a mistake unless you don't learn from it. Next time I know you will be more prepared."

Much of Smith's popularity with rank-and-file employees results from his genuine concern about their welfare. He travels tirelessly, visiting his far-flung operations and stops to chat with workers from the loading dock to the division president's office.

The first question is always the same: "How's your leadership?"

That sort of ad hoc reverse performance evaluation, in which workers are asked about managers' performance, creates an environment that quickly exposes incompetents. There are few secrets in Evergreen. Everyone knows the objective is customer service and performance; no one can rest on his or her laurels for long.

The second question is: "How are you doing in finding a replacement for yourself?" Smith believes good people find other good people, and he encourages them to replace themselves to move up the promotional ladder. John Irwin, the thirty-five-year-old who heads up insurance for Evergreen International Aviation, credits much of the company's success to Smith's confidence in young people.

"Del likes to give people an opportunity. He is willing to let us do it, to let us make our own mistakes. He recruits many people just out of college and trains them in his way of doing things. They often go through a one-to two-year management training program and then are given more responsibility than they ever dreamed possible at their age.

"Mary Simmons is a good example. In her mid-twenties, she is one of Del's right-hand people. He trusts her completely, and she has a great deal of responsibility. When he is unable to go somewhere, he often sends Mary to represent him."

"Mr. Smith often uses me as a sounding board," Simmons says. "He asks me what I think and I tell him. He doesn't like yes-men around him. He wants an honest answer. He believes that everyone teaches everyone else. We learn from each other, so he asks our opinion. But discussion is not a substitute for action. Everyone knows that with him, results are the only thing that matter. He insists on performance and accountability. If you want his advice, he is always available. He has a complete open-door policy, but if you commit to something, he expects you to get it done.

"He is very perceptive, which makes him good at evaluating people. He is sensitive to their feelings, and he listens to what they are *not* saying as well as what they *are* saying. He is completely trustworthy and with him there is no pretense. He is exactly as he appears, always. He is very consistent, not one way today and different tomorrow," Simmons said.

He also likes deadlines. If the response is vague, he talks it through with the employee until they agree upon a date. A goal isn't a goal unless it has a completion date attached to it.

Smith maintains several houses on the thousands of acres he owns around the McMinnville facilities, which are used to house employees awaiting permanent assignment elsewhere or those in training at headquarters. Evergreen provides cleaning and cooking services at accommodations that are much friendlier than at an impersonal hotel. The chairman frequently drops by to chat and to welcome new arrivals to the Evergreen family.

"We can learn from you," he tells newcomers. "If you see a better way to do something, tell your supervisor or call me. Sometimes we get too close to things to see every opportunity. You may be more objective. We're interested in learning everything we can from you."

When a new employee offered a suggestion about computerizing a portion of the scheduling during one of the kitchen table chats, Smith probed. Satisfied the new man knew what he was talking about, Smith said, "Call me in the office on Monday and we'll set up a meeting with the right people to talk about it further. Tell my assistant that I asked you to call and that she should put you through."

It's an accepted fact at the company that there are Evergreen people and there are those who are not. A description is not written down in a manual, but it is generally accepted that an Evergreen person is one who shares Smith's values. They have a penchant for hard work, they enjoy challenges, and they are highly motivated.

"Our philosophy is never limit yourself or the company," says Joe Sharp, the forty-one-year-old president of the Evergreen Holding Company. Sharp spent two years as an English teacher and a few years with a public-utility company before joining Evergreen as business manager of Smith's agricultural investments in 1984. After three years of growth that exceeded thirty percent annually, Smith tapped him for the post of vice president of materiel of Evergreen Airlines. Soon afterward, he was named executive vice president of the airline before assuming the presidency of the holding company in 1989.

"Del is a great teacher and mentor," he says. "He works with you instead of kicking you in the behind. One day when we were driving around looking at the farm property, we got the idea to build an athletic complex on the property. It will be finished next year, and will feature the very latest in fitness equipment. We're also going to build an air museum on land Evergreen owns, and we are exploring the possibility of developing an air show featuring Del's collection of antique airplanes that will travel around the country. If it's a good idea, Del will support it. He is determined to be successful in everything he does, and he insists that we do the same. He believes that if we work hard, do the right things, and believe in ourselves, we cannot fail. There is no excuse for not performing. Instead of faking being sick to avoid going to school, his kids faked being well so they could attend! He will not accept excuses for not performing.

"Despite his strict performance standards for himself and those around him, he is a very kind and giving person. He helps many people who have no idea who their benefactor may be," Sharp says.

Echos Mary Simmons, "He is like a dad that anyone would be proud of. When we were in Washington, D.C., for a few days, we got to know the people in the hotel.

One of the waitresses in the hotel restaurant was a young African girl who told us she was working there to earn the money to bring her family to America. Mr. Smith didn't say anything about it, but when we checked out of the hotel he left an envelope for her with a thousand dollars in it to help pay her family's expenses. That's the kind of person he is; he believes God wants him to help others."

When a McMinnville bank of which Smith was a director got into trouble because some of the local borrowers were unable to repay their loans, several of the directors thought the best course of action was to declare the bank insolvent and go out of business.

"Del wouldn't consider it," Joe Sharp recalled. 'We are not going to let down our investors and the citizens who have money on deposit here,' he said. He provided the cash necessary to keep the bank afloat and put two or three key people on the board to make sure management maintained the kind of business practices that would not allow such a situation to occur again.

"He's an absolute capitalist, but he truly believes that in the end we will all be measured by what we've given back, not by what we've taken. He's a man of action. He says, 'Let's get the job done and not worry about congratulations and frills. Our job is to take care of our customers and not spend too much time worrying about who gets the credit for a quality job. If the organization looks good, we all look good.

"Del is committed to Napoleon Hill's principles of success and frequently talks about them to us. I know that he practices them all, but I would say that he is especially good at Applied Faith and Teamwork. He teaches us to believe in ourselves. Sometimes we may be disappointed in our fellow man, but we always know we can count on ourselves, our team members, and especially Del. He pulls harder than anyone.

"He is so excited about our possibilities that it's infectious. He is totally committed to quality, and he is on top of every detail, every minute of every day. He is totally focused on his goals and he encourages us to be the same. Although he is often accused of being a workaholic (as most of us at Evergreen are), he also understands and appreciates family values. Even though we work long hours, he gives us opportunities to travel and take our kids places that we would not otherwise have been able to do."

As a father, Smith encouraged his boys to explore the world and to test themselves. When they weren't racing go-carts, they were free to hop an Evergreen flight to Alaska for a weekend of salmon fishing or hunting, activities that Mike especially enjoyed. "We went everywhere," he says, "sleeping on airplanes on the way home so we could get back in time for school on Monday."

With a father qualified as a commercial pilot and an instructor, both boys quickly learned to fly themselves. Mark learned in one day, taking his first lesson at 8 A.M. and soloing later that same day. Today he holds both airplane and helicopter pilot licenses. Mike holds a commercial license with an instrument-rating and an air-transport rating. When his brother is competing nearby, he may fly his antique biplane to the track to watch Mark race.

The elder Smith devoted a great deal of effort to making sure his sons didn't grow up as spoiled rich brats. He got them involved in scouting and lists his sons among his achievements, citing their Eagle Scout ratings along with their other accomplishments. He made time for their scouting activities himself, and at the end of a canoe trip the scouts might find the elder Smith hovering overhead in an Evergreen helicopter while someone tossed watermelons into the river for the tired, hungry troop.

Smith still lives in the home where he raised the boys and points with pride at the recreation center the boys helped build as teenagers. He provided the materials; Mike and Mark contributed their labor. The result was a spacious game and exercise room adjoined by an indoor pool, a retreat where a group of spirited boys could burn up some excess energy.

They joke about what a tough taskmaster their dad is, but they share his work ethic and his commitment to helping others. Mark donates half of his earnings from professional racing to The Seeing Eye, Inc., and the National Society to Prevent Blindness. In an interview published in the April 7, 1991, issue, *Parade* magazine reports:

" 'I was just sitting down one day with my dad and some of the people who handle my sponsorship,' Smith recalled. 'I just mentioned how lucky I felt to be able to do what I'm doing, and the conversation turned to the idea that we should do something for others. We decided instead of just talking about it to do something about it.' "

Recalling his own treatments to overcome "lazy-eye syndrome" to get to twenty-twenty vision, Mark suggested helping blind people. *Parade* continued:

"It was, in many ways, a natural decision. The young racer's father is Delford Smith, a self-made millionaire who founded one of the world's largest aviation-leasing and maintenance firms. The elder Smith and his company, Evergreen Aviation Inc., have long donated time, money, and equipment to the fight against river blindness, the devastating parasitic illness that has blinded millions in West Africa. They also contributed several helicopters to a medical group that fights high-altitude cataract blindness in Nepal. Smith was eager to follow in his father's footsteps. 'My dad is a really amazing guy,' he said. 'I really admire him.' "

The words *amazing guy* have often been used to describe Smith. He is truly a driven man—in the best sense of the word. He is obsessed, but with all the right things. He makes money not simply for the sake of making money but for the good it can accomplish. He helps many charities and contributes generously to the less fortunate, but like Napoleon Hill, he places far more value on helping others help themselves by realizing their true potential.

Any discussion with an Evergreen "old-timer" invariably leads to a conversation about the number of people who have left the company to go out on their own. It is a part of leadership, they believe, to allow others to grow, and they know that people will inevitably grow in directions that will be impossible to predict at the outset.

"I couldn't even guess how many people we have helped go into competition with us," Smith says. In an environment where information is freely shared and everyone is encouraged to develop to the limits of his or her capabilities, it is an inevitable consequence that some will leave and join competitors or start businesses of their own. It is a source of pride when they do well; Smith knows that today's Evergreen will be different tomorrow, anyway. The company must constantly innovate to stay ahead of the competition. He believes that it's not what you do as much as how well you do it.

His managers are repeatedly told that there are no secrets in the company. They share information to build competence and confidence. Smith distributes the company's objectives throughout the organization to make sure that every employee knows what the chairman's goals are. His list for the fiscal year ending in 1992 included:

- Definiteness of purpose
- Quality without compromise
- Competitive cost and service advantage in each marketplace
- Dynamic leadership and accountability
- Total teamwork with magnifying motivation and enthusiasm
- Weekly measurement of dedication to management development and training
- Serious regular review of results in every market arena
- Constantly measured operational production efficiency
- Team commitment to budget disciplines
- Worldwide quality alliances
- Recruitment of team members with outstanding ability and character
- Creative and prudent market expansion
- $500 million in revenues
- Ten percent pre-tax profit through better tariff management, cost, and debt reduction
- Responsiveness to global opportunities and emergencies
- Promotion of global peace, goodwill, and free enterprise

Part of every leader's responsibility, Smith believes, is

to develop character as well as ability. "One without the other is unacceptable," he says.

The leaders he most admires are Jesus, Gandhi, Mohammed, Churchill, W. Clement Stone, and presidents Lincoln and Eisenhower. He considers visionaries Howard Hughes and Bill Boeing outstanding leaders in aviation, and names football coach Vince Lombardi as one of the most noteworthy contemporary leaders, citing his attention to basics as an essential characteristic of a good leader. "Attention to the basics is fundamental to the success of any endeavor," he says. "It doesn't matter what field you are in, you cannot succeed unless you are good at the basics."

Smith's commitment to Evergreen's growth is a commitment to creating jobs and extending opportunities to those that deserve them but might not get them if not for driven entrepreneurs such as himself. Those commitments sustain his drive and allow him to maintain a relentless schedule that includes working sixteen-hour days, six and seven days a week, year in and year out.

Evergreen Senior Vice President of Administration Donna Nelson has run the office for Smith for seventeen years, yet still marvels at Smith's drive and his capacity for work.

"The greatest statement he often makes," she says, "is 'God gave us a life. We owe him our best performance!' That is a powerful statement and why communicating our creed, managing by measurement, and maintaining our family spirit are essential. To be part of the Evergreen family is truly an honor, but with the honor comes responsibility and accountability.

"We have such a strong philosophy of leadership and management of the Six M's (management, money, men, machines, material, and market) that teaching this discipline is the finest corporate college in America," she states.

It is an atmosphere of mutual respect. When asked about Nelson, Smith responds: "I worry about her. She works too hard. She is raising a family on her own, and she spends too much time at the office; sometimes we have to make her go home."

Nelson has worked closely with Smith for so long that she knows instinctively how he will respond in a given situation. She is the glue that holds the Evergreen family together when he is away, and maintains order in the chaos that characterizes a mobile empire going in several directions simultaneously.

She says that for Smith, going the extra mile extends beyond his employees and his business.

"We are so dedicated to make the world a better place to live that our work is really a joy—fighting blindness (including asking all chiefs of state we meet to declare that sight is a basic human right), battling the plague of drugs, and promoting and perpetuating the free-enterprise system—and has substantial meaning for us all. Del backs us in these missions without hesitation."

Nelson is committed to being a lifelong teacher and "encourager" like Smith. "The principles are firm," she states emphatically. "Our Mastermind Alliance with those mentioned in this chapter, along with Ron Lane, vice chairman of the airline, and John Kiesler, who runs the helicopter operations, are the same principles we practiced when we only had the helicopter company. We are committed to safety, quality, financial stability, reliability, agility, and total compatibility—with the profitability that makes it happen.

"W. Clement Stone told us: 'Do it now!' " she recalls. "and Mother Theresa told us when we started her first drug-rehabilitation program in India: 'All we ever need to know is: the time is now!' Del encourages our young managers—and us—to take heed. That's a great, great lesson."

Despite his tireless commitment to his Evergreen "family," and their charitable missions, Smith somehow finds time to contribute to the aviation industry. He has served as chairman of the board and president of Helicopter Association International and founded the economics committee. He is a director of the Airlift Association and is a member of the National Defense Transportation Association and the National Air Carrier Association.

When one of his Bell-205 helicopters lost its tail-rotor

control, he didn't simply repair the problem and get on with the business. He researched similar problems and discovered that the cause of the failure was a faulty heat treatment in the manufacturing process. His persistence in tracing the problem to its cause made the entire industry safer. In 1991, estimates placed Smith's net worth at $600 million. That year Evergreen posted revenues of some $477 million and owned a fleet of aircraft worth between $900 million and $1 billion. His fleet includes sixteen 747s, eleven DC-8s and DC-9s, eleven 727s, a hundred helicopters, and scores of other fixed-wing aircraft. He also owns twenty-three antique aircraft—including a mint condition WWII B-17 Flying Fortress bomber and a Ford Tri-Motor—all in flying condition. He plans to exhibit them as "The Heritage Collection" along with a collection of antique military guns and WWII Russian tanks in the museum that he intends to build in McMinnville.

Del Smith has been a positive influence on countless people whose lives he has touched. By believing in them, he has helped them to believe in themselves and encouraged them to become achievers. He has accumulated great financial wealth, but he has also found the true riches of life: the respect of his family, his friends, and his business associates. He has made the world a better place for his having been a part of it.

EPILOG

On October 25, 1986, at the Fairmont Hotel in Dallas, W. Clement Stone, president of the Napoleon Hill Foundation Board of Trustees and the founder and chairman of Combined International Corp., presented Delford M. Smith with the Foundation's Gold Medal for Entrepreneurial Achievement.

In his distinguished career Smith has received hundreds of awards and honorary degrees, but none was more fitting. Smith has been a tireless proponent of Napoleon Hill's principles of success and the values for which he stood. Smith's personal jet has placemats that feature a photograph of the aircraft surrounded by the seventeen principles of success, and he often sponsors Science of Success courses for his employees.

Success hasn't changed Smith much. He still works harder than most of his employees and never asks others to do something he hasn't or wouldn't do himself. He is as comfortable with senators and celebrities as he is with a new college graduate who has just joined his airline. He genuinely likes people.

When the Napoleon Hill Foundation Board of Trustees set out to find an individual whose example might inspire others to higher levels of achievement, they chose Del Smith. His life, they believed, was an excellent model to follow.

The true measure of a man, it has been said, is not how he handles failure. His real worth is determined by how he handles success. Most of us have more experience with failure; we learn from our mistakes, we dust ourselves off, and we get back into the fray. But what happens when we have reached levels of achievement that allow us to do whatever we wish?

Smith still clings to the values that brought him success. The principles he learned many years ago when he found a copy of *Think and Grow Rich* at the orphanage sustain him today. He quietly goes about performing acts of kindness and generosity, sharing the wealth that he has earned, while helping others to achieve levels of success they never dreamed possible.

As you study his life, read about it not with envy but with joy and anticipation. The principles he practiced, the success attributes he developed, are yours for the taking. The secret of his success—and many others—are contained in the pages of this book.

You have only to take them and apply them in your own life.

POWER PLUS
MOTIVATION:
EPIGRAMS

Included in this book are many epigrams to help you condition your mind with Positive Persuasive thoughts. They will increase your power for self-discipline, and will motivate and rekindle the flame of desire in your life. These short verses have been called by many names: success vitamins, distilled wisdom, epigrams, proverbs. Regardless of the name you choose, you will definitely be able to increase your power for success by means of the principle of auto-suggestion. Some of these statements have been gleaned from the Napoleon Hill *Golden Rule Magazine, The Science of Personal Achievement,* old manuscripts, and the memory bank of the mind. At one time Dr. Hill had written over six thousand of these to be used in a program of human relations for one company.

These proverbs are based on the experience of more than five hundred of the outstanding leaders who have been responsible for the development of the American Way of Life.

They have proved sound and practical because they have worked successfully for those who tried them. They have been reduced to the fewest words possible, for the benefit of all who sincerely wish to find their place in the world.

The collection was prepared with the hope that each person who reads it may be enriched in body, mind, and spirit; for as the great philosopher Socrates has said: "Wisdom adorns riches and softens poverty."

These proverbs are mind conditioners. Read them thoughtfully and make them your own, then observe how other people definitely and quickly give you their friendly cooperation.

As this book draws to a close, the Napoleon Hill Foundation extends to you the hand of friendship. Through the written word, we wish you an abundance of courage and peace and faith. If you have these states of mind, all other things that you need will come to you when you need them.

ACCURATE THINKING

How can you judge others accurately if you have not learned to judge yourself accurately?

Did you cheat the other fellow, or yourself? Be thoughtful before you answer.

The person who thinks before he acts seldom has to apologize for his acts.

Trying to convince a man who doesn't think is love's labor lost.

Thinking your way through your problems is safer than wishing your way through.

The fellow who thinks the whole world is wrong might be surprised at what the world thinks of him.

Many men who think they have arrived are surprised to learn that they have been traveling in reverse gear.

You may as well not listen if you don't think.

Be careful not to tangle with the man who thinks before he acts.

ACTION

Watch the man ahead of you and you'll learn why he is ahead. Then emulate him.

If you wish a job done promptly and well, get a busy

man to do it. The idle man knows too many substitutes and short cuts.

The man who doesn't reach decisions promptly when he has all necessary facts in hand cannot be depended on to carry out decisions after he makes them.

The man who only does enough work to "get by" seldom gets much more than "by."

Good intentions are useless until they are expressed in appropriate action.

It takes more than a name on a church membership to make a Christian.

BELIEVING

You can do it if you believe you can.

A man comes finally to believe anything he tells himself often enough even if it is not true.

If you don't believe it yourself, don't ask anyone else to do so.

Might throws itself on the side of those who believe in right.

The common "hobo" works harder and pays more for what he gets out of life than any other person, but he kids himself into believing he is getting something for nothing.

CAUTIOUSNESS

Be cautious of the man from whom dogs and children shrink with fear.

Over-caution is as bad as no caution. It makes other people suspicious.

Look carefully to see if the pasture on the other side of the fence appears greener, for there may be plenty of thistles mixed with the grass.

When a man says: "They say so and so," ask him to name who "they" are and watch him squirm with embarrassment.

When a stranger appears too eager to do something for you, take care that he doesn't do something to you.

Look the fellow over carefully who is trying to sell you
his way of life, to make sure his way is as good as
yours.

Beware of the fellow who tries to kid you into believing
he is doing so much better than you.

CHALLENGE

Render more service and better service than is expected
of you if you wish to attract quick and permanent
promotion.

Every time you perform a task, try to excel your last
performance, and very soon you will excel those
around you.

Who told you it couldn't be done, and what great
achievements has he performed that qualified him
to set up limitations for you?

Henry Ford is reported to have offered twenty-five thousand dollars to anyone who would show him how to
save a single bolt and nut on each automobile he
made.

Show me how to save a thin dime on any operation in
the plant and I'll show you how to get quick and
adequate promotion.

Where will you be and what will you be ten years from
now if you keep on the way you are going?

Never tear down anything unless you are prepared to
build something better in its place.

In the hour of defeat many men have discovered their
true greatness by accepting defeat only as a challenge to try again.

CHIEF AIM OR GOAL

What do you want from life and what have you to give
in return that entitles you to it?

The successful man keeps his mind fixed on what he
wants in life—not what he doesn't want.

Peggy Joyce Hopkins married four millionaires, one after
another, because she knew what she wanted and re-
fused to accept substitutes.

Never mind what you have done in the past. What are you going to do in the future?

The only permanent thing in the entire universe is that which a man sets up in his own mind.

If you don't know what you want from life, what do you think you will get?

Be sure about what you want from life and doubly sure of what you have to give in return.

Examine most carefully the things you desire most.

Wisdom consists in knowing what not to want as well as what to want.

Keep so busy going after what you want that you have no time to fear what you don't want.

Don't be afraid to aim high when choosing your life's goal, for no matter how high you aim, your achievements may fall below it.

If you don't know what you want, don't say you never had a chance.

COOPERATION

Unless you are an army officer, you can get better results by requests than you can by orders.

No man is capable of giving orders unless he knows how to take orders and carry them out.

Willing cooperation produces enduring power, while forced cooperation ends in failure.

Try telling your foreman about the things you like and see how willingly he will help you get rid of the things you don't like.

Friendly cooperation will get a man more than unfriendly agitation in any market.

No man can succeed and remain successful without the friendly cooperation of others.

Cooperation must start at the head of a department if it is expected at the other end. Ditto for efficiency.

Friendly cooperation is never any part of the devil's work. He is working on the other side.

Most men will respond more freely to a request than they will to an order.

A man who can't take orders graciously has no business giving them.

Remember that no one can hurt your feelings without your cooperation and willingness.

COURAGE

If you don't know, have the courage to admit it and you will be well on the road toward learning.

Courage is often one jump ahead of fear.

The man who complains he never had a chance probably hasn't the courage to take a chance.

CRITICISM

One way to avoid criticism is to do nothing and be a nobody. The world will then not bother you.

Never fear unjust criticism, but be sure it is unjust.

Never criticize anyone you don't understand. Better put in the time trying to learn something about him, then criticism may be unnecessary.

If inventors feared criticism, we would still be traveling by ox cart and wearing homespun clothing.

Don't be afraid of criticism, but be prepared to accept it if you have a brand new idea to offer.

Never criticize another man's deeds unless you know why he performed them. The chances are you would have done the same under the same circumstances.

If you can't take criticism, you have no right to dish it out to others.

If you can't stand criticism, you may as well not begin anything that is new.

Before criticizing the coffee, remember that you may be old and weak yourself sometime.

If you haven't done so well with overgenerous criticism of others, why not reverse your philosophy and give praise a trial?

Before you start criticizing, you had better do a little softening up by praise.

Praise more freely than you criticize if you wish to be popular.

DEEDS

If you are really great, you will let others discover this fact from your deeds.

Count that day lost whose descending sun finds you with no good deeds done.

Medals and titles will not count when you get to heaven, but you may be looked over carefully for the sort of deeds you have done.

The only safe way to boast is by constructive deeds and not by words.

When you have talked yourself into what you want, right there is the place to stop talking and begin saying it with deeds.

Self-praise is a credit only when it consists of deeds helpful to others and not of mere words.

Deeds, not words, are the greatest means of self-praise.

If you really are smarter than other men, you will let others find this out from your deeds.

The safest and best way to punish one who has done you an injustice is to do him a kind deed in return.

Waste no words on a man who dislikes you. Deeds will impress him more.

By all means tell the world how good you are—but first show it!

The man who thinks he can buy his way into heaven with money alone may regret that he didn't convert it into good deeds instead.

Perhaps you can say it in words of eloquence but deeds will be remembered longer.

It's not the epitaph on your tombstone but the record of your deeds that may perpetuate your name after death.

Remember this: the world pins no medals on you because of what you know, but it may crown you with glory and riches for what you do.

Faith is a combination of thoughts and deeds.

If you appreciate the kindness shown you by others, say it with deeds as well as words.

What you do is more impressive than anything you might say.

The right sort of deeds require no embellishment of words.

DEFINITENESS OF PURPOSE

This is a fine world for the man who knows precisely what he wants of life and is busy getting it.

A man without a definite major purpose is as helpless as a ship without a compass.

All riches consist in the habit of clear thinking. If you have no major purpose in life, your minor purpose will amount to nothing but a scant existence.

Willpower is the outgrowth of definiteness of purpose expressed through persistent action, based on personal initiative.

A rudderless ship and a purposeless man are eventually stranded on a desert sand.

Honesty and hard work are commendable traits of character, but they will never make a success of the man who does not guide them toward a definite major purpose.

Living without a definite major purpose promises nothing but a scant living.

If you have no major purpose, you are drifting toward certain failure.

Constancy of purpose is the first principle of success.

EDUCATION OR LEARNING

Education means development of the mind from within so it will help one to take his problems apart and put them to work for him and not against him. All education is self-acquired since no one can educate another.

That which you learn from your job may ultimately be more valuable to you than the immediate pay you receive.

If you are not learning while earning, you are cheating yourself of the better portion of your just compensation.

A man may learn by listening, but not by talking. Before

anything can come out of the mind, something must be put into it.

No man is properly educated until he has read Emerson's essays and understands them.

A good teacher is always a good student.

An educated person is not necessarily the one who has the knowledge, but the one who knows where to get it when he needs it.

Studying another man for constructive ideas pays off better than looking for his faults.

Knowledge is not power; it is only potential power that becomes real through use.

You may learn many useful facts by studying the honeybee, provided you don't try to show it how to do its job.

Learn to do some one thing better than anyone else can do it, and you can forget your financial problems.

If you are not trying to learn all about your foreman's job, you are tossing away the possibilities of promotion to his or a better job.

Where does the philosopher learn so much about the mistakes men make? From those who make them!

The ability to ask intelligent questions made Socrates the best-educated man of his time.

Knowledge, intelligently used, attracts greater knowledge.

The more you learn about your job, the more you may earn from your job.

The person who learns while he earns is being paid to go to school.

Knowledge is useless until it is transformed into benefit through action.

EFFECTIVE SPEECH

Remember, every word you speak gives someone a chance to find out how much—or how little—you know.

Not always is it what you say, as much as the way you say it, that counts.

Have you noticed how natural it is for a man to modify his tone of voice so it pleases when he asks a favor?

Speak gently and you will not need to weigh your words so carefully.

The man who speaks gently is heard further.

Carelessly expressed words often have an embarrassing rebound.

The most biting pain comes from a sharp tongue.

Can you imagine our Lord slandering anyone for any cause?

Think what you please, but be careful how you express your thoughts.

ENTHUSIASM

Where *enthusiasm* is a *habit,* fear and worry do not hang around.

If you are without enthusiasm, you are without a definite major purpose.

Enthusiasm starts the wheels of the imagination to turning.

A man without enthusiasm is like an automobile without gasoline.

The happiest men are those who have learned to mix play with their work and find the two together with enthusiasm.

Enthusiasm often makes dull conversation interesting.

THE EXTRA MILE

A peacemaker always fares better than an agitator.

Remember that every time you go the extra mile you place someone under obligation to you.

The end of the rainbow is reached only at the end of the second mile.

Only those who have the habit of going the second mile ever find the end of the rainbow.

Every time you influence another person to do a better job you benefit him and increase your own value.

A good fisherman goes out of his way to bait his hook with what fish prefer, which might not be a bad tip for those who wish to succeed in human relationships.

You cannot make all people like you, but you can rob them of a sound reason for disliking you.

The most important job is that of learning how to negotiate with others without friction.

Ferdinand the Bull has some good qualities, but you can't bring them out by shaking a red cloth in his face. Ditto for men.

Remember, you can place anyone under obligation to you whom you can induce to *accept favors* from you.

The man who does more than he is paid for is sooner or later paid willingly for more than he does.

Start going the extra mile and opportunity will start following you.

Don't push the other fellow around if you have corns on your own toes.

He is richest who gives most in service to others.

Only the highway of useful service leads to the city of happiness.

FAILURE

Edison failed ten thousand times before perfecting the incandescent electric light bulb. Don't worry if you fail once.

Drifting, without aim or purpose, is the first of thirty major causes of failure.

Edison failed ten thousand times before he perfected the modern electric lamp. The average man would have quit at the first failure. That's why there are so many "average" men and only one Edison.

Men may have found opportunities in failure and adversity which they could not recognize in more favorable circumstances.

Making life "easy" for children usually makes life "hard" for them in adulthood.

Men don't mind being told of their faults if one is generous enough to mix in a few of their virtues as well.

Success requires no explanations—failures must be doctored with alibis.

There is a vast difference between failure and temporary defeat.

No one may succeed until he recognizes the nature of this difference.

A man is never a failure until he accepts defeat as permanent and quits trying.

Most failures could have been converted into successes if someone had held on another minute or made one more effort.

Success attracts success and failure attracts failure, because of the law of harmonious attraction.

The man who tries to get something for nothing generally winds up by getting nothing for something.

The man who gambles for money is a potential cheater, for he is trying to get something for nothing.

Isn't it peculiar that a man often is so clever at inventing alibis and so dull at doing the job that would make alibis useless?

The other fellow's mistakes are a weak alibi for your own.

Failure is not a disgrace if you have sincerely done your best.

If you have no major purpose, you are drifting toward certain failure.

Don't blame children who are bad. Blame those who failed to discipline them.

Human faults are like garden weeds. They grow without cultivation and soon take over the place if they aren't thinned out.

Remember that the faults of man are pretty evenly distributed among all of us.

Self-pity is an opiate.

A wise man watches his faults more closely than his virtues; others reverse the order.

Failure is a blessing when it pushes one out of a cushioned seat of self-satisfaction and forces him to do something useful.

Failure seems to be nature's plan for preparing men for great responsibilities.

Your failure may prove to be an asset, provided you know why you failed.

If you don't know why you failed, you are no wiser than when you began.

FAIRNESS

Don't overlook small details. Remember that the universe and all that is in it is made from atoms, the smallest known particles of matter.

The best way to get favors is to start handing out favors.

FAITH

Faith cannot be created, but it can be *appropriated* by all who have prepared their minds to receive it.

Faith never diminishes through use, but it increases thereby.

No man can destroy your faith in anything unless you consent.

The greatest of all miracles is the power of simple faith.

Misfortune seldom tangles with the man whose constant bodyguards are *hope* and *faith*.

Faith needs a foundation on which to stand. Fear exists without a base.

Faith is born of *definiteness of purpose* operating in a positive mental attitude.

Faith is a state of mind that often makes the word "impossible" obsolete.

Faith will not bring you what you desire, but it will show you the way to go after it for yourself.

FEAR

Loud threats often indicate deep fears.

Defeat will respect you more if you learn to accept it without fear!

Don't temporize with fear, just go ahead and kill it.

Remember that a policeman is the only sort of man who gets satisfactory results with fear and force. Others do better with persuasion.

Fear is the devil's greatest weapon and man's greatest enemy.

Fear is the most costly of all the human emotions, although most fears have no foundation in facts.

Men with a clear conscience seldom fear anything.

Every bargain based on fear or force is a bad bargain for the one who drives it.

Go to bed praying and get up singing, and notice what a fine day's work you will do.

Neither a dog nor a mule has any respect for the person who fears it.

Keep so busy going after what you want that you have no time to fear what you don't want.

Close the door of fear behind you and see how quickly the door to faith will open in front of you.

Tell me what a man fears most and I'll tell you how that man can be defeated at will.

Freedom and fear cannot co-exist in any person's life.

Fear is bombastic: faith works in silence. But it works. When the two meet head-on, faith always is the master of fear.

Bad luck seems to prefer those who fear it.

Keep your fears to yourself. The other fellow has his own.

Hope and fear *don't* travel together.

The man who *fears* poverty will never be rich.

Fear kills more people than do most things which men fear.

You needn't fear the man who fears himself, unless you are that man.

Faith needs a foundation on which to stand. Fear exists without a base.

FRIENDS

The man who calls on his friends only when he goes after something soon finds himself without friends.

Friends must be grown to order—not taken for granted.

If you wish "acquaintanceship," be rich. If you wish friends, be a friend.

If you must let someone down, be sure it isn't the friend who helped you up when you were down.

A friend is one who knows all about you and still respects you.

Friendship needs frequent expression to remain alive.

Friendship recognizes faults in friends but does not speak of them.

GRIPE

Some men "gripe" when they have a just cause and others just gripe.

It is better to earn a promotion than to gripe for it.

If you must gripe in order to be happy, in heaven's name do it in a whisper so you'll not disturb others.

Don't be too hard on the fellow who is always griping, for he is making life pretty tough for himself as it is.

If you must gripe, why not gripe for a bigger opportunity to be useful to others?

Whine about your misfortunes and thereby multiply them, but keep still and starve them out.

Give a griper plenty of rope and he will hang himself without your help.

HABIT OF HEALTH

When you feel sluggish, try nature's doctor. Just quit eating until you are hungry again.

The best time to "doctor" is before you become sick.

If you would have good health, learn to quit eating before you are entirely satisfied.

Keep your mind on your physical ills and you will always be sick. Ditto for health.

Some athletes endorse cigarettes, for a price, but they don't smoke them at any price.

Ripe fruit and raw vegetables constitute a healthful diet of which one can never overeat.

You know what to feed your automobile for good service; now learn what to feed yourself for good health.

Don't try to cure a headache. It's better to cure the thing that caused it.

A big appetite doesn't always lead to sound health.

Do you have the cigarette habit, or does it have you?

Pills will not cure toxic poisoning, but plenty of water will.

Proper diet and elimination will serve better than an apple a day to keep the "medico" away.

Watch your eating habits and save a doctor's bill.

HANDICAPPED

A blind boy paid his way to a master's degree at Northwestern University by taking notes on class lectures in the Braille system of shorthand, writing them out on a typewriter, and selling copies to his classmates who had stronger eyes but weak ambition.

If you become discouraged, think of Helen Keller who, although deaf, dumb, and blind, made a good living by writing books to inspire her more fortunate fellowmen.

The man who starts at the top is greatly handicapped because then he can move in but one direction—downward!

HAPPINESS

Some people accumulate money so they can convert it into happiness, but the wiser ones accumulate happiness so they can give it away and still have it in abundance.

Happiness can be multiplied by sharing it with others without diminishing the original source. It is the one asset which increases when it is given away

A smile is a little thing that may produce *big results*.

Happiness is found in doing—not merely in possessing.

You can't find happiness by robbing another of it. Ditto for economic security.

A smile helps one's looks and makes him feel better without cost.

Any person can be won by affection quicker than by hatred.

The man who gives freely of happiness always has a big stock of it on hand.

You can laugh off worries that you can't scare off with a frown.

HARMONY

The orderliness of the world of natural laws gives evidence that they are under control of a universal plan.

There is harmony throughout the universe, in everything except human relationships.

Friction in machinery costs in terms of money. Friction in human relations impoverishes both the spirit and the purse of man.

If you cannot agree with another, you can at least refrain from quarreling with him on that account.

There are three sides to most of your disagreements with others: your side, the other fellow's side, and the right side, which may be somewhere between the other two sides.

The man who inspires harmony in human relationships goes up: the man who stirs up friction goes down. The order is never reversed.

The loss caused by friction in human relationships, if it could be prevented, would make all men tax-free and pay for the world wars in a single year.

The most important job is that of learning how to negotiate with others without friction.

Remember it takes at least two people to carry on a quarrel.

Unlimited power may be available when two or more men coordinate their minds and deeds in a spirit of perfect harmony for the attainment of a definite purpose.

Mutual confidence is the foundation of all satisfactory human relationships.

A good fisherman goes out of his way to bait his hook with what fish prefer, which might not be a bad tip for those who wish to succeed in human relationships.

The man who creates good fellowship among men will never be short of friends.

The person who loves harmony usually knows how to maintain it.

All enduring success is founded upon harmonious human relationships.

If you must meddle in human relationships, try to be a peacemaker among men and you'll not find too much competition.

Anything that disturbs harmony among men is apt to have originated with those who profit by mistrust.

HOPE AND ENCOURAGEMENT

If you look around, you can always find someone who is worse off than yourself. Be grateful you aren't in his shoes.

Time is the greatest of all doctors. If given a chance, it can cure most of the ills that men gripe about.

When things become so bad they cannot become worse, they usually begin to be better.

Misfortune seldom tangles with the man whose constant bodyguards are hope and faith.

Hope and fear don't travel together.

When hope dies, opportunity seldom attends the funeral.

Hope and faith are the willing servants of successful men.

Opulence without effort is a hope without fulfillment.

HUMAN RELATIONSHIPS

Jealousy is temporary *insanity*.

You can't be perfect but you can be honest.

Clothes may not make a man, but they may go a darned long way toward giving him a favorable start.

It takes more than a title and a mahogany desk to make an executive.

The man who *builds* a house always gets more for his work than does the man who *tears it down*.

Harmony in human relationships is a man's greatest asset. Don't permit anyone to rob you of your share.

One thing that gets the goat of an angry person is a smile when he expects a frown.

When you can't win, you can at least *grin*.

Your job will do for you no more than you do for it.

Revenge is a trait of the *primitive* man.

If you are looking for trouble, someone will be meddlesome enough to help you find it.

Begin looking for symptoms of illness and the disease itself will soon put in its appearance.

One bad habit often spoils a dozen good ones.

Your *reputation* is made by *others*, your *character* by *yourself*.

Never mind what you have done in the past. What are you going to do in the future?

Remember that the faults of man are pretty evenly distributed among all of us.

Discourtesy to a subordinate is a sure sign of an inferiority complex.

Suppose you do get another man's "goat"? What are you going to do with it?

Ability is greater than money because it can be neither *lost* nor *stolen*.

Hatred and justice cannot occupy a small mind at the same time.

IMAGINATION

The man who dipped a chunk of ice cream in chocolate and called it "Eskimo Pie" made a fortune for the five seconds of imagination required to create the idea.

Clarence Saunders made $4 million in four years by borrowing the self-help cafeteria for the grocery business and naming it Piggly-Wiggly. Imagination pays!

The imagination is the workshop of the soul, where are shaped all the plans for individual achievement.

Your job will never be any bigger than your imagination makes it.

IDEAS

Just omit your opinions and give me the facts so I may form my own opinions, and you may serve me better.

An opinion is no sounder than the judgment of the person offering it.

If you have a better way of doing anything, your idea may be worth a substantial fortune.

INSURANCE AND PERSONAL

You don't have to do more than you are paid for, but you can push yourself ahead mighty fast by doing it *voluntarily*.

Life insurance helps to kill the fear of poverty in old age.

A man's love for his family can be pretty accurately measured by the amount of life insurance he carries for their protection.

The man who spends all he earns will die a pauper if he neglects to carry life insurance.

No man should go into debt for anything greater than the amount of life insurance he carries.

JUDGING

Don't judge the entire church by its worst members. All wheat is surrounded by some chaff.

Would you take a chance on being judged in heaven by the same rules that you judge your fellowmen?

JUSTICE

Justice keeps an accurate record of all debits and credits and it balances its books with regularity if not with speed.

Justice has the uncanny habit of catching up with people when they are the least prepared for it.

LAW OF COMPENSATION

The man who does no more than he is paid for has no real basis for requesting more pay because he is already getting all he is earning.

The man who does more than he is paid for is sooner or later paid willingly for more than he does.

If you are looking for trouble, someone will be meddlesome enough to help you find it.

Some men appear to be "allergic" to honest work, but opportunity is equally allergic to them.

The man who does his job precisely as he would do it if he owned the business for which he works may see the day when he will own that business or a better one.

Remember that most troubles men get into overtake them when they are in bad company or at places where they should not be.

Columbus didn't know where he was going when he started, didn't know where he was when he got there, nor where he had been when he returned; so his neighbors had him chained in prison on suspicion.

The man who deliberately gets in the way of opportunity by being on the job all the time sooner or later is crowned by opportunity.

Henry Ford became rich, not from the sale of Ford cars, but from the service he rendered through his cars.

Every time you influence another person to do a better job, you benefit him and increase your own value.

Do your job precisely as if you were your own boss, and sooner or later you will be!

The man who can give his employer a good reputation nearly always is given a good reputation by his employer.

Don't be satisfied with being good at your job. Be the best, and you'll soon be indispensable.

The law of compensation isn't always swift, but it is as sure of operation as the setting of the sun.

Make your money work for you and you'll not have to work so hard for it.

First a man takes liquor or cigarettes of his own choice; then they take him with or without his choice.

Hurting another man's reputation will add nothing to your own, so why bother yourself without compensation?

The more you are promised for nothing, the less you will get for something.

The misfortune you wish for others may become the pattern of your own life.

Never bear down too hard on a man just because he is subject to your authority, for the order of the authority sometimes is reversed.

When you start giving out, you'll soon begin taking in.

The eternal law of compensation balances everything throughout the universe with its opposite of an equal force.

If you have something you don't need, give it to someone who needs it. It will come back in one way or another.

LEARNING FROM ADVERSITY

Before opportunity crowns a man with great success, it usually tests him out through adversity to see what sort of mettle he is made of.

If you don't want your life to be "messed up," don't fool around with those who have messed up theirs.

When adversity overtakes you, it will pay you to be thankful it was not worse instead of worrying over your misfortune.

You never know who are your real friends until adversity overtakes you and you need financial cooperation.

If life hands you a lemon, don't complain, but convert it into lemonade and sell it to those who are thirsty from griping.

LIBERTY AND FREEDOM

No man is free until he learns to do his own thinking and gains the courage to act on his own personal initiative.

Thinking accurately makes a man free, but nothing else does.

No man is free who holds a grudge against another, for he is under bond to his own emotions. Don't be too hard on the "boss," for you may be a "boss" yourself some day.

High taxes with plenty of freedom are more desirable
    than no taxes without freedom.
Freedom and fear cannot co-exist in any person's life.
A free man fears nothing.
No man can be entirely free until he is entirely honest
    with himself.

LOVE

Love is just a game to an old bachelor, but it's a tonic
    to an old maid.
There is something good about any man who is loved by
    his dog and his family, for they know him as he is.
Only one thing will attract love, and that is love.
Love, courtesy, and friendship are three priceless assets
    that cannot be purchased with money, and *must be
    given away* before they are valid.
Poets may rave about "love in a cottage" but others
    know that love goes out the back door when poverty
    knocks at the front door.

LOYALTY

Two things money cannot buy are love and friendship.
    These are gifts of the gods and have no fixed price.
One great lesson to be learned from a dog is that of
    enduring loyalty.
The truly great man is a servant—not a master.
The dog that doesn't wag its tail when its master comes
    home had better be looking for another master.
If all men had the loyalty and gratitude of all dogs, this
    would be a pretty fair world.
In heaven's name, don't bite the hand that feeds you.
The man who owns a good dog is never without a friend.
Friends must be grown to order—not taken for granted.

MASTERMIND

The mind grows only through use, and it atrophies
    through idleness.

A man is no greater than the thoughts that dominate his mind.

There is something about truth that makes it easily recognizable by all who are searching for it with open minds.

A closed mind stumbles over the blessings of life without recognizing them.

Take possession of your own mind, and you may soon make life pay off on your terms.

Henry Ford's mind was precisely like every other normal mind, but he used his to think with and not to harbor fear and self-imposed limitations.

Remember that the mind grows strong through use. Struggle makes power.

Beware of the man who tries to poison your mind against another under a pretense of helping you. The chances are a thousand to one he is trying to help himself.

The keenest minds are those which have been whetted most by practical experience.

A quick decision usually denotes an alert mind.

Control your own mind, and you may never be controlled by the mind of another.

No one can make you angry unless you open the door of your mind to him.

A man's progress in life begins in his own mind and ends in the same place.

Your real boss is the one who walks around under your hat.

The mind serves best which is used most.

The mind never becomes tired but sometimes it becomes "bored" with the sort of food it gets.

Know your own mind and you will be as wise as the sages.

Your mind is your own, and so is the responsibility as to how you use it.

If you know your own mind, you know enough to keep it always positive.

MENTAL ATTITUDE

The quality and quantity of the service you render, plus the mental attitude in which you render it, determines the amount of pay you get and the sort of job you hold.

The man with a negative mental attitude attracts troubles as an electromagnet attracts steel filings.

If you are worried or afraid of anything, there is something in your mental attitude that needs correction.

Remember that no one is ever rewarded or promoted because of a bad disposition and a negative attitude.

Quick promotions are not always the most enduring.

Trying to get without first giving is as fruitless as trying to reap without having sown.

No man is ever rewarded by promotion because of a negative mental attitude.

It is better to imitate a successful man than to envy him.

It is always safe to talk about other men as long as you speak of their good qualities.

You either ride life or it rides you. Your mental attitude determines who is rider and who is "horse."

Instead of complaining of that which you don't like about your job, start commending that which you do like and see how quickly your job will improve.

Sometimes it is wiser to join forces with an opponent than it is to fight him.

No man could ride a horse if the horse discovered its real strength. Ditto for a man.

The man who has more enemies than friends needs to examine his own mental attitude.

Your mental attitude determines the sort of friends you attract.

Before trying to master others, be sure you are the master of yourself.

It isn't defeat, it's your mental attitude toward it that whips you.

If you haven't the will power to keep your physical body in repair, you lack, also, the power of will to maintain a positive mental attitude in other important circumstances that control your life.

A man's best recommendation is that which he gives himself by rendering superior service, in the right mental attitude.

Character is accurately reflected in one's mental attitude.

A negative mind spawns only negative ideas.

It doesn't pay to look at others through a foggy mental attitude.

A positive mental attitude is an irresistible force that knows no such thing as an immovable body.

Remember your mental limitations are of your own making.

If you are sure you are right, you need not worry about what the world thinks.

Most illness begins with a negative mind.

Men with positive mental attitudes are never found in a rut.

If you are an American citizen, don't let any plug tell you that you are downtrodden.

MENTAL ATTITUDE AND THE MIND

The physical body is a mechanical house in which the mind dwells.

No one has yet discovered the limitations of the power of *his own mind*.

Good manners begin with a positive mental attitude.

A negative mind never attracts happiness or material success, but it will attract their opposites.

Every brain is both a broadcasting station and a receiving station for the vibrations of thought.

A well-disciplined mind recognizes but a few limitations.

Look for the good in others and they will look for the good in you. Ditto for the "bad."

Your mind belongs to you exclusively. Take possession of it, direct it to specific usage, and make life pay off on your terms.

A man's likes and dislikes come back to him from unexpected sources and often *greatly multiplied*.

If your mind can make you sick—and it can—remember it also can make you well.

One optimist may wield more constructive influence than a thousand pessimists.

Unfed worry soon dies of starvation.

Your true age is determined by your mental attitude, not the years that you have lived.

If you aren't on good terms with your conscience, take time out and read the Sermon on the Mount (Matthew, Chapters 5–7).

Your mind is the only thing you *control exclusively*. Don't give it away too freely through useless arguments.

Most illness begins with a *negative mind*.

Life has a habit of giving everyone that which he *believes* he will get.

A bad disposition is like yeast. It makes everyone "sour" who comes near it.

Men with positive mental attitudes are never found in a rut.

Chickens come home to roost and so do men's thoughts, so be careful what sort of thoughts you send out.

The odds are a million to one that you have no worries you couldn't eliminate by merely changing your mental attitude.

A man is more apt to "rust" out his brain from disuse than he is to wear it out from use.

A young mind makes a young body.

When a free thinker is born, the devil trembles with fear.

A well-disciplined mind works while the physical body sleeps.

Your own *mental attitude* is your *real boss*.

Only an open mind can grow.

Self-praise usually is a definite indication of an inferiority complex.

Your mind is your own, and so is the responsibility as to how you use it.

A sick mind is more dangerous than a sick body, for it is a form of sickness which is *always contagious*.

Some people are never free from troubles, mainly because they keep their minds attuned to worry. The mind attracts that which it dwells upon.

Keep your mind fixed on what you want in life: not on what you don't want.

Change your mental attitude and the world around you will change accordingly.

A positive mind finds a way *it can be done.* A negative mind looks for all the ways *it can't be done.*

If you can't manage your own mental attitude, what makes you think you can manage other people?

The mind is filled with mental dynamite. Be careful how you touch it off.

When you close the door of your mind to *negative thoughts,* the door of opportunity opens to you.

Your *mental attitude* is the most dependable key to your *personality.*

You can't control other men's acts, but you can control your mental reaction to their acts, and that is what counts most to you.

You can think your way into or out of almost any circumstance, good or bad.

Most stumbling blocks are the handiwork of a *negative* mind.

You can always see in other people whatever traits of character you are looking for.

There has always been a shortage of men who get the job done on time *without excuses or grumbling.*

Opportunity has a way of getting near the man with a positive mental attitude.

Wise men think twice before speaking once.

Life never is sweet to the man who is sour on the world.

Remember this—troubles generally go where they are invited.

The worst thing about worry is that it attracts a whole flock of its relatives.

Enthusiasm starts the wheels of the imagination to spinning.

OPPORTUNITY

Opportunity has a queer way of stalking the person who can recognize it and is ready to embrace it.

The man who is quick to see his limitations generally is slow in seeing his opportunities.

Another man's mistakes may be a rich field of opportunity for you if you know what caused his mistakes.

Speaking out of turn may ease your pride, but it may also play havoc with your opportunities.

If you are an able-bodied American, don't ever admit that the world has not given you an opportunity.

If it isn't your job to do it, perhaps it is your opportunity.

Opportunity frowns upon selfish monopolies.

Key yourself up with expectation, and opportunity may give the key a turn.

Opportunity will let you down if you aren't strong enough to hold it up.

If you could see an opportunity as quickly as you see the faults of others, you'd soon be rich.

A sharp tongue may cut the line of communication with opportunity.

When you close the door of your mind to negative thoughts, the door of opportunity opens to you.

Opportunity often knocks only to find no one in.

A resourceful person will always make opportunity fit his needs.

Opportunity wastes no effort looking for the person who is wasting his time through idleness or destructive action.

Opportunity will not interest itself in the person who isn't interested in it.

OPINIONS

Most opinions are mere hopeful wishing, not the result of careful analysis of facts.

Never express an opinion unless you can explain how you came by it.

It is more beneficial to ask intelligent questions than it is to offer free opinions which have not been requested.

If your opinions are worth anything, why give them away so freely?

Just tell me the facts and omit the opinions.

Your opinion may be safer if you don't express it as a
    fact.

ORGANIZED THINKING

Ponder the fact that one has complete control over but
    one thing, and that is the power of one's own
    thoughts.
You are where you are and what you are because of the
    food you eat and the thoughts you think.
Some nuggets of thought are worth more than nuggets
    of gold.
It may do no good to "stop, look, and listen," unless
    you also think.
If you are really smart, you know when to stop talking
    and start listening.
Think your way through—then push the body through.

PEACE OF MIND

Don't take yourself too seriously if you wish to get any
    joy out of life.
Nothing that causes a man to worry is worth what his
    worry costs him in peace of mind and physical
    health.
A man who is at peace with himself is also at peace with
    the world.
Unless you have peace of mind, you are not a free
    person.
Get on good terms with yourself, and see how quickly
    others get on good terms with you.
If you are not at peace with yourself, you can't be at
    peace with others.
If you are truly at peace with yourself, you'll never be
    at war with others.

PERSONAL INITIATIVE

The best job goes to the man who can get it done without
    passing the buck or coming back with alibis.

Act on your own initiative, but be prepared to assume full responsibilities for your acts.

That which stifles personal initiative is definitely an enemy of individual achievement.

PLEASING PERSONALITY

Men like you better when you greet them with a smile instead of a frown.

Three little words—"if you please"—carry the power of great charm.

You'll always be welcome if you bring a smile with you and leave your worries at home.

I have heard men say they never mistrust a man who whistles or sings when he works.

Life never is sweet to the man who is sour on the world.

One thing that gets the goat of an angry person is a smile when he expects a frown.

When you can't win, you can at least grin.

PRAYER

The greatest and most resultful of all prayers are those offered as gratitude for the blessings we already have.

It is better to give thanks for the blessings we already have than to pray for more blessings.

Prayers expressed with fear or doubt always produce only negative results.

The art of being grateful for the blessings you already possess is of itself the most profound form of worship, an incomparable gem of prayer.

PROCRASTINATION

Procrastination is the bad habit of putting off until day after tomorrow that which should have been done day before yesterday.

The habitual procrastinator always is an expert creator of alibis.

Suspense is the child of indecision, and it is the first cousin of procrastination. It is also the "pet" that keeps many people in poverty.

REALITIES

The five known realities of the entire universe are time, space, matter, energy, and the intelligence that gives these orderliness.

Today's dreams become tomorrow's realities. Do not belittle the practical dreamer, for he is the forerunner of civilization.

There are no such realities as good or bad luck. Everything has a cause that produces appropriate effects.

There is no such reality as passive faith. Action is the first requirement of all faith. Words, alone, will not serve.

The only permanent thing in the entire universe is change. Nothing is the same for two consecutive days.

RESPECT

Self-respect is the best means of getting the respect of others.

Sound character begins with keen self-respect.

It takes more than a loud voice to gain respect for authority.

RESPONSIBILITY

High wages and the capacity to assume responsibilities are two things that belong together.

If you do a job another man's way, he takes the responsibility. If you do it your way, you must take the responsibility.

Big pay and little responsibility are circumstances seldom found together.

The privilege of bringing children into the world carries with it the responsibility of teaching them the fundamentals of sound character.

Don't covet the other fellow's job if you are not prepared
to accept the responsibility that goes with it.

SELF-CONFIDENCE

Self-confidence may be mistaken for egotism if it is not
accompanied by humility of the heart.

Too much self-confidence often inspires too little
caution.

SELF-CONTROL

An educated man is one who has learned how to get
what he wants without violating the rights of others.

Before trying to master others, be sure you are the master of yourself.

No man is a free man until he learns to do his own
thinking and gains the courage to act on his own
personal initiative.

Develop your ego but keep your foot on its neck.

When you get hot under the collar, you'd better keep
cool about it.

If you have limitations, take care to keep them to yourself, for enemies have the habit of mastering men
through their weaknesses.

Independence starts with self-dependence.

Hotheads don't produce cool thoughts.

Hatred may not injure others, but the damage it does to
the hater is *unescapable*.

When you get yourself under *complete control*, you can
be your own boss.

SELF-DISCIPLINE

Self-discipline is the first rule of all successful leadership.

When angry, whistle for three minutes before speaking
and observe how your anger will take on the quality
of reason.

Have you ever tried to be angry while you were smiling?
Try it!

You can't control other men's acts, but you can control

your mental reaction to their acts, and that is what counts most to you.

True wisdom begins with self-understanding based on self-discipline.

Self-discipline makes discipline from the outside unnecessary.

When you get yourself under complete control, you can be your own boss.

SILENCE

Sometimes the man whom you think you have bested by talk has outwitted you by silence.

Silence has one major advantage: It gives no one a clue as to what your next move will be.

Silent thought is more powerful than spoken words.

SLEEP

When you don't know what else to do with your problem, try sleeping on it for a night or so.

A friendly conscience is a mighty good cure for sleeplessness.

If you cannot sleep, have a look at your stomach or a confidential talk with your conscience.

SOUND PHYSICAL HEALTH

Eat right, think right, sleep right, and play right and you can save the doctor's bill for your vacation money.

If you think you are sick, you are.

Begin looking for symptoms of illness and the disease itself will soon put in its appearance.

Searching for symptoms often leads to physical and mental illness.

STUBBORNNESS

Definiteness of opinion without tolerance generally turns out to be only stubbornness.

Plain stubbornness is often mistaken for "pride."

SUBCONSCIOUS MIND

The record of every person's life is indelibly recorded in his subconscious mind.

The subconscious mind often works out one's greatest problems when the conscious mind is asleep.

Keep your conscious mind fixed on what you desire, and your subconscious mind will unerringly guide you to it.

SUCCESS

That man is rich indeed who has more friends than enemies, fears no one, and is so busy building that he has no time to devote to tearing down another's hope and plans.

It will pay anyone to stand on the sidelines of life and watch himself go by now and then, so he may see himself as the world sees him.

The greatest of all schools is popularly known as the university of hard knocks.

Two kinds of men never get ahead—those who do only what they are told to do and those who will not do what they are told to do.

Money may not make a man a success, but it does give him a mighty good reputation.

The greatest of all success rules is this: Do unto others as you would if you were the others.

No man ever becomes so successful that he doesn't appreciate a kindly word of commendation for work well done.

The surest way to promote yourself is to help others get ahead.

Don't be in too big a hurry to get to the top of the ladder of success, for then you can move in only one direction—down.

The successful leader makes decisions quickly but changes them slowly if they must be changed.

Most successful men in the higher brackets of success did not strike their best stride until they passed the age of forty.

The man who has only time for gossip and slander is too busy for success.

Anyone can stand poverty, but few can stand success and riches.

Find out how to get production up and it will drag you and a bigger paycheck along with it.

Save expense for the company and the company will save money for you in proportion.

If a man worked as hard at the task he desires to do as he does at the task he must do, he could go places.

In a well-managed business all promotions are self-made. The employer's only part in the transaction is to check carefully to make sure the promotion has been earned.

If you were your own employer, would you be entirely satisfied with the day's work you have done today?

The man who tries to promote himself by demoting others cannot stay on top if he gets there.

The greatest known cure for loneliness, discouragement, and discontentment is work that produces a healthy sweat.

A "successful" politician is one who is long on promises, but short on keeping them.

Success attracts success, as evidenced by the fact that you can get what you want when you don't need it more easily than when you are in urgent need.

Man seldom ever begins to succeed in the higher brackets of success until he is past forty, mainly because most of his early years are spent in unlearning things that aren't true.

Some men are "smart," others are "wise." The difference is this: the "smart" man can make money, the "wise" man can make it and use it wisely.

If you can show how time or materials can be saved, you can easily show how your paycheck can be increased.

Remember the door to opportunity swings two ways—*in* and *out*.

No one can keep you down except yourself.

Defeat doesn't discourage the man who *knows* he is right.

The man who complains he never had a chance probably hasn't the courage to take a chance.

Success that comes easily is apt to go quickly.

When you learn to take life as it comes, it usually comes the way you wish it.

It is a sure thing that you'll not finish if you don't start.

If you put all your eggs in one basket, be sure to see that no one kicks the basket over.

Never mind what the other fellow didn't do. It's what *you do* that counts.

If you are a shepherd, be the *best* and you may live to own the herd.

You can always become the man you would have liked to be.

Sooner or later the world will find you out and reward you or penalize you for *exactly what you are.*

If you were offered the best job in the plant, are you ready to fill it?

Are you waiting for success to arrive or are you going out to find where it is hiding?

Remember, it is not necessary for others to fail in order that you may succeed.

Life says: "Make good or make room, but don't make excuses."

When a job chases a man, it usually picks a man who is employed.

If it isn't your job to do it, perhaps it is *your opportunity.*

Keep your conscious mind fixed on what you desire, and your subconscious mind will unerringly guide you to it.

The world stands aside and makes room for the person who knows where he is going and is on his way.

The climb upward will be easier if you take others with you.

There are no dead-end roads for a persistent man who knows what he wants and where he expects to find it.

Before worrying about how to get more pay, try thinking how you can do a better job, and you may not need to worry.

Remember, a kite flies against the wind, not with it.

The person who will not take a chance seldom has one thrust upon him.

It's better to *excel* another than to waste time envying him.

No man can make life pay unless he knows definitely *what he wants!*

The ladder of success is never crowded at the top.

Opportunity is something that permits one to get his foot inside the door of success, but it doesn't break the door down.

Nature yields her most profound secrets to the man who is *determined* to uncover them.

No man can succeed and remain successful without the friendly cooperation of others.

Opportunity never slips up on the man who straddles the fence through indecision.

If you expect something for nothing, you are doomed for disappointment.

Never argue over unimportant details, for if you win, you will have gained no advantage.

You'll not get much out of life if you allow others to live it for you.

Great achievement is born of struggle.

Constancy of purpose is the first principle of success.

The best possible way to get a transfer from the job you don't like to one you like better is to do your present job so well the management will desire to use your skill on a more important job.

The job you like least to do may provide you with the experience you need for promotion to a better job.

Many a parent has made life hard for his children by trying, too zealously, to make it easy for them.

When the going is hardest, just keep on keeping on and you'll get there sooner than someone who finds the going easy.

Poverty may not be a disgrace, but surely it is not a recommendation.

Don't look to the stars for the cause of your misfortunes. Look to yourself and get better results.

The man who works harder when the boss isn't around is headed straight for a better job.

Work must have been provided as a blessing, since every living creature must work or perish.

It is easier to keep ahead than to try to catch up with back work.

Have you noticed that the most efficient workman is generally the busiest?

Rejoice with the man who is succeeding and he may let you in on the secret of his success.

Are you waiting for success to arrive or are you going out to find where it is hiding?

Never mind how much you know! The important thing is what you can do with what you know.

There isn't much one can do for the man who will not try to do something for himself.

If one gets something for nothing it generally turns out to be worth to him about what it cost.

The man who does not systematically save a definite percentage of all he makes is apt never to acquire economic security.

A little job well done is the first step toward a bigger one.

Don't become excited over temporary success, for it may be only a bait to determine how much you can manage.

You'll never be a success until you train your mind to be success-conscious.

A man never gets very far ahead until he becomes his own "fortune-teller."

The quality and the quantity of the service you render fixes your wages and determines what sort of experience you are getting.

The chances are that your job likes you precisely as much as you like it, but no more.

Loafing on your job hurts your employer, but it hurts you more.

Don't ask your employer why you are not promoted. Ask the person who really knows best—yourself.

If you have more enemies than friends, the odds are a thousand to one you have earned them.

It isn't what you earn as much as what you save that counts in the long run.

The quality and quantity of the service you render is the only standard by which your pay can be fixed.

The greatest of all riches is just plain common sense.

The American system of free enterprise not only makes riches, it also makes successful leadership.

SUCCESS-CONSCIOUSNESS

If you don't have the full approval of your conscience and your reason, you had better not do the thing you contemplate.

An apology is a healthy indication that a man still is on speaking terms with his own conscience.

If your conscience isn't clear you'd better start housecleaning from within.

The conscience speaks, not in audible words, but through that small voice from within.

TACTFULNESS

A truly big man never tries to impress others with his bigness and never tries to "keep up with the Joneses."

There can never be any harm in speaking about other people provided you speak of their good qualities.

It is better to request a man to perform a service than it is to order him to perform it.

When the other fellow's facial expression looks pained, it's time to stop talking or change the conversation.

When you don't know anything good to say about a man, just button up your lip and you'll feel better.

You can get close to any man by the simple process of taking a keen sincere interest in what he is doing.

Merited praise will gain reciprocal interest from any man.

If you must talk about your good qualities, try not to cover too much territory.

TEAMWORK

A good football team consists in harmonious coordination of effort more than in individual skill.

When you ask another person to do something, it may
  help both him and you if you tell him—what to do
  why he should do it
  when he should do it
  where he should do it
  how he may best do it.

TEMPER

A temper is a good thing to have provided one does not
  try to give it to someone else.

Temperament is a state of mind consisting of nine parts
  "temper" and one part "mental" energy.

When you lose your temper, you'll be better off not to
  go back to find it.

Hot heads don't produce cool thoughts.

When you become so angry you don't know what to do,
  it will be safer to do nothing.

THOUGHT CONTROL

If a man gave spoken expression to every thought that
  came into his mind, he would have no friends.

Thoughts are contagious. Therefore be careful of the sort
  you release.

TIME

Tell me how you use your "spare" time, and I will tell
  you what and where you will be ten years hence.

Time is a wonderful healer. It tends to equalize good
  and evil and to right the wrongs of the world.

You might discover how to save enough time and materials in your department to insure you an increase in
  pay and add a better job. Why don't you try?

You will find time for all your needs if you have time
  properly organized.

The most profitable time any man spends is that for
  which he is not directly paid.

The man who wastes his own time may be no less a thief
  than the man who steals other people's property.

Time ultimately cures all the ills and rights and wrongs of the world. Nothing is impossible with time.

There has always been a shortage of men who get the job done on time without excuses or grumbling.

The time some men devote to giving others bad reputations might be better spent in doctoring their own.

The length of time a man sticks to a job is a pretty accurate measure of his dependability.

Don't waste time on the man who forms his opinion before he examines the evidence.

The man who fights with his wife at meal time usually fights with his associate workers the rest of the time.

The best time to sell a man anything is right after dinner. (Women, please copy.)

Hurry, brother, hurry! The sand in your hourglass is running lower every second, and the glass can't be refilled.

Time is too precious to be wasted in foolish arguments or discontent.

Time is one thing that is rationed to everyone and it has no black markets at any price.

Just what are you waiting for, and why are you waiting?

Indecision and lack of a major purpose are the greatest of all thieves of time.

If your time is of no value to you, perhaps you can make it of value to others.

No man is paid for his time, but he may be paid for the use he makes of it. Only used time is of value.

The use of one's time determines the space one occupies in the world.

Every time you think in terms of benefit to your employer, you come one step nearer an equal benefit for yourself.

If you cannot forgive, don't ask to be forgiven, for you'll be wasting your time.

Time will cure worries which respond to no other treatment.

Live each day as if it were your last and you'll develop a keen respect for time.

When defeat overtakes you, don't put all your time on counting your losses. Save some of it to look for your gains, and you may find your gains are greater than your losses.

Some mistakes can be corrected, but not the mistake of wasted time. When time goes, it has gone forever.

The poet cries, "Backward, turn backward, oh time in your flight," but he cries in vain, for time flows only ahead.

The most beneficial use of time is that which one devotes to silent meditation when searching for guidance from within.

Time spent in silent thought may yield fabulous riches through the creation of sound ideas.

When there is no work for your hand to perform, let your mind be employed so not a second of time will be wasted.

Every minute of time saved on any job is a step on the road to promotion.

It isn't sufficient just to arrive. You should be on time.

Most misfortunes are the results of misused time.

The lowest type of time-waster is known as a "bum," and sometimes he is found temporarily in respectable company.

Time, the great universal doctor, can cure all human ills, and most of them very quickly.

Remember there is always an ending for everything except time and space.

TONE OF VOICE

Remember the tone of your voice often conveys more accurately what is in your mind than do your words.

WILLPOWER

The most interesting thing about a postage stamp is the persistence with which it sticks to its job.

Anyone can quit when the going is hard, but a thoroughbred never quits until he wins.

Victory is always possible for the person who refuses to stop fighting.

Nature yields her most profound secrets to the man who is determined to uncover them.

WISHING

If I had but one wish that could be granted, it would be for more wisdom with which to enjoy the many blessings I possess under the American form of government.

If I had one wish and it could be granted for the asking, I would ask for more wisdom.

The scientist is the only type of man who does no hopeful wishing and accepts all the facts as he finds them.

TRAITS OF CHARACTER

Dependability is the first foundation stone of good character.

You can tell by the company a man chooses what sort of character he has.

Your reputation is that which people think you are, your character is that which you are.

Every thought a man releases becomes a permanent part of his character.

Sound character is a man's greatest asset, because it provides the power with which he may ride the emergencies of life instead of going down under them.

Some men resemble a cheap watch. They are not dependable.

Pick out some person whom you admire and imitate him or her as closely as you can. This is hero worship, but it improves character.

Boastfulness generally is an admission of an inferiority complex.

Profanity is a sign of inadequate vocabulary or unsound judgment, or both.

If you must be deceitful, be sure you never try to deceive your best friend—yourself.

Money is either a good or bad influence, according to the character of the man who possesses it.

No man is so good that he has no bad in him, and no man is so bad that he has no good in him.

The man who is honest only for a "price" should be rated as dishonest.

A lazy man either is sick or has not found the work he likes best.

The man with sound character generally does no worrying over his reputation.

Attend well to your character and your reputation will look out for itself.

Falsehood does evermore have a way of publishing itself.

A man is either honest or dishonest. There can be no compromise between the two.

Bankers often lend money on character, but seldom on reputation alone, for they have learned that not all reputations are deserved.

Honesty is a spiritual quality that cannot be evaluated in terms of money.

It's mighty easy for one to justify dishonesty if he makes his living from it.

Too much truth will make some men madder than too little.

Politeness usually begins at home or it doesn't begin at all.

WORRY

Never stop to think about your worries, for they will catch up with you quickly enough unless you outrun them.

Success-consciousness is a death warrant for worry.

Worry and success simply can't live together in the same house.

You can laugh to death many worries you can't get rid of otherwise.

Unfed worry soon dies of starvation.

Before worrying about how to get more pay, try thinking how you can do a better job and you may not need to worry.

When enthusiasm comes in at the front door, worry runs out at the back door.

Today's worries may become tomorrow's priceless experiences.

Worry will kill one quicker than work.

Never listen to a doubting Thomas unless you are willing to become one, for doubt is contagious.

Take possession of your own mind and worry will have to look for another boarding place.

Old Man Worry's relatives are: fear, ill health, ill temper, indifference, procrastination, jealousy, envy, hatred, selfishness, bad judgment, poverty, premature old age, and discouragement. *What a flock of bums!*

Let the *other fellow* do the worrying if he has no better sense.

Worry thrives on self-pity.

You don't have to open the door every time worry knocks.

Most worries are not half as serious as their owners think they are.

If you have time to worry, you haven't enough time to succeed in your job.

If you are too busy to visit with worries, they'll be too discouraged to hang around.

Worries generally go where they are most welcome.

Only the weak crave sympathy!

Forget your worries and most of them will slap back by forgetting you.

HELPFUL HINTS ON HOW TO SPEND YOUR MONEY

NO CREDIT REQUIRED: HOW TO BUY A HOUSE WHEN YOU DON'T QUALIFY FOR A MORTGAGE
Ray Mungo & Robert H. Yamaguchi

This book provides a simple step-by-step procedure on how to purchase a home even if you don't qualify for credit. This indispensable guide proves that, with some creativity and simple common sense, anyone who wants a home can own one.
175646

To order call: 1-800-788-6262